TRAUMA, BONDING
&
FAMILY CONSTELLATIONS

Green Balloon Publishing

Professor Dr. Franz Ruppert is Professor of Psychology at the University of Applied Sciences in Munich, Germany. He gained his PhD in Work and Organisational Psychology at the Technical University of Munich in 1985.

Since 1995 he has focussed on psychotherapeutic work and specifically on the causes of psychosis, schizophrenia and other forms of severe mental illness. He has combined with this his interest in bonding and attachment theories and modern trauma work to understand better the effect of traumatic events, not just on those who suffer the event but on whole bonding systems, especially families.

His publications include: *Verwirrte Seelen* (2002, Kösel, Munich), (*Confused Souls*, not available in English) followed by the German version of the current book: *Trauma, Bindung und Familienstellen: Seelische Verletsungen verstehen und heilen* (2005, Pfeiffer bei Klett-Cotta, Stuttgart). His next book, *Seelische Spaltun und innere Heilung Traumatische Erfahrungen integrieren* (Pfeiffer bei Klett-Cotta, Stuttgart) was published in 2007 and is currently being translated for the English market under the title *Healing the Split in the Soul: the Integration of Traumatic Experiences*.

Ruppert facilitates workshops in Germany and many other countries, furthering his insights into the deeper transgenerational effects of trauma in different cultures, and researching the methodology of constellations to understand better its powerful effect on patients.

This is Ruppert's first book available in English.

TRAUMA, BONDING
&
FAMILY CONSTELLATIONS

Understanding and Healing Injuries of the Soul

Franz Ruppert

Translated from German by
Sally Tombleson, Oliver Fry and Alexandra Chalfont

English-language version edited
by Vivian Broughton

Green Balloon Publishing

First published in the United Kingdom in 2008
by Green Balloon Publishing

Klett-Cotta
© 2005 J.G. Cotta'sche Buchhandlung Nachfolger GmbH
Stuttgart
For the English language translation:
© 2008 Franz RuppertCopyright © Franz Ruppert 2008

Green Balloon Publishing
An imprint of Constellations Work Trainings Limited,
Frome, Somerset, BA11 5DG
www.greenballoonbooks.co.uk

ISBN 978-0-9559683-0-3

Book production by Action Publishing Technology Ltd, Gloucester
Printed and bound in Great Britain

Contents

Contents

Foreword

Thank you!
It takes the contribution of many hands to bring a book to successful fruition. First of all I would like to thank all the patients who offered me their trust and allowed me a glimpse of their souls, those who allowed me to publish in this book a small part of the many different things they experienced, and those who afterwards gave their honest feedback, both verbal and written, as to which things helped them and which didn't.

I would also like to thank all the participants in my constellation seminars for the courage shown in treading this unorthodox path together with me. Adapting to a new method – one that goes far beyond the usual understanding of how psychological and spiritual processes come into being and work – is no simple matter. It is also no simple matter to play the roles of the representatives in a constellation and to step into another person's life. Many have shouldered enormous burdens, while in the role of the representative, in order to allow others to recognise and understand themselves better. My express thanks therefore go to the participants in my advanced training groups and workshops for their strong backing and help with my own personal development. I would also like to thank my colleagues from my inter-vision group.

All the case studies in this book are authentic. To preserve the anonymity of the patients, however, some of their names have been changed. Behind every "case" there exists a real person, with his own unique family and life history. I selected from these histories those parts I thought best illustrate the theoretical background and the therapeutic process. It goes without saying that these case studies will never do justice to the complexity of each individual, his or her unique psychological and spiritual make-up; indeed, every one of them has his or her own unique spiritual world.

I wrote this book for a specialist readership – those who wish to help people suffering from psychological disorders – as well as for therapists and counsellors who work with family constellations. It is also intended to provide the reader, friends and family as well as others with access to a new understanding of deeply bonded relationships. For this reason, where possible I have avoided Latin and Greek terminology and limited the use of scientific jargon. In naming people and groups, I have moved randomly between the male and female grammatical forms.

Franz Ruppert

Foreword to the English Edition

Much time has passed since the publication of this book in German. During this time, I have found further opportunities to expand my learning through practical work with clients as well as increasing study of the literature. As a result, I have revised the original German text in a number of places in order to formulate these correlations with improved precision. Where new insights were gained and I deemed it important to the understanding of mental disorders, I also expanded on the original. I can now see the extreme importance the discovery of mirror neurones in the human brain has for the understanding of mental processes. They appear to provide the physical basis for the development of the bonding processes. They may also facilitate the transfer of trauma experiences from one generation to the next and probably allow the phenomenon of representation in constellations to be much better understood.

In the bibliography section, wherever possible I have given the English language titles and publishers of the German reference works.

Finally, I would like to thank Vivian Broughton, who invited me to communicate my theories and apply my practical therapeutic work in England. Without her active and caring support, I would not have been able to complete this book. She is more than the editor of this book. She is an expert in psychotherapy and constellation work and a woman with a very friendly and warm heart.

Franz Ruppert 2008

Editor's Foreword to the English Edition

Editing a translation of a book such as this is a challenging task. Not only is one undertaking editing and proofing, one has also the responsibility of producing a version which is congenially readable for an English-speaking audience and at the same time honours the author's intentions as expressed in the original language. Additionally, the complexity of the subject matter, and the innovatory nature of some of the ideas required particular care.

I was helped in this by extensive first hand experience of the author's work and by my own background as a constellations facilitator.

I want to acknowledge in addition the help and support of colleagues, in particular the translators Sally Tombleson, Oliver Fry and Alexandra Chalfont; the proofreaders Barbara Morgan and Tony Glanville; and Clare Kavanagh for preparing the index.

I want to express particular thanks to John Mitchell for co-ordination of the proofreading and his support throughout.

Vivian Broughton 2008

PART I:
Trauma, Bonding and a Multigenerational Perspective

1
Psychological Disorders

1.1 The Unexplained Origins of Psychological Disorders

The most difficult disorders to understand are those for which we can find no appropriate event or circumstances in the person's life to account for the severity of the condition that is suffered, where there is no obvious event to relate the condition to, or the symptoms displayed and the severity of the condition are out of all proportion to any possibly associated events.

Anxiety, Fear and Panic Attacks

Anna had her first panic attack when she was in fact feeling quite well. She was sitting in the sunshine by a window in her room studying for an examination that was not difficult for her. Suddenly a deathlike fear arose within her, a fear that, since that first time, she has made every effort to suppress, deadening almost all her emotions. She is terrified of going mad and ending up in psychiatric care, and so far no therapy has helped her.

Ralph, on the other hand, has always known fear. It has tortured him ever since he can remember. Going to school was hell as he hated leaving his mother and it was impossible for him to participate in any school outings. Doctors and psychologists had treated him since his childhood but no form of therapeutic care had led to the disappearance of his fears. He just learnt to conceal them from others, and to some extent to keep them under control.

If we are actually threatened, it is natural to experience fear, as when one is threatened with a gun. But why are there some people who are gripped by unexplained fears not restricted to a given situation? Why does panic and terror sometimes strike as if out of nowhere? And why do some children seem to be excessively fearful right from birth?

Depression

Depression often presents a similar puzzle. Why does Mr S. develop a serious clinical depression after separating from his wife? Why, a year after the separation, does he then suffer a complete mental breakdown and become as fearful and helpless as a small child? Why does his state not follow the course of the normal pain of separation as expressed in disappointment, anger and grief? Why does he isolate himself voluntarily, although there is nothing he fears more than loneliness? How does it come to such a point that he can only get through the day using tranquillisers?

When we lose someone or something of value and importance to us, or when nothing seems to go right, then it is understandable that we may get depressed. Courage deserts us, we withdraw, we cannot sleep properly at night any more, and we lose our appetite. The world seems grey and pointless. But what is the origin of serious clinical depression that seems to emerge without an identifiable external cause? Is it really just our genes?

Mental Breakdown

Other unexplained psychological breakdowns are not uncommon. Maria had moved to another country far away

4

from her parents, where she was professionally established, recognised and popular. However, she suddenly began to experience phases of shortness of breath, which became more and more frequent, increasing pains in different parts of her body, and she found herself struggling to keep her head above water until finally she suffered a complete collapse. She had to give up her job and became more and more isolated, tortured by fear, pain and feelings of anger. She could no longer contain the emotional turmoil going on inside her.

Something similar happened to John. His schoolmates' teasing resulted in him descending into increasing emotional chaos. He had to break off his education, and finally ended up in a residential community for the mentally ill. What happened to him? How could he have maintained stability for seventeen years and then suddenly collapse, feeling within himself powerful urges to throw himself in front of a subway train?

Laura had always suffered psychological disquiet and had never really felt normal. As a girl she tried drugs and then became anorexic.

Case Study 1:

"It always seemed to me that I was different."

"I thought it was normal to have practically no memory of one's childhood. As a child, I was seen as shy. I don't remember my pre-school years at all and I know very little about my time in primary school. I do have a few images that are anchored in my mind – a dress, a fall, my parents' bedroom with its dark floral curtains and bright blue carpets beside the bed. These images have stuck and they make me feel afraid. I have a memory that as a child I always imagined that behind some curtains there was a hidden and secret room that protected me. I often wished to go into this room. I never felt I belonged to my family. I often thought I might perhaps have been adopted."

5

Every individual has problems and crises in life which often provide an opportunity for growth. Why is it that some people fail to cope? Why does a crisis take these people deep into an emotional and psychological abyss? Why, for some people, does every new relationship end in chaos?

Psychosis and Schizophrenia

Even less comprehensible at times are the cases of children who do not manage to become independent and adult when they grow up. These children may seem to have a normal development, are intelligent and perform quite well at school. Suddenly, however, their personality begins to change. They may withdraw and perform bizarre rituals, talking incomprehensibly. Some become suddenly confused as if out of nowhere, or after having smoked cannabis or taking other drugs, while others become deeply confused when they have their first intense emotional and sexual relationship.

Many young women and men affected in this way reject help, although their problems are obvious. They want to be left alone by their parents and the doctors and psychotherapists who are concerned about them. Yet they are deeply confused in their hearts and minds. For some, vivid images of war, scenes of rape or other horrors may arise within them and they may increasingly retreat into a delusional world. In contrast to the flood of pictures and emotions inside them, they may agonise constantly in an abstract way over good and evil, increasingly losing contact with reality. They may be incapable of completing their schooling or other career training, and for years they may alternate between spending time in psychiatric institutions and their parental home, taking psycho-active drugs in high doses, spending their lives without any prospect of real improvement.

Can we say with certainty that problems and difficulties with school friends, conflicts with teachers, insecurity at emerging sexuality can really be the grounds for such developments? The taking of cannabis can indeed trigger psychotic conditions, but why doesn't everyone who uses cannabis or other recreational drugs become psychotic or schizophrenic? Why some and not others? The real reasons must lie deeper. Psychosis often suddenly erupts in adulthood. This may happen within the context of a new love and sexual relationship or pregnancy. Thus for Eva, separating from a man was suddenly a matter of life and death. For her it signalled the start of a twelve year period of mental illness, with periods of hospitalisation and schizophrenia in the care of psychiatrists and psychotherapists.

Case Study 2:

A matter of life and death

"I loved a man very much. For me it was the ideal relationship. We went to South America together. It was the first time that I really trusted a man. In South America he became a different person – the precise opposite of what he had been – evil, utterly evil. He rejected me. He came close to killing me, leaving me in a seriously ill condition for days without water or medication. He did not want me to be there. I was close to never getting back to Germany. My life was hanging by a thread. My lifeline was R., my best woman friend – a fixed point to which I could return and survive the long flight. At Munich airport I broke down in her arms. It was my most serious psychosis."
(see also Case Study 46, page 212).

A Multiplicity of Symptoms

Whether the sufferer is adult or adolescent, the symptoms of psychological suffering are many and varied, characterised by fear, anxiety, panic attacks, serious depression, dissociative identity problems (e.g. borderline personality disorder), together with innumerable forms of destructive behaviour, directed either towards the self or others. Schizophrenia and psychosis, symptomatised by delusions, hallucinations, disorganized speech and behaviour, are the most serious forms of mental illness. The great variety of pathological compulsions, addictions and dependencies make a long list, ranging from alcohol and drug dependency to work addiction, compulsive stealing and many more.

The symptoms of "psychological illnesses" or "mental disorders" are compiled and classified in the standard works: *International Classification of Diseases and Related Health Problems* (ICD–10, WHO, 1992) and the *Diagnostic and Statistical Manual of Mental Disorders* (DSM IV, APA, 1994). There are currently 395 possible diagnoses for mental disorders listed in the DSM IV.

Psychological disorders manifest differently in men and women. For example, women are more susceptible to depression, while statistics show men are more likely to have alcohol-related problems. Eating disorders are more prevalent among young girls, and hyperactivity more prevalent among boys. Significantly more women than men seek help and advice from doctors and psychotherapists (at least in Western industrialised countries) (World Health Report 2004: *Changing History*).

In Europe the average suicide rate is 28 per 100,000 men and 7 per 100,000 women. Four times as many women as men make suicide attempts. Men who want to commit suicide are more likely to be successful than women. For men it is a final act of self-destruction, whereas for women it is often a cry for help (European Health Report, 2005).

Psychological problems may also underlie many physical symptoms. Many people suffer from physical complaints, such as chronic headaches, persistent breathing problems, skin diseases or rheumatic inflammations, for which doctors cannot provide a satisfactory explanation of the origins, and for which conventional medical therapies rarely provide solutions. Physical pain is often an expression of suppressed emotional pain. Sometimes it is only through the physical manifestation of their complaints that some people can get some of the attention for their suffering that they otherwise lack.

Lastly, it is important to mention those who would never refer to themselves as suffering from any kind of mental illness, but whom we recognise as such by their actions: people who commit the acts of rape, sexual abuse, murder and manslaughter that fill our newspapers. The perpetrators of these acts, indeed anyone who seriously injures another physically or emotionally, thereby even destroying their lives, undoubtedly has serious psychological problems. Reports of court proceedings show that perpetrators of violence often do not have any sense of having done anything wrong. Lack of any moral sense, ethical standards and capacity for sympathy cannot be considered indications of psychological health (cf. Antisocial Behaviour Disorder, DSM IV). The question here is: why do some people develop in this horrifying way?

Case Study 3:

The perplexing psyche of the offender

Although there have always been people who commit murder and other atrocities, there are other forms of behaviour, which also strike us as completely inhuman. Many serious offenders show no feelings of guilt or remorse: "On Thursday, at Bochum's Higher District Court, men accused of murder and drug dealing casually chewed gum while contemplating their defence lawyers' activities. The brother of the principal defendant, Eugen N., could not suppress a grin. And indeed there was something grotesque in the way the six gang members' lawyers opened the trial for a brutal series of murders. The facts of the case were so terrifyingly stark: six men, mostly Russo-German, ranging in age between 21 and 27 were accused of having executed five individuals between December 2003 and January 2004. Their motives involved quarrels with Dutch dealers concerning drug quality, turf wars, debts and the gangs' internal disagreements" (Süddeutsche Zeitung 15 October 2004).

Another reported court case: "Prosecutors produced a

ten-page document outlining the suffering of Sylvia B., who since 1986 (when three years old) had been continuously sexually abused by her father. The abuse increased over the years to the point of daily rape when in 1997 Sylvia B.'s mother was hospitalised for a year for depression. During this time Sylvia B. had to assume her mother's role and submit to the accused's perversity. Karl Heinz B. could not leave his daughter alone, even when she herself was hospitalised following a suicide attempt. Sylvia B., by then seventeen moved to a sheltered residential community but still visited her parents. On these visits her father carried on abusing her" (Süddeutsche Zeitung 23 October 2004). After the sentence was passed the father who had confessed in full did not express one word of regret.

1.2 Inadequate Theories and Treatments

We know the symptoms of psychological and emotional suffering; we can list, reference and catalogue them. However, can we say that we really understand their causes, how they develop in all of their variety and complexity? Can we really alleviate these conditions in a targeted and systematic way through the use of medical treatment (medication or operations), or by educational measures (instruction, education and advice), or with psychological therapies (listening, interpreting and understanding)? Or in the final analysis do we have to endure the situation, perhaps easing people's suffering a little, but never really healing them or helping the suffering disappear altogether?

All cultures traditionally have tried to understand and influence the dark and mysterious sides of human behaviour and experience. In older, more traditional cultures healers, shamans and holy men acted on a variety of ideas as to why members of their tribe, clan or nation might demonstrate permanent or periodic unusual behaviour. The various concepts behind many healing rituals include possession by evil spirits, bewitchment by magic, and loss of the soul. In these contexts treatment for depressed or confused people might include necromancy, prayers, witch-hunts, voodoo magic, anointing with herbs, magic potions, music or shamanic travel. In industrialised societies there are many modern-day healers who use the thinking, ideas and rituals of traditional societies.

Modern societies in the mainstream, however have looked to science to provide answers as to why mental disorders exist and what can be done to counteract them. The different disciplines of medicine and psychology have been involved in trying to understand the mentally ill for over 150 years. The scientific approach can be characterised as regarding as real only what can be observed, counted, measured or corroborated by experiments; for science, when it comes to mental illness, it is facts and proven theories that must replace belief and philosophic speculation.

The Concept of Psychiatric Illness

Over time, science has generated many theories of mental illness. The application of the concept of pathology to unusual psychological phenomena is itself the result of a scientific initiative to separate body from psyche, soul and spirit. The concept of illness conveys the idea that the psychological and spiritual nature of a person can be subject to illness or disorder in the same way as the body can, and that the body is in the end the true reason for mental and spiritual crisis. According to the concept of psychiatric illness, our psycho-spiritual nature is to be understood solely in terms of the state of the physical and material processes upon which the functioning of normal health depends.

The resulting approach leads to the search for substances and material structures upon which the "pathological" in an individual's psyche is based. Psychiatry sets the tone in this area (e.g. Bäuml, 1994; Rahn and Mahnkopf, 2000), where the scientific endeavour has produced many hypotheses concerning the function of genetic building blocks, brain structures and metabolic processes, both in the body and in the brain. This is the main theoretical foundation upon which psychiatric therapeutic treatment is based. People with mental disorders are treated with psychotropic drugs, or surgical intervention to the brain (e.g. lobotomy), or shock treatment (e.g. insulin-shock or electric-shock). These treatments are applied in the framework of clinical institutions or outpatient medical care.

The weakness of the medical initiative lies in the fact that psychiatry, even in the 21st century, cannot prove the hypothesis that depression, personality disorders or schizophrenia even exist in a medical sense. There are indeed mental incapacities and dementias, where there is a close and causal link between physical and psychological symptoms, which can be proved with a high degree of probability, categorized as the organically based disorders in the DSM IV. However, there is an enormous number of psychological disorders where, despite intensive research, no physical symptoms are to be found. Psychiatry's concept of pathology therefore rests on very insecure foundations. It is more a question of belief – an agreement between psychiatrists to share a point of view. A German psychiatrist openly admits that: "The pathology concept, particularly for those of us involved in psychiatry, is a strictly medical one. Illness only exists in the body, and we call the psychological abnormality 'pathological' when it can be traced back to pathological organic processes. We thus base our pathological concept in psychiatry exclusively on pathological changes in the body ... The pathological processes behind cyclothymia and schizophrenia are not known to us – that they are based on pathologies is an assumption that is well subscribed to ... The fact that, apart from abnormal variants in psychological nature and psychological abnormalities where physical illness is the cause, there are also these 'endogenous psychoses', is a difficulty for human psychiatry ... We stand by ... in the sense of a heuristic principle ... the hypothesis and thus the notion of the 'pathological' ... The occurrence of mania is a symptom of admittedly unknown aetiology but an illness can be postulated. ... If possible the description of a system should not only be an agreement with myself but one made collectively with others (colleagues)" (Schneider, 1992).

In essence, the theoretical foundations of biological psychiatry are now refuted. None of the arguments put forward concerning the genetic or biochemical causes of psychiatric illnesses stand up to logical or empirical examination. Peter Breggin has thoroughly investigated these lines of argument and research in biological psychiatry and comes to the following conclusion: "In the world of modern psychiatry, where assertions are made as to truth and future prospects in the light of goals already achieved, propaganda is regarded as science. Nowhere is this more apparent than in the claims psychiatry makes in relation to genetics, biology and the physical treatment of depression and mania." (Breggin, 1996). Ty Colbert outlines the following net result: "Although billions of dollars are spent on research, and although there are hundreds of biochemical theories on the question of the causes of psychological illnesses, we can now render the results of these investigations quite simply:

- Psychotropics do not correct any biochemical imbalance; they make the emotional-cognitive capacities of the human brain unusable.
- Genealogical and family studies do not provide any proof of genetic inheritance and, with correct analysis, actually indicate an environmentally/psychologically related explanation.
- Further genetic markers might be found but they are no proof of the existence of defective genes.
- Photographs of the brain have, in relation to schizophrenia, merely highlighted differences in the area of the lateral ventricles. These small differences, which are often within the range of what is regarded as normal on the scale of values related to the human brain, can easily be attributed to stress, nutritional deficiencies, medicines or other factors" (Colbert, 1999).

The discoveries of modern gene research refute, rather than confirm, the pathological concept of psychiatry. The effect of genes is not unalterable; they are situation-dependent and are engaged and disengaged by interpersonal relationships.

Digression 1: Sick genes, or relationship patterns that make you ill?

The brain as an organ is of central significance for emotional and psychological events. It is, however, not true to say that psychological illness is caused by genetic defects that manifest as disturbances in brain metabolism. There is no scientific proof whatsoever that psychological illness is inherited, as it is in the case of, for example, Huntington's chorea. So far, no one has discovered genes that cause schizophrenia, depression, pathological fear or hyperactivity. The assumption of a genetic component in the emergence of psychological illness is pure speculation resting on an out-of-date understanding of genes as a person's unchangeable basic make-up.

Modern gene research now assumes that all humans are up to 99.9% genetically identical, i.e. everybody has approximately the same 35,000 genetic building blocks. What, however, is not genetically inheritable, is genetic regulation, that is the way in which existing genes are engaged and disengaged. The so-called "transcription factor" is responsible for the decision as to whether a gene on the DNA string is read or not, the extent to which this occurs, and whether or not a protein is generated by this. These "transcriptions factors" are controlled by signals that come either from one's own body, or from the environment, and perception and experience are of central significance for the brain's gene activity. "It is the non-material signals that have the greatest influence on the regulation of genes in the brain. Interpersonal situations registered by the nerve cell systems of the five senses are continuously changed in the brain into biological signals, which in their turn have substantial effects on the action of transcription factors. This explains why emotional experiences can activate and deactivate numerous genes within a very short time. The period from activation of a gene to completion of the protein can be in the region of a few minutes" (Bauer, 2002, p. 38 ff.).

This discovery is of enormous significance to our understanding of psychological illness because it means that:

- *Our mood or psychological state is dependent on our external environment and how we perceive it.*
- *Our mood is also determined by our inner psychological world and the experiences that we have had and have stored within our body.*
- *Experiences which positively modify our perceptions, thought habits and memories, are not only healing for the mind or soul, but also for the body.*
- *Medicinal treatments can only modify the biological inner world – they modify neither patterns of experience nor memories in any lasting way.*

For us humans it is nature and the people in our environment that constitute the external dimensions of influence. Everyone understands the healing influence of good weather; however, interpersonal relationships are of even greater significance for our psychological state. We all experience how well we feel when in good company, and what a relief it is to remove ourselves from the presence of people whom we experience as psychologically stressful. That is why when people return to their original social environment, e.g. after a stay in psychiatric hospital, they will often revert to their usual negative relationship patterns. Certain relationships can actually make people ill.

Case Study 4:

Reverting to an old relationship pattern

A woman wrote to me as follows: "At 58 years of age I left home in a very serious plight. I had tried any number of medicines, had sessions with psychologists, had been hospitalised three times and I had also been to spas for cures several times, where in fact I always felt very well. Once I left home, I was quite like my old self. I felt happy with life and full of ideas and pleasure. Over a period of 5 years I pulled myself out of the 'mire' thanks to positive thinking and my own initiative and enterprise. I was able to enjoy nature and for the first time in my life, I was truly happy.

"But when I returned home, the past always caught up with me very quickly. My husband continually calls me names, and puts me in a negative light in front of the children whenever he can. ... My daughter came to visit me for the first time in 20 years. On the first day of her visit we immediately had to call the emergency doctor. My whole body went into cramps, I was freezing cold, I was limp, my entire strength drained away and I felt as bad as ever. I now feel worse than I did when I was out searching for help."

In light of the fact that the assumptions and contradictions in the theories of medical psychiatry have now been scientifically proven as arbitrary (Bentall, 2004), the search for alternative explanatory approaches must be followed. Even more so, considering the failure that confronts modern psychotropic psychiatry in its current treatment of the "psychologically ill". Considering the hopeless state to which many people with psychological problems are reduced by our current understanding and treatment of psychiatric illness, searching for better explanations and therapeutic approaches is imperative.

Case Study 5:

"... unbearable, additional torment ..."

"My sister has suffered with "schizoaffective psychosis with manic-depressive episodes", as described in her most recent diagnosis, for more than twenty years. At first she was diagnosed as having a cyclothymic disorder, then schizophrenia and since then her diagnosis has expanded to the above six words. When I was an adolescent, I already felt that her psychiatric treatment, principally medication, was an unbearable additional torment for my sister and that it was completely useless and thus pointless. For my sister, who is now almost 39 years old, periods in psychiatric institutions and on medication have resulted in no improvement whatsoever.

"For 10 years I got worked up about her treatment but finally, as do probably many patients themselves, I reconciled myself to the fact that our society knows of no better solution for psychological illness and simply follows the same path to nowhere out of pure helplessness. ... Why do people who receive a psychiatric training, certainly originally undertaken with the good intention of wanting to help the psychologically ill, not have the insight to see that their therapising completely bypasses the psychologically ill? Why do they not see that their own investment is in having their narrow view confirmed, regarding it as a kind of personal insult when their treatment methods regularly turn out to be utterly wrong?" (extract from an e-mail letter to me, dated June 2004).

An example of another letter (August 2005): "My wife (36 years of age, with 3 children) has been suffering for several months from panic attacks and anxiety states. The problem came on quite suddenly and without warning. After a ten-day stay in hospital (nothing was established as being physically wrong) my wife was transferred to the hospital's psychiatric department. My wife was discharged after eight weeks. Her discharge was at her own wish, as my wife could no longer bear being under psychiatric care. The treatment methods, as far as I can evaluate these things, left a lot to be desired. First, my wife was restrained using Tavor (4x 0.5mg) and simultaneously she was given Cipralex, which was increased to 30 mg. As neither really achieved much after 5 weeks, the Tavor was gradually reduced (in the course of which my wife suffered very pronounced withdrawal symptoms with violent shivering and vomiting). A variety of medication was then tried to counteract these symptoms (Atosil etc.). I would also like to mention that my wife does not like taking medicines one bit and that taking them was an additional strain. After my wife was home again, and with the agreement of her general practitioner, she gradually reduced the Cipralex to zero (because of continuous feelings of dizziness and impaired vision)."

In psychiatry and psychotherapy mistaken theories are by no means harmless. In the most favourable instances, they can simply result in people not being helped. However, in the worst cases they can mean that the psychologically ill are made worse. Richard Bentall, a psychology professor at Manchester University, expressed this very clearly as follows: "At the beginning of the twenty-first century, it is easy to dismiss these excesses of the past as products of more primitive times. However the abuses to which psychiatric patients were subjected in all countries in the West, reaching a crescendo in Nazi Germany, were enabled by assumptions about psychosis that are the main elements of the Kraepelinian paradigm. [Emil Kraepelin assumes that severe mental illnesses fall into discrete types such as 'schizophrenia' and 'manic depression', and that there is a clear dividing line between madness and normal functioning]. Without regarding madness as solely the product of a damaged brain, it would not have been possible to devise a therapeutic system that relied exclusively on physical treatments at the expense of treating people with warmth and humanity. Without the hypothesis that this brain damage is genetically determined, killing would not have been regarded as a rational treatment by a generation of well-trained nurses and physicians in Germany. Above all, by regarding psychosis as not understandable (to use Jasper's terminology), psychiatric patients were denied a voice, which might otherwise have been raised in protest against these horrors." (Bentall, 2004)

Freud and the Power of the Unconscious

The point of view put forward in the work of Sigmund Freud at the start of the 20th century was that unconscious emotional conflicts, not physical defects, were the real causes of "neuroses" and "psychoses". Freud made it clear that negative life experiences generate "psychological illness". Among other things, he recognised the destructive effects of sexual abuse. However, under pressure of criticism from colleagues, he dismissed his insights, and from then on looked for the causes of psychological illness more in the inner psychological processes rather than in outer events (Dulz, 2000). At the time in which Freud lived, the then male-dominated society was not ready to confront its own actions and the devastating psychological consequences for children and women, and disputed it.

Psychological and scientific research from then on has had a very pronounced focus on what happens *within ourselves* – on our abilities and strengths and what takes place within us consciously and unconsciously. Psychological illnesses are explained in terms of the individual not managing their internal psychological processes.

Thus, in an irony of fate, Sigmund Freud, the great pioneer, diverted for at least a further fifty years psychotherapists' attention away from the external causes of psychological suffering to the internal processing of those causes. As revealing as the understanding of "repression", "sublimation", "reaction formation", "transference" and "projection" might be, they are concepts in limbo insofar as the understanding of psychodynamic connections are concerned if attention to external causes is missing. Inasmuch as psychotherapy, no

19

matter what style or school, does not address the actual causes of psychological disorders in the external world of the individual, it is inevitable that psychotherapy itself will remain stuck at a halfway stage. Thus, it often reinforces the original problem, leaving patients without hope that they can ever be helped. This approach also protects the perpetrators and in the end blames the victim. This critique also applies to, for example, cognitive behavioural therapy, where, when confronted with self-destructive behaviours, the primary focus is to get the symptoms under control without addressing the question of causes, which, in my experience in most cases, relates to a history of sexual abuse of the client.

Professional Helplessness

Even in modern Western societies, it is often the experience of those suffering from serious mental illness that the help given by scientifically and well-trained specialists is unsatisfactory. Psychotropic drugs might bring mild relief in the short term, but taken over the longer term they become increasingly less effective, generating addiction and generally causing more harm than good. Achieving psychological stability by means of chemical anaesthetisation of feelings cannot be the best wisdom. If the removal of anxiety and confusion means the removal of feelings, then the zest for life is also gone.

Even conventional psychotherapy, which can last for years, often may only extend to improving the client's ability to manage the symptoms of suffering. The fear, depression, inner emotional chaos or schizophrenia often does not go.

It is often the case that instead of recognising that current science is still not in a position to adequately explain psychological disorders well enough to lead to effective therapeutic methods, psychologically ill patients themselves often get blamed. Patients are accused of not accepting the diagnoses that are made, or are accused of not being prepared to go through with the proposed therapeutic measures – in short, they are accused of refusing to be healthy. Instead of helping emotionally damaged people to understand themselves better, things are often reduced to power games between therapist and patient, whereby the patient in the final analysis draws the short straw.

Case Study 6:

"therapies, therapies, therapies"

"For over twenty years my life was determined by appointments with doctors and therapists. Looking back, just the time involved was a nightmare. It is particularly discouraging to anyone having to re-organise his or her life because of depression. A brief summary of my therapies: bad, incompetent diagnoses, always new concept-less treatment attempts using medicines and talking therapies – finally, wrong, time-consuming treatments without any previously determined content or time framework" (Reimer, 2002).

Admittedly, we still do not know the true causes of many psychological disorders, above all the more severe forms of psychological disorder, but it seems to me that there is an initial major step we can take towards moving out of this unsatisfactory situation. We must dare to question the old explanations radically, and be on the look out for new theories. Why should psychological illness be different from any other phenomena? In my view we can only see and understand the development of psychological illness, and be able to exercise systematic influence on these apparently very multi-layered psychological processes when we have:

- recognised the real *causes*,
- understood the beneficial, as well as the obstructive, *conditions* that establish the illness,
- learnt to clearly differentiate between *causes* and *conditions,* and
- separated *causes* from *consequences,*

21

Anything else is simplistic. "Common sense" and "wanting to help" are as insufficient as theories are, masking essential realities and diverting attention to psychological phenomena rather than helping to promote clarity.

The fundamental difficulty is always that those who want to understand the emotions and experiences of others have their own emotions and experiences. In order to fully understand the enigma of others' psyches, we have to be aware of our own, including our shadow side. There is a considerable danger that in the assessment of another, our own cultural imprints, prejudices, blind spots and invested attitudes (ideologies) influence us. On a mental and emotional level there is so much that is unconscious that none of us can really be free of the danger of being blind to that to which our own unconscious is blind.

In my opinion we as doctors, psychologists, psychotherapists and social workers in the actual situation do not need endless new methods or remedies, or structural reforms in methods of dealing with patients and clients. What is needed are fundamental insights and a much deeper understanding into how serious psychological disorders develop, and why individuals often can no longer manage their psychological processes themselves – why individuals become victims and why they also become perpetrators. It is only then that treatment, relief from or healing of psychological disorders will be significantly more effective than it currently is. It is only from appropriate theories which understand the causes of symptoms that helpful practice will follow.

2

Multigenerational Systemic Psychotraumatology (MSP)

2.1 Basic Assumptions for Multigenerational Systemic Psychotraumatology (MSP)

With this book I am attempting to make my contribution to a better understanding of disorders. In doing so, I am including research in which I am engaged into the causes of psychological wounding, my theoretical argument, and my practical and therapeutic experience over the last ten years. I am extending the work I began with the book *Verwirrte Seelen* (*Confused Souls*, Ruppert, 2002).

There are two theoretical building blocks and one practical method for accessing confused systems that have proved to be exceptionally useful in my experience for understanding the mysteries of psychological and emotional disorders. These are:

1. the concept and theory of bonding,
2. trauma theory, and
3. the methodology of constellations work.

1) John Bowlby (1907–1990), the English psychiatrist, was persistent in pointing out the profound significance of bonding (attachment) for our emotional health and his work has borne fruit in professional circles (Bowlby, 1973, 1995, 1998, 2006). Bowlby's theory on the existence of a psychological bonding

system and its far-reaching consequences for human experience and human behaviour is gaining more and more acceptance worldwide. It is resoundingly confirmed in numerous examples of scientific research. (Brisch, 1999, Grossmann and Grossmann, 2004, Brisch and Hellbrügge, 2006, 2007).

2) In my opinion, perhaps for the first time in the history of man, the concept of trauma provides a scientifically based, theoretical framework that clarifies and renders comprehensible which particular events injure a person's mind, maybe even destroying it. (Fischer and Riedesser, 1999; van der Kolk, McFarlane and Weisaeth, 2000; Huber, 2003 a and b; Herman, 2003).

Whilst traditional approaches see the symptom itself as the problem, current trauma theory enables a radical change in perspective: the symptom is seen as a necessary protective mechanism for overcoming a traumatic experience. That is why we cannot simply erase symptoms through therapy. We have to understand their actual function: the symptom as an expression of the fact that feelings are stymied in order to prevent the re-traumatisation of the individual. So it is only when the true causes are understood and therapeutically processed that the symptom can come to rest or transform into another healthier psychological structure.

3) For me it was vital, for an improved understanding of the symptoms of psychological injuries, to see them on the one hand as being symptoms of bonding disorders and, on the other, as the consequences of traumatisation. A decisive step forward for me was linking these two concepts together. Further insights into the causes of emotional and psychological problems can then be gained by considering the possibility of the transmission of the consequences of traumatisation via the emotional bonding process. The riddle as to why individuals who have not had traumatic experiences themselves still display the associated symptoms (e.g. extreme fear, panic states, deep depression or confusion) then becomes soluble.

2.2 Bonding and Trauma: Three Principles

Working with the methodology of family constellations (see Part II) enabled me to clearly identify the connection between bonding and trauma. In the light of an understanding of bonding theory, the methodology of constellations reveals, with the help of representatives who play out relationships within the family, the unconscious but active bonds between individuals. The method also reveals that some bonds are extremely tangled, and that entire families can be living in an emotional turmoil of symbiotic needs and aggressive attempts at boundary-making. Serious forms of bonding disorder follow from an inability to integrate certain events within family systems – events that can therefore never come to a place of emotional resolution. Bert Hellinger, the founder of the method of family constellations (Hellinger, 1994), pointed to important issues in bonding relations, but did not develop any systematic classification of the type of event that can deeply shatter a family bonding system. However in his work he grasps intuitively from case to case which events are significant in their ongoing effect on a family over generations. In the light of trauma theory however, it is immediately apparent that these events are traumatic ones, for example parents who die early, children given away for adoption, sexual abuse, etc. Such events disrupt relationships between family members so painfully that they generate psychological turmoil in every individual family member.

Combining the theory of bonding with the theory of trauma means that we can formulate a general principle as follows:

A mother who has suffered trauma will inevitably pass her traumatic experience on to her child in some form.

Thus a traumatic experience *always* has some effect over several generations. Fathers, and the trauma they might carry, are also involved in the trans-generational transmission process. They also pass on their trauma to their children in a slightly different way from the mother.

25

First Principle of MSP:
For me, the recognition stated above contributes to the *first principle* of a model for Multigenerational Systemic Psycho-traumatology (MSP):

Traumatic experiences are handed down to the next generation via the emotional bonding process.

A Systemic View
Before working with constellations, it had already become clear to me that the isolated observation of psychological problems (when one looks only at the individual concerned) is inadequate. Psychological systems are created within relationship systems, and the latter's complex dynamics are expressed through communication and interaction. Working with constellations brings the far-reaching effects of bonding in early childhood into focus, showing how early bonding patterns are replicated in all further relationships that an individual has. A child who bonds with parents who hold unresolved trauma becomes entangled in that unresolved trauma, and will repeat

Traumatic experience in generation 1

Bonding disorder in generation 2,
Increasing the high risk of more
trauma experiences

Bonding disorder in generation 3,
with very high risk of trauma
experiences

Fig. 1: Multigenerational sequence: trauma – bonding disorder –
trauma

the entangled relationship pattern in all their subsequent relationships, thereby perpetuating the entanglement. These patterns of entanglement may continue over generations, carrying the hidden danger of generating renewed traumatisation in subsequent generations. The experience of trauma can create such serious bonding disturbances in turn increasing the likelihood of an individual suffering traumatic experiences, and subjecting others to trauma.

Case Study 7:

When will it stop?

M. is a young woman with punk hair, punk leathers and a pierced nose. She is unstable, feels herself unloved and has a very poor relationship with her mother. Many years before, an acquaintance raped her repeatedly. Now she is pregnant by a man who, among other things, deals in drugs. Ms. M.'s mother, as a small child, was sexually abused by her father and her mother's mother was also repeatedly raped during the Second World War. What are the chances of M.'s own child developing a healthy and secure bonding to their father and mother? Will the child get through life without traumatic experience? Might the child become a perpetrator, particularly if it is a boy, another victim of sexual abuse if it is a girl? What might prevent this happening?

Second Principle of MSP: The second principle of Multigenerational Systemic Psychotraumatology states that:

The human psyche is a multigenerational phenomenon.

According to this principle a person's physical, emotional and psychological problems are very often the consequence of entanglements in bonding relationships that stretch back over three or four generations. Thus, symptoms of mental illness can only really be understood and resolved if we take into consideration the system of entangled relationships from which

27

the patient must release himself in order to heal himself. Thus, the diagnosis of mental disorders inevitably has to include a diagnosis of the patient's family system over multiple generations. Otherwise it is totally incomplete and misleading! A genogram should be included in every diagnostic process.

Seeing the human psyche in a trans-generational context had a prominent forerunner in Carl Gustav Jung, and the idea is currently being developed by different theoreticians and practising psychotherapists independently of one another.

Digression 2: Other views on multigenerational perspectives

The multigenerational perspective is not new in psychotherapy. In the light of Freud's attempt to explain the origins of the human psyche and its symbolic expression in "Totem and Taboo", one might even cite him as one of the originators of a transgenerational perspective. "An event like the killing of the original father by his sons would have to have left ineradicable traces in the history of mankind, and generated ever more substitute forms the less it was to be recalled" (Freud, 1972).

Carl G. Jung formulated the theory of a collective unconscious that imprints archetypes in the individual psyche (Jung, 1979). In his idea the collective wisdom of humankind is transferred in symbols, emotional states and types of male and female attitudes from one generation to the other.

Further approaches are to be found in the work of Ivan Boszormenyi-Nagy (Boszormenyi-Nagy and Spark, 1973) and Anne Ancelin Schützenberger (1993). Boszormenyi-Nagy (a family therapist) emphasised, amongst other things, the existence of a deep sense of a balancing of give and take within a family over the generations (ibid), and Anne Ancelin Schützenberger concerned herself in particular with the hidden and secret areas of family genealogies, people lost and missing. She uncovered events in families, the effects of which proved to be problematic over many generations, as if they were unconscious inheritances (ibid.).

Furthermore, consideration should also be given to the work of Nicolas Abraham and Maria Torok (1994), Serge Tisseron (2001) and Elisabeth Troje. In an essay by the psychoanalyst Elisabeth Troje, we find her thinking about placing psychoses in the context of the traumatic experiences of earlier generations: "There have apparently been traumata in the life of the mother or the life of the father, secrets that the family keeps, which the family preserves, the injustice of which causes the family to feel ashamed, originating in the parental generation, or that of the grandparents" (Troje, 2000).

In connection with their contributions to a multigenerational perspective, reference should also be made to Leopold Szondi, Horst Eberhard Richter and Helm Stierlin (von Bülow 2004). I will expand later on the exceptionally significant insights of the psychoanalyst Christa Schmidt (Schmidt, 2004, case study 18, p. 103). Trauma researchers also increasingly converge in seeing traumatic psychological injury not as a phenomenon that concerns only the individual, but as one that generates process patterns that continue to have an effect over generations (St. Just, 2005).

Third Principle of MSP:

The healing of psychological injuries must be sought through maintaining sight of the entire trauma-disturbed bonding network in which the individual is entangled.

It is insufficient in psychotherapy to guide the client to an isolated solution for herself alone. She can only really release herself from the entanglements within her soul (as the internal emotional and psychological matrix of relationships) when she knows that all those with whom she is bonded in love and in trauma can best help themselves and she is neither able nor responsible for their healing.

Above all it is when the natural love of the parents for their children, no longer spoiled and confounded by the effects of traumatic experiences, can flow within the client, and can be experienced by her that a sense of peace returns. In the soul of a child this process of longing for their parents' love must come to a satisfying end without falling into extremes of illusion or despair.

Psyche and Soul: a Differentiation and Definition

The multigenerational point of view prompts me to differentiate and explain the terms "psyche" and "soul". I connect the term "psyche" with the notion of various processes that flow within an individual: perception, feeling, imagining, thinking, remembering including the sensorimotor control of our activities. I use the word "soul" if it concerns processes *that occur between people and that are generated when individuals are in contact with one other*. There is a sentence in Boris Pasternak's *Dr. Zhivago* that expresses precisely what I mean: "The person in other people that is the actual soul of the person." In other words I hold the other in me and he is a part of me. In this sense we are not really individuals but always part of a human community at the deepest level of our psychological existence. My concept is that the soul has its origin in the interconnectedness between those people who are descended from each other. The soul, however, also goes beyond kinship and connects people who share common feelings, ideas and activities.

Processes in Theory and Practice

The present book is the result of an empirically supported process of developing theory. For me constellations work with patients, both individually and in groups, always yields fresh insights into the psychological structures and processes of the soul, while at the same time raising new, unanswered questions. These questions lead to a search for further theoretical understanding, and in turn this often leads to corresponding discoveries discussed in the available specialist subject literature. It is reflexive learning and theory making. This means that new possibilities emerge for refining the work done in constellations and introducing new elements. The practice is therefore theory-led and theory formation is directly oriented to the problems that arise in practice. Formulating this in terms of scientific theory means that inductive and deductive paths of forming theory complement one another. An individual case shows general patterns, and from general insights that have been gained prognoses for the individual case become possible (cf. Chalmers, 1999).

The methodology of Constellations seen in this way, as far as my work is concerned, performs the function of scientific experiments, which can confirm or contradict hypotheses. The usefulness for practice in this approach lies in the fact that patients and clients participate in the development of method and theory, which can be corrected at short notice if success in treatment and interventions is not forthcoming. It is only the constant challenges resulting from practical work that make vagueness in theory clear and force continuous revision.

In the next chapters, I initially present the theoretical contexts (bonding and trauma) and then the method (constellations), through which I make most of my discoveries. Use of a method can in my opinion only be sensibly discussed on the basis of the theoretical considerations which underlie it.

3

Psychological and Emotional Bonding

3.1 Bonding Relationships as the Basis of Human Existence

Humans live in groups and it is in groups that we survive, flourish or perish. We are born into a group of people, our family and relatives, and in that group we grow up. We become specialists, through our body, soul and senses, in maintaining and configuring our lives within human groups.

Our life begins through the unification of a male sperm cell and a female egg cell, and so life is passed on to us. For us the origins of sperm and egg are our mother and our father, our parents, embodying the roots of our unique identity. Normally we grow for nine months within our mother's belly, and then we come into the world naked and bare, in extreme need of protection and help. Without intense nurturing, provision of food and warmth, without the extensive protectiveness of our mothers, we would quickly die of hunger or cold, or be at the mercy of our environment in some other way. In turn, without the support of her man or her community our mother would quickly become enfeebled, overtaxed and helpless.

The better things are for the mother, the better things will be for the child. The mother is also better off the more love she herself received as a child, and the more support she experiences from the community in which she lives, from all the men and from all the women. Psychological foundation stones are laid in these basic conditions of human existence.

The reverse is equally true: that from the start anything that causes stress to or is missing for the mother, to the same extent causes stress to and is missing for the child. If the mother receives no support from her partner, from her mother or from other relatives, she is more subject to pressure and stress. If in addition she experiences contempt and violence at the hands of others, the effect of this will invariably be transferred to her child. So nearly every psychological problem starts in the early developmental mother-child relationship.

Babies depend completely on their mothers, on their love and care from the moment of birth. They also depend on the communities of people into which they are born. In respect of the foundations of the emotional development of a person, the modern world has not changed very much. The newborn child has to orient herself to her mother using all her strength and all her senses. Her mother is the source of her physical, emotional and psychological development. She is the most important person for the child. Mother and child, from the moment of procreation are an emotionally and psychologically interwoven unit. An easy ability in adapting positively to mother-child relationships is an innate part of our nature. In cases of successful mother-child bonding, the chances of the child's emotional and psychological development being positive are high. In cases of unsuccessful bonding, this becomes more precarious and can lead to serious psychological and emotional problems.

Attachment Theory

It was about 50 years after Freud that the English psychiatrist and psychotherapist, John Bowlby (1907–1990), was able to move scientific attention to the phenomenon of bonding (attachment), and consequently to what happens not only *within* but *between people*. Bowlby first made his name through a study of 44 thieves. This study seemed to support

33

the claim that maternal deprivation in early childhood could lead to very severe problems in social and emotional adjustment later in life.

After the Second World War, he was commissioned by the World Health Organisation (WHO) to research the psychological health of homeless children. In this study, he combined his knowledge of the bonding need in childhood with some striking features of the psychology of children who had not had any secure bonding to a primary person (Holmes, 2002).

Bowlby's realisations can be summed up in the statement: bonding patterns are established primarily to the mother from birth onwards. Emotional bonding to the mother by the child is necessary for survival. Spitz and Wolf (1946) recognised that newly born children waste away and even die without loving contact with a primary person, and that this happens despite sufficient provision of food and personal care.

Bonding is a universal principle of nature. Living creatures that survive together are drawn to one another through bonding forces. There are different ways in which bonding can come about:

- by immediate contact, e.g. skin and body contact,
- by sensory perception, e.g. smell, taste, sight, hearing,
- by emotions, e.g. love or fear,
- by thoughts and memories,
- by speech.

Different types of animals, perhaps also different types of plants, will use different bonding channels. Bonding develops in a mutual process of adaptation, each of the participants in the bonding process leaving a lasting impression on the other, the resulting combination of the bonding then making both into one larger living entity, a bonded unit.

Animals that reproduce via two sexes and rear the subsequent offspring by caring for them, develop specific bonding relationships between the parent generation and the offspring generation. Mammals that live in social groupings, e.g. in packs like dogs, or herds like cows, show particularly pronounced bonding behaviour. The more highly developed the care of the offspring and the social behaviour of a species, the more similar it becomes to that which we observe in ourselves. This is why animals can bond to humans and humans to animals. For animals, humans function as substitute parents or pack leaders. For many people, animals are substitute parents, children, siblings or friends. Deep bonds can develop between humans and animals, and therefore entangled bonding relations are also possible between humans and animals (Rüggeberg and Rüggeberg, 2003).

Qualities of Human Bonding

The maternal bond is the primary form of bonding for humans. The child registers the fact that the mother is present most clearly through direct physical contact, registering her particular smell and the specific taste of her milk. Eye-to-eye contact is also of fundamental significance for the confirmation of the bond. Hearing the mother's voice and understanding her words consolidate this mutual familiarisation process. It is via the mother that the child experiences herself – I am here, I have a body, I have needs and feelings. Bonding to the mother is the foundation of psychological patterning for every human being. Conversely, this means that, if this original bonding is missing or is seriously disrupted, then the psychological and emotional foundations of an individual are exceptionally unstable and subject to disturbance. The child has no orientation and no security about herself.

Interpersonal bonding is highly emotional. It is not just a question of whether the other person is there, but *how* she is there, whether she is there with her feelings, above all, her love. Human emotions – fear, love, anger, grief, pain, shame and guilt – have their origins in the bonding process and the exchange of feelings is an essential component of the process of bonding. Feelings that people share with one another inform the way in which they react to one another and become

35

emotionally and psychologically dependent on one another. What one person feels is also significant to the other; individuals who are emotionally bonded can easily empathise with each other.

Thoughts also influence the bonding process, but in individual development they become important much later and not before the age of two. Later in life a majority of our thoughts centre on the ties that we have to our parents, children, partners, friends and work colleagues. People who are very closely connected exchange their thoughts together. This can even stretch to reciprocal telepathy.

In extreme cases of lack of emotional quality in the relationship of a mother to her child, the child can feel like a machine.

Case Study 8:

Like a machine

Mrs B. comes to a constellation seminar because of her psychotic daughter. She is willing to understand and explore what she might have to do with her daughter's psychosis. As in many cases of psychosis I have worked with, in this case the roots of the problem lay in denied sexual violence and loveless parent-child relationships stretching over some generations.

In a constellation, the representative for Mrs B.'s daughter was placed a long way away from her mother. She reacts like an automaton to everything her mother's representative says and does. "Machine now switching on, machine sees, machine now thinks ..." is an example of the representative's commentary. It is only when a true feeling flows backward and forward between the daughter's representative and her mother that she feels released from this insane condition in the constellation and feels human.

Pre-natal Bonding and the Sensitive Phase immediately after Birth

Beyond the theories of John Bowlby it is assumed now that bonding develops between mother and child even before birth. The child reacts sensitively to the mother's movements, contacts, moods, heart sounds and speech melody. She notices her mother's joys and sorrows. She tunes into the relationship during pregnancy (Janus, 1997, Hüther and Krens, 2005). In the case of twins or multiple babies there is a good case for assuming that the children even develop mutual bonding through their close contact to one another before birth.

The process of giving birth is an act of opening of the mother's body. A woman can best open her body, when she opens her feelings for her child. When the mother is anxious, or in extreme cases, when she does not want the baby at all, then her body physically locks, and delivery can become a long and painful experience. All violations of a woman's sexuality by rape or sexual misuse heavily disturb the natural instincts during delivery and thus disturb the bonding process.

Immediately after birth, the bonding process between child and mother is supplemented and reinforced via external sensory communication. The child recognises her mother's unique smell and feels her skin. She learns to differentiate her mother's face from other faces. She is happy when she sees her mother's face and feels seen by her mother's eyes. Finally, the mother-child bond is consolidated through physical handling and different forms of verbal and non-verbal interaction, which give this bonding its own unique quality. The mother is in her uniqueness irreplaceable for the child, just as the child is irreplaceable for the mother (Zimmer, 1998). The mother and child together form a psychological and emotional dyad in which they are mutually oriented and interwoven.

Unfavourable circumstances for building up a secure and supportive bond between mother and child include premature birth, use of incubators, presence of machinery and equipment, medicines, narcosis, early separation of the newborn from the mother, minimal physical contact between mother and baby and abstention from breastfeeding. If the experience of the birth is marked by fear and pain for the mother and child, there is a danger that the distressed anxious baby will later feel insecure and alone despite the mother's intense caring. The formative impression of his very first relationship can be that of an unanswered need for proximity and security, and this may later be transferred to all his subsequent relationships.

Research by Klaus and Kennel (1987) and Daniel Stern (1991) clearly indicates the importance of direct bodily contact as well as eye contact between mother and newborn child. Skin to skin contact in the sensitive phase immediately after the birth, and sucking at the mother's breast will stimulate important vital functions in the child's body and help to make the child feel unafraid.

From birth, every baby reacts to facial expressions, imitating them, reacting strongly to a laughing, crying or angry face. Eyes for the child are the windows to the mother's soul and the main dialogue between mother and child happens in the play of facial expressions and the dance of eyes.

If a child repeatedly looks into a mother's eyes that are dead or empty, he is subject to distress, and, over time, becomes vulnerable to desperation and hopelessness. Mothers who feed their child with an expressionless face are likely to cause panic to the child. In experiments in which mothers wore face-masks and remained silent while feeding, the babies drank less of their mothers' milk and even, after some days, behaved in a disturbed manner.

Bonding Need and Bonding Ability

An individual's ability to bond and their essential need for bonding lead to particular bonding behaviour fostering a reciprocal bonding and then maintaining it. Bonding behaviour is activated when the distance between persons bonded to one another becomes too much, if notice is given of separation, or if there is a danger that one person loses the other.

Complementary to the bonding need of the child, which is basic and necessary for the child's survival, is the bonding ability of the parents. In bonding or attachment research the ability of parents, and in particular the ability of mothers, to create secure bonding to the child is described as "sensitivity". According to Mary Ainsworth, a sensitive mother is in a position to:

- perceive the child's signals attentively and immediately,
- interpret correctly the signals from the baby's perspective, and know whether, for example, the crying means hunger, feeling unwell, pain or boredom,
- react appropriately to the child's signals, and
- do so within a tolerable period of frustration for the child.

To summarise, psychological damage results if mothers are urged not to turn to face their children, remain inflexible, leave them to cry and unrelentingly ignore their feelings (Harrer, 1940). It is no accident that this was among the many crimes committed by National Socialism in Germany in the early part of the last century (Chamberlain, 1996), as Hitler himself had a severe bonding disorder because of his mother's inability to respond due to her own unresolved trauma. Hitler's subsequent ideology could only find fertile ground with other similarly bonding-disordered people.

Mothers should be encouraged and supported to handle their newborn child in the initial highly sensitive and formative phases as lovingly as possible. It is children who cannot access a mother's love who may become tyrants and may never truly be independent. Karl-Heinz Brisch assumes, in the light of his research, that the sensitivity needed by mothers in dealing with their children is something that can be taught and enhanced (Brisch, 1999). This would have a great impact on the prevention of future emotional disturbances for the child. Since the sensitive, empathic mother is the mirror for the child as he gradually develops a growing awareness of himself, if she is too preoccupied with her own needs and state of being, she will lack, or only partially develop, this sensitivity towards her child. In this case, she is likely to project her own needs onto the child rather than recognising the child's needs; for example she may stimulate the child too much or too little, feed him too much or too little, hold him tight for too long or leave him alone too long. She may either set the child excessively rigid boundaries or no boundaries at all. The child then is likely to develop a distorted perception of his needs and existence, and will be unable to develop his independence, instead becoming a replica of his mother's damaged or confused narcissistic personality. He will be unable to free himself from his symbiotic entanglement with his mother, and his process of individuation will be threatened. Later in his life, the child will repeat this bonding pattern in his relationships with others.

Therefore, it is my conviction gained from my therapeutic experience with many clients that the roots of psychological problems are primarily bonding disorders between mother and child. Bonding disorders between father and child are mostly subsidiary.

The Case for a 'Bonding-Sense Faculty'

The ability to receive bonding-relevant data and the ability to transmit bonding-relevant data to others probably involves a unique bonding sense faculty, which all humans must have, and which has yet to be researched. It is presumably independent of our other recognized senses. In my opinion, what supports this idea is the fact that, mothers and children react to one another even if they cannot see, hear, physically feel or smell each other. Many mothers report, for example, that they have sensed when something has happened to their child, even when the child was far away. Rupert Sheldrake, the English biochemist and philosopher of science, has collected records of many such experiences, all of which point to a telepathic transmission of feelings, moods, and images; the genuineness of these reports has been checked and confirmed using scientific methods (Sheldrake, 2003). Phenomena observed in constellations, in my opinion, also support the case for a very pronounced intrinsic bonding sense in humans. It is not uncommon for mothers to tell me that after a successful psychotherapeutic treatment their children sought contact with them again, even when this contact had been interrupted for many years.

In addition, I see a confirmation for this thesis of the existence of an intrinsic human bonding sense faculty in the discovery of mirror neurones. In my first book on the methodology of constellations, I assumed that constellations worked because we, as humans, have our own apperceptive sense for bonding and relating (Ruppert, 2001). Representatives in constellations do not think themselves into their roles analytically, they immediately and directly perceive and experience the psychological and physiological conditions of the person they are representing (ibid). Since then, I think this has been confirmed by the revolutionary discovery of "mirror neurones" in brain research by the Italian physiologist Giacomo Rizzolatti (Rizzolatti, Fadiga, Fogassi and Gallese, 2002). Rizzolatti discovered, initially in animal experiments and subsequently in experiments with humans, the existence of specific nerve cells, which always fire within a person when they perform a specific action. However, he discovered that these nerve cells also fire in an *observer* of a person performing an action. The nerve cells in the observer mirror the environment and fire like the brain of the acting person. Once these particular nerve cells had been found, brain researchers discovered this principle of mirroring in other areas of the brain connected with other significant psychological functions. "There are networks of the pre-motoric system which serve action planning, and networks of bodily sensation which make use of our senses so that we know how an action feels or would feel for another person. The latter networks function in conjunction with the emotional centre of the brain. There are mirror nerve cells here, which, like a kind of simulator, activate in us what initially were only the emotions and feelings of the other. Resonance triggered by mirror nerve cells means that if we can feel in ourselves the intended actions, sensations and feelings of another, we gain a spontaneous and intuitive understanding of what motivates the other. The resonance pattern, of summoning up within ourselves what is physically and psychologically close to us, becomes a fixed installation within a short time. There is then a dynamic inner configuration of the other, composed of their living qualities – their conceptions, sensations, physical feelings, longings and emotions. To have available such an inner representation of a person who is standing close to us is something like having the other person inside us" (Bauer, 2005).

Reactions to Separation

That the phenomenon of bonding actually exists is seen most clearly when the bonding process is interrupted or comes to a standstill. As long as we feel involved and integrated, we take the phenomenon of bonding as a matter of course. It is only when the bond is lost that we realise whom and what we miss. Within seconds, we feel an acute inner turmoil.

In small children separation immediately results in a stressful situation, and in fears of being abandoned. If the mother moves out of sight, the child immediately starts to become restless, crying and protesting. This behaviour normally triggers in the mother the impulse to return to the child. Having the mother in sight, or having bodily contact or hearing her voice pacifies the child's fearful feelings. Most mothers are also anxious and disturbed if they are separated from their dependent children.

Thus, what children most want to avoid is a long separation from their mother. Separation causes extreme emotional distress to the child, causing the child to go through different emotional stages. These emotional stages in children separated from their mothers were observed by John Bowlby (1998) as almost always occurring in the following sequence:

- **Fear and panic:** fear is the child's first reaction to separation and the imminent threat of the loss of bonding to the mother, which is why he screams and cries in the hope that he will get her back again. A child that is left alone experiences a profound fear, a mortal fear. If you recall that in the wild young animals will die without their mother's protection, it is obvious that this feeling of fear is rooted in an experience of extreme threat to existence.

- **Rage and fury:** the child's second reaction to separation from the mother is a protest at being left alone in the form of rage and fury, and this provides a further demand that the mother return. If the mother does not come back, this protest is in vain, and it stops after a while.

- **Despair and apathy:** the third phase is characterised by the child being utterly exhausted by his previous efforts to re-establish contact with his mother. He then whimpers and moans, until he finally withdraws into himself in pain about the separation. He subsequently reacts less and less to his environment and at this stage, there is a great danger that the will to live in the child dies, and the child enters a state of extreme depression.

This stage of emotional despair and withdrawal is mostly followed by somatisation of the emotional and psychological pain in the body. Emotional pain becomes physical pain, expressed in physical tension, cramps and, in time, in chronic illness (e.g. constrictions in the chest, ongoing headaches or back pain). The origins of the emotional pain are no longer accessible to the conscious awareness, and if help are sought from a doctor or physiotherapist, the most that can be expected is short-term relief for those types of pain.

Case Study 9:

Tense and cramped

Mr K. (30 years of age) takes part in a constellations seminar. Despite numerous courses of medical treatment, he has such massive tension in his back that he can hardly walk or sit straight. He chooses and sets up a representative for himself who increasingly assumes Mr K.'s tensed and cramped posture. The representative twists himself into a hunched over position with his head bent back at an angle, staring straight up, and says he sees bars in front of his eyes.

Mr K. relates that the background to this is that after his birth his mother put him into a home. When he was three years old, he returned to his mother. The back tension mirrored the traumatic experiences of the child, who, deserted by his mother, lay in his cot in the home staring apathetically at the bars of the cot. Any negative relationship experiences re-activate these memories in Mr K. and lead to his ongoing physical tensions.

Bonding Patterns

Mary Ainsworth was a colleague of John Bowlby and made her name in attachment research with her experiment "The Strange Situation". This classic experiment investigates the manner and quality of attachment behaviour. The experiment was staged as follows:

1. A mother and child are introduced to a laboratory play-room where there are interesting toys. The mother encourages the child to play and sits on a chair in a corner of the room.
2. A stranger to the child enters the room. She sits for one minute on a chair in another corner of the room. She then makes contact with the mother for one minute and converses with her.

3. The stranger then plays with the child for one minute.
4. The mother now gets up and leaves the room.
5. The stranger comforts the child in a manner appropriate to the child's distress and tries to encourage the child to play again.
6. After three minutes, the mother returns and the stranger unobtrusively leaves. The mother is again available for the child.
7. The mother leaves the room once more and the stranger returns.
8. The mother returns and the stranger leaves.
9. The mother leaves and comes back after 20 seconds.

In this experiment, there are two variables:

• presence or absence of the mother,
• presence or absence of the stranger.

The following features of the child's behaviour are observed:

• his play behaviour and his exploratory behaviour,
• his reactions to his separation from his mother,
• his reactions to being comforted and distracted by the stranger,
• his reaction when the mother returns, and
• his non-verbal expression of stress.

So how does a child behave when separated from his mother? Is he reduced to confusion and panic or does he remain calm? Does he allow himself to be comforted and distracted by the stranger? How does he react when the mother returns – is he happy, calm or rejecting?

Based on her experiments Mary Ainsworth (1973) differentiates three types of attachment:

• **Children with secure attachment:** these children seek proximity to their mother during or after a stressful situation, e.g. when she leaves and when she returns. They exhibit grief if they are left alone, which is clearly related to missing the mother. Strangers are not able to comfort them. They greet the mother upon her return and seek close physical contact and comfort. They resist being put down by their mother.

- **Children with insecure-ambivalent attachment:** these children also seek and maintain contact to the mother; however, they resist attempts at contact and interaction by the mother. They cry vehemently and are furious when they are left alone with the stranger, and when the mother returns. In the pain of separation, they cannot differentiate between the desire to go to the mother or to stay away from the mother. They are disappointed in her because they have been abandoned and they want to protect themselves from more disappointment. Therefore, they vacillate in their conflict of deciding between disappointment and the wish to be comforted.

- **Children with insecure-avoidant attachment:** when the mother returns, these children noticeably avoid proximity with her and resist her offers of contact by turning away, looking away or moving from her. They do not cling when picked up nor resist being put down. They do not show grief at having been left, if anything they show displeasure at being alone. Mother and stranger are treated in almost the same way. These children have decided to withdraw, as if the child has no expectation of getting anything positive from his mother. He cuts himself off from his painful feelings of fear, anger or grief.

Research has shown that 50–60% of children demonstrate secure-attachment behaviour, 30–40% are insecure-ambivalent and 10–20% insecure-avoidant (Brisch, 1999).

The scientific work of Mary Main and Erik Hesse resulted in the above three attachment categories being supplemented by another, namely "disorganised attachment", as opposed to secure and organised attachment. Children with disorganised-attachment patterns, when in separating and reuniting situations "run toward the mother, remain standing halfway, turn around and run away from the mother increasing the distance from her. In addition, they may stiffen in the middle of a movement sequence ('freezing'). Apart from that, stereotypical movement and behaviour patterns were to be observed" (Brisch, quoting Main and Hesse). Mary Main and Erik Hesse place disorganised-attachment behaviour in the context of a child's having suffered a traumatic loss or in circumstances where the child is being traumatised by the parents (e.g. by physical violence or sexual abuse).

Further research into child attachment behaviour has yielded a multiplicity of interesting results (Brisch, Grossmann, Grossmann and Köhler, 2002):

- The classification of children under the headings "secure", "ambivalent-insecure" and "insecure-avoidant" attachment can be clearly established at the age of 6–12 months. The classification is also applicable to 2–4 year olds – they simply express their attachment behaviour differently. They cry less, when they are left alone and they seek contact less through physical proximity and more by speech.
- Children under 1 year experience longer separation from their mother much more acutely than 2 year olds.
- In the case of children who switched from secure to insecure attachment during the second year of life, stress in the family could be identified as the cause.
- The classification of attachment patterns can also be applied to the father-child bonding (attachment). Children develop different attachments to mother and father.
- Secure-attachment children show positive development intellectually and socially (e.g. they are more cooperative); attachment-ambivalent children show slower intellectual development, and attachment-insecure children develop disorders in their social behaviour.

- The child's increasing independence is related to his attachment experience. The attachment-secure child risks going further from his mother when exploring objects and making contact with other people than an attachment-insecure child does.
- The mother's mere absence, e.g. as a result of working away from home, is not in itself decisive of the quality of the attachment.
- Children who are cared for by other people, for example, half the day spent with a child minder, form their attachment primarily to their mother. In the case of children in group care (e.g. in a kibbutz) findings revealed more ambivalent-insecure children than in family care.

Bonding Patterns and Relationship Styles

One of Bowlby's central theories is that a child's relationship to her mother and father in the first years of life are of crucial significance throughout the rest of her life. Parents are and remain the most important people for the child, to whom she can and must orient herself. According to Bowlby, a child develops an "internal working model for relationships" based on her experiences with her mother and father. In later life, she transfers these experiences onto other people (Bowlby, 1995). Positive experiences lead to positive expectations and corresponding behaviour in later relationships. Negative relationship experiences lead to negative expectations of other people. Studies of children's development support the idea of the parent-child-attachment pattern's durability in the child's relationships to people other than their parents (Bretherton, 2002).

Bonding and Belonging

Bonding creates a sense of belonging and identity; without our emotional experiences, which stem from bonding, we do not really contact other people and we remain indifferent to our fellow human beings. In most societies it is through paternal bonding that the child understands and takes her place within the family structure, and, depending on how the family is integrated within the wider community, the child also finds her place in that community. Only when a child feels a sense of belonging, does she recognise the rules and laws of her given society, and then develops a conscience as to what she may and may not do in that society. In order to belong, the child will necessarily adapt to society and attempt to become a useful member of that society; she is ready to make herself useful in society because society is useful to her.

The sense of belonging can be destabilised, for example by migration and emigration, which affects both parents and children. When parents lose their familiar social structure, they have to put energy into asserting themselves in the new environment, and the children are also subject to this stress of finding their place in the new community. Refugee or economic migrant families suffer from being outsiders. Thus their children also feel like outsiders.

For children, adoption can mean the loss of the sense of belonging; they lose their family of origin and, in the case of adoption from abroad, their country of origin. They lack a basic security, which can be expressed as follows: "I belong to my family and to the society to which my family belongs." They miss their social and emotional roots, therefore building up a stable identity and a feeling of self-worth is much more difficult for them.

For some individuals this process of being distanced from their original culture can on the other hand enhance their emotional and psychological development. Symbiotic relationships, which rely on customs, rituals and religious and ideological interpretations, have to be surrendered in favour of greater individual autonomy and responsibility. It is not only the need for personal freedom, but also the drive for independence from protective social constraints that can determine a person's individuation.

Attachment & Relationship

Relationship and attachment are by no means identical phenomena and should not be confused as such. There are relationships without attachment and attachments without relationship. Whoever has a relationship to another person can have, but does not have to have, an attachment with that person. In the case of some attachments, the relationship may not exist anymore, as in the case of a strong attachment to a person who is absent or dead.

Relationships that are based on bonding and attachment, I call "bonding relationships". Relationships that are based for example on legal contracts or agreements could be described as work relationships. You can terminate a work relationship, however you cannot simply terminate a bonding relationship. A mother cannot give notice to her child of the termination of the maternal bond, and a child cannot renounce his bond to his parents or siblings. A person is more likely to succeed in his own development if he is growing out from a secure attachment, as opposed to an insecure-ambivalent attachment. The release from an insecure bonding, especially if the bond to the mother has been an agonising experience, is very hard for a child and usually only successful with therapeutic assistance.

3.2 Types of Bonded Relationships

Maternal Bonding

For everyone the maternal bond is the prototype of all bonds. What happens in this first and most important bond influences all future relationships in a person's life. Maternal bonding determines the underlying structure of a person's psychological makeup as well as the person's later patterns of bonding and relationship.

In my opinion, natural instinct is the main factor in the unconscious process of psychological and emotional bonding between mother and child. The bonding process is independent of will and intention. A mother and child instinctively seek emotional contact with each other. This process of unconscious bonding can only be destroyed permanently by some kind of massive influence.

From the start, mother and child live in a continual process of emotional exchange, an emotional stream flowing between them in both directions. However, the mother's feelings are stronger and so she must take the lead. For the child this emotional experience forms the basis of his emotional world. The mother's emotional world and the experiences and memories contained in it become the child's primary building blocks for his emotional and psychological development and identity formation (Fig 2).

In a sense, the child *is* the mother. It is in the maternal bonding that the child discovers the prototype for his identity.

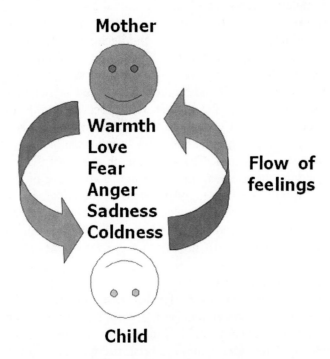

Fig. 2: Mother and child exchanging emotions

He is what his mother is. At the beginning of his life, the child is an extension of the maternal psyche. The child expresses through his sensations and behaviour what is inwardly affecting the mother. Nothing in the mother's psyche remains hidden from the child's receptors, because the child is constantly monitoring his mother's emotional state. Is she there? Is she awake or asleep? Is she well disposed or should I be afraid of her or be afraid for her?

In this way, the child touches those feelings that are unresolved for his mother; even if the mother herself is not fully aware of some of her own feelings (for reasons which will become clear in the chapter on trauma), the child will experience her deepest emotional and psychological state. The child also actively attaches to those feelings that are hidden from the mother herself. The child is the mirror of the mother's soul – her complete psychological and emotional structure.

The readiness on the part of the mother to be wholly there for the child, together with the child's unconditional loving and devotion for the mother can, under more difficult circumstances, result in an experience of deprivation or loss for the child. This is likely if the mother is confused or her feelings are unavailable, and she cannot really accept and love her child, even if she truly wants to. Then the child is in a state of continual stress, feeling he has to try to persuade his mother to love and stay with him. The more the child senses the danger of rejection, the more he clings to his mother. Children have their own will to survive, independent of their mother, and if his mother is emotionally unavailable, or consciously or unconsciously withdrawing from him, the child will then have to strengthen this will to survive to a greater extent.

Mothers and daughters
There is no bond as close as that between mothers and daughters. The mother can empathise best with her daughter, and in her mother the daughter has a person whom she knows completely. Therefore symbiotic relationships between mother and daughter are common and mothers and daughters find it

difficult to separate. Through their mothers, daughters experience what it is like to be a woman, and if the mother is comfortable with her gender identity then the daughter will also be comfortable with hers. If the daughter perceives in her mother only the negative aspects of being a woman, the result will be insecurity in her own life as a woman.

Mothers and sons
In many traditional societies, it is expected of women that they bear a son to be the heir. Thus through their sons many women may feel more valued, looking at their male child with pride. However, as a woman it is more difficult to understand a male mind, and mothers may tend to experience and educate the boy as if he were a girl. Therefore, a boy may have to find a way of reconciling the internal conflicts that are likely to result from having to develop his male identity in the sphere of a woman's influence. That task is difficult to resolve without the presence of a father. One could say that a mother alone cannot turn a son into a man.

If a woman has had poor experiences of her father, or men generally, she is likely to try and teach her son to be more sensitive, responsible, and stronger generally than the men that she has known. However, since she does not respect the men in her own bonding system, she is likely to criticise and speak badly of them, so is more likely to make her sons frightened of becoming men. Sons of mothers who have been disappointed by men may feel over-burdened. They are required to perform or deliver something that, in the eyes of their mothers, their fathers and grandfathers could not, and they are to do that without any real male role models. The result is usually that such sons may not fully become adult men either, taking refuge in pseudo-male roles, the philanderer, or the "macho" isolated hero, never in truth knowing how a man should rightly interact with a woman, or how as fathers they are to bear the responsibility of children. Later in this book there will be much more about the multiplicity of possible entanglements between mothers and sons. Even if grown men do not like to hear it, the fact is that these entanglements can mean utter and complete attachment to mothers for the rest of their lives. Moreover, what sons were unable to resolve in their maternal relationship as children becomes the burden they bring to all their subsequent personal and professional relationships. They very often treat their partners as if they were their mothers.

Paternal Bonding

In modern life in families, where many women want professional independence, the result is the expectation that fathers will participate more in the children's care and education. Increasingly women want to return to professional life as quickly as possible after the birth of a child, and additionally it is no longer the case that a mother will necessarily get support from her female relatives. However, even if a father does take on these responsibilities and does help more with child rearing and education, if maternal and paternal bonding are seen as the same in relation to the child, the reality of the differences of these parent-child relationships may be ignored. Maternal bonding, because of the particular biological conditions, is inimitable for the child and cannot be compared to any other form of bonding, or be substituted by the paternal bonding. Paternal bonding has its own particular quality and is quite different.

Paternal bonding is of enormous importance for the emotional development of all children. For all of us the father is as unique as the mother. It is from the father that the child receives the second part of his identity. This fact was long overlooked in science: "Information on the father's significance in relation to the child's bonding development is rare in bonding research. ... In our research, the quality of father and child interaction during play had as much predictive significance as the mother's sensitivity over the first two years of life. In partner interviews both parents in their own way contribute to the representation of bonding" (Grossmann, Grossmann, Winter and Zimmermann, 2002).

For the child the father is a different mirror from the mother, offering the child an alternative view of the world to that offered by the mother. He supplements and expands the female view of things with that of the male. For the child the father opens up the world in play, he sets different limits, and gradually he removes the child from exclusive symbiosis with the mother by fully occupying his position beside the mother as her husband. The father's particular functions for the child are shaped by cultural and social conditions. A secure bond to the father supports the child's emotional growth.

A child's first psychological and emotional inclination is toward the mother. However, if she is psychologically and emotionally inaccessible (especially if she is suffering the consequences of trauma), the child will often turn to the father. For example, if a mother is occupied with a more recently born child, the older child will often seek out relationship with the father who, in this situation often feels equally "orphaned" and will gladly accept the child's move to a stronger bonding relationship. In this way the child, as she bonds with her father, may become entangled with his emotional problems or, (most frequently with fathers and daughters) a situation can arise where the emotional proximity is too great, and may result in too much, even inappropriate, physical closeness. In therapy as an adult, the "father's daughter" may initially let go of her strong ties to her father, and then what surfaces is that she actually misses her mother. Maternal bonding, despite any difficulties, is always present as the source of emotional and psychological life. It is the working through of disordered maternal bonding that is often decisive for the daughter's emotional recovery. It is only through psychological and emotional contact with her mother that a daughter learns to be a woman. If she stays within the father's sphere of influence, she will remain a child.

Missing fathers:
A "missing father" has a significant influence on the psychological development of a child. Approximately 25% of children

born in Germany between 1930 and 1945 had to cope with their fathers' lengthy or permanent absence. As a representative investigation shows, these individuals are still suffering as a result: "The overall results of research into those adults who suffered an absent father show that they have a negative existential orientation, higher symptom load and more pronounced social limitations" (Decker, Brähler and Radebold, 2004).

A father who is missing has not simply disappeared. Through her connection and intimacy with her mother's psychological and emotional being, the child perceives her father. The child senses her father in respect of how he is emotionally anchored in her mother's being, how her mother "holds" the sense of her father:

Examples:
- in the mother's grief, if the father died young (e.g. in war),
- in her disappointment if the father left her,
- in her panic, rage and impotence, if the father was brutal and violent or
- in her happiness that she created a child with a man she loved.

The latter was, for example, the case with a patient who was the result of an extra-marital relationship of his mother. Although it was during his therapy that, for the first time, it became clear to him that his mother's husband was not his birth father, he had always had a strong image of his mother being ecstatically happy with a man other than his father. However, he also felt within himself his mother's guilt and fear that her infidelity would be found out. It is not a co-incidence that his own life had hardly been joyful; before his therapy, he had been unable to sustain relationships.

Fathers are more than mere procreators or suppliers of genetic material. The significance of the father for a child's development is too great to be ignored in therapy, so the question as to who the child's father is, is of great importance. Unclear or dubious paternity will always have an impact on the child, who will sense his mother's uncertainty and will express it, not in articulate terms but by his behaviour or in the symptoms of illness. Every person needs their father, and therefore has a right to know who their birth father is.

In the same way that maternal bonding forms the basis for perception and feeling in other bonding relationships, so the quality of the bonding to the father acts as a model for many later relationships in a person's life – to friends, teachers, partners, work colleagues and for sons, to their own children.

Fathers and daughters
For daughters, stable paternal bonding facilitates their search for a reliable partner, and "unhealthy" paternal bonding will inhibit successful partner relationships. Another man hardly has a chance compared with an "admired and wonderful father" who jealously binds his daughter to himself. Daughters who worship and adore their fathers because they lack the attention of their mothers will often entangle their husbands and sons in this dynamic, because most of us seek partners who will reflect the emotional and psychological makeup of our child self.

Case Study 10:

Father, husband or son?

Mrs M. says that she does not have a close relationship with her mother who seemed absent when she was a child, and hardly showed any interest in Mrs M. So from the beginning Mrs M. turned towards her father, whom she experienced as very loving. She worshipped him and was decidedly a "father's daughter". Later she even went on holiday with her father, taking her mother's place. Of her relationship to her future husband, she said, "When I saw my husband for the first time I immediately fell in love with him. I was fascinated by him, particularly by his size. After the birth of our first son, I was only interested in our son. I suddenly saw

57

my husband as someone who was in fact very weak." In her partner, she had looked for a copy of her father, and when the son came along, he then became the father substitute.

Emotionally unavailable fathers who humiliate or act violently prevent their daughters from becoming mature enough for an adult partnership; the daughter often will seek out violent and uncontrolled partners who are incapable of forming a good bond. It is well known that daughters of alcohol-dependent fathers often seek partners who are also alcohol dependent. Sometimes daughters who are attached to emotionally withdrawn and depressive fathers will seek out husbands whom they experience as weak and in need of help, in order to look after them.

In later partnerships, the woman attempts to complete or balance out whatever remains unfinished from the paternal bonding, for example by attempting to save her father from his addiction. However, as one relationship cannot be substituted for another, and as what is in the past cannot be undone in the present, such attempts fail without exception and lead to more unhappy relationships.

Fathers and sons
In societies dominated by men, sons are usually the pride of their fathers; they bear their names and guarantee the continuation of the ancestral line. Sons represent the legacy of the father, and so in some traditional social structures daughters may suffer because their fathers value them less.

Ideally for the son, the father is a model of manliness, power, reliability, cleverness and humour. He is the opposition against whom they can rub up and measure their physical and intellectual strength. In sparring with his father, the son grows into society. The father gives the son, among other things, professional orientation, but sons also look to their fathers, not just for recognition of their endeavours, but also for love and warmth, and the son learns love for women from his father.

In some circumstances, for the father, the son may represent a competitor for the love of the mother. After the birth of a son, some fathers feel rejected by their wives. If the mother gives her son precedence over her husband, an unhealthy rivalry develops between father and son. A wife and mother who repeats her unresolved relationship with her own father in her relationship with her son does injustice to her husband and her son; she is likely to be raising another generation of emotionally immature men.

If a woman feels more entangled in love to a man other than the father of her child, e.g. to an former lover, the son may become a barrier in the relationship between the mother and father, because the son is representing the rival of his father. Furthermore, women who did not actually want to get married and have children, but let themselves be persuaded by their husband or their parents, may turn their children into obstacles between themselves and their husband. In their exclusive concern for their children, they make themselves inaccessible to their husband, additionally preventing the children's access to their father.

Emotionally undeveloped or incapable fathers are a heavy burden on their sons, being either weak and unstable, in which case they cannot give their sons support in life, or hard and intractable, in which case they may become their sons' torturers. The sons may themselves become closed, uncommunicative and devoid of feeling, in turn influencing a subsequent generation of men who again cut themselves off from their feelings. Men who are cold and emotionally closed off within themselves, are likely to inflict emotional pain on other people, transferring the pain that they themselves cannot bear.

Sibling Bonding

Every child has a different temperament at birth and this is influential as the child seeks her place in the family, in relation to not only her parents and their parents, but also in relation to any brothers and sisters she might have. Every newborn child will modify the system of relationships within the family, and equally the child has to adapt to the prevailing family dynamics. From this, children develop their survival strategies, which then become their established personality style.

Thus, siblings have a particular emotional relationship to one another, which arises from their direct contact with each other. However, even more than these shared experiences, it seems that the special bonding that siblings have with one another is particularly shaped by the quality of the maternal and paternal bonds to each individual child. When mother and father love all of their children, the children then love one another. If, however, they love one child but reject another, rejection and rivalry will also occur between the children.

When a mother is bonded to a child that dies early, the next-born child may unconsciously be bonded to the dead sibling. If a mother cannot develop a bonding relationship to any of her children, the children will then not find loving relationships with each other; they may often quarrel, and as adults will remain internally bonded to each other in this unsatisfying relationship, even if externally they go their separate ways. If there are quarrels and arguments concerning inheritances, the parents' unresolved conflicts with each other may often flare up again.

Case Study 11:

Brother-sister conflict

Mrs S. sees her brother as "nothing but a trial". She recalls arguments with him throughout her entire childhood. He pestered her, but also worshipped her and was at times servile, and when she rejected him, he became furious and abusive, and subject to attacks of uncontrolled fury.

Mrs S.'s mother had been sexually abused by her own father, and she had married in order to get away from home. Her first child was Mrs S.'s brother, but because of her own trauma she was not emotionally available to him, and the brother found neither the warmth and stability he needed from his mother, nor the recognition he needed from his father. The father advanced in his career seeking from it some compensation for the lack of attention received from his wife. Sexual abuse, as had happened with the mother, was repeated with the second child, the daughter (Mrs S.) who, experiencing no support from her mother, rejected her mother and looked for support from her father, which then developed into an abusive relationship, repeating the sexual abuse that her mother had experienced.

Through his own instability, the brother had a distorted relationship to his sister, which put her in a state of even greater panic because she experienced it, without being aware of it, as a re-stimulation of the abuse. She did not see herself as able to resolve her relationship with her brother, and it was only in therapy that the unconscious connections in her family became clearer to Mrs S. Understanding them better finally led to a more relaxed relationship with her brother.

Substitute Bondings in Childhood

If the mother is under stress and minimally available for bonding with her children, younger siblings will sometimes bond to an older sibling as a mother substitute. However, in order for this to work the older sibling must have a good enough bonding to his or her mother. In the absence of this possibility, the younger child will often turn to a grandmother, where again, successful bonding depends on the grandmother's availability. Sometimes grandparents feel more relaxed in caring for their grandchildren than they did with their own children. Aunts can also serve as substitutes for the child's bonding need if necessary, but ultimately, for the child, no one can really replace the mother for maternal bonding.

Nor can foster parents or adoptive parents truly replace the mother, even if the child is handed over to the adoptive mother immediately after birth. Even then maternal bonding has been established, because the child has already experienced the most intense contact with his birth mother – this includes nine-months of pregnancy, the birth itself, and after the birth contact through smell, touch and eye contact. All this is suddenly interrupted by being separated from his mother, the child then suffers a separation trauma (more on this in Chapter 6). This separation trauma has a permanent effect on the child's further emotional development no matter how loving the adoptive mother might be. If the adoptive mother ignores the fact of the separation trauma then she cannot support the child in coping with the trauma.

Bonding with Partners

The existence of the two sexes, male and female, and our sexual reproduction ability, is the most important existential principle of the human species. Nothing shapes a person more than their gender identity and their experience of the polarity between man and woman. Whether we are born male or female is of fundamental significance for everything that follows in our life. The differences in the sexuality of man and woman and the different functions of male and female sexuality affect and inform the bonding behaviour of men and women in their own respective ways. The ability to enter into emotional bonding and maintain it is normally more pronounced in women than in men, where men's more pronounced competitive and dominant behaviour reduces their bonding ability. Whereas women try to tie men to themselves with emotions, men more often try to convince women to enter a lasting relationship through physical strength, sex, money, material gifts, cleverness and power. Social role attributions like being a "proper woman" and a "proper man" reinforce these tendencies, for example, women are likely to feel more responsible for the emotional quality in bonding and men are more likely to take responsibility for the external material framework of a partnership.

Men in the main are less tolerant of emotional injury than women, tending to act out their emotional pain through aggression toward others, whereas women are more often likely to direct their aggressiveness against themselves, and occasionally also against others who are weaker, for example their children.

These fundamental differences between men and women can make their cohabitation a paradise of desire in some phases of the relationship, but over time, they may also lead to enormous problems. Of course, men and women sexually attract one another, but whether they stay together, and for how long after the sexual act, and whether they love one another and accept one another in their difference is a question of their readiness to grow together emotionally.

Women see men through the filter of their female psyche, and men also see women through the filter of their male psyche, and neither, therefore, see the other as he or she really is (Brizendine, 2006). On this basis, the disappointment of not having found the "right" man or woman is unavoidable. For a relationship to work, a high degree of readiness on the part of the couple to accept their differences, particularly between male and female patterns of perception, thinking and ways of doing things, is necessary. It is not easy for a man and a woman to accept their sexual and personal differences. Often both will feel like the victim of the other, overlooking their own role as perpetrator. It requires a constant willingness to adapt and compromise for the relationship to develop into a stable and loving relationship.

The quality of couple bonding is, in my experience of couples' therapy, to a high degree dependent on the quality of the maternal and paternal bonding that the man and woman bring to the relationship. If in general the maternal bonding was good enough, then the couple's bonding process has a good chance of growing and flourishing. If the man or woman looks for a replacement for their own failed maternal bonding in their partner, all the feelings of frustration, anxiety, doubt and anger from that bonding will be acted out in this 'substitute' relationship – and subsequently with the children. People with good maternal bonding do not cling symbiotically or addictively to their partner, and do not flee into emotional withdrawal or blind acting out of fear and anger whenever there is the smallest problem.

Similarly, although less strongly and prominently, the pattern of the paternal and sibling bonding may be lived out in the couple's bonding relationship. Good bonding in childhood enables good relationships in the present, earlier bonding experiences forming the foundation for later relationships. A daughter learns about being a woman from her mother, a son learns about being a man from his father. Good experiences of this can be built on, whereas with negative experiences the foundations are missing. If a "father's daughter" and a "mother's boy" get together as a couple, the start of the relationship might be exciting and interesting, but over time there will be a lot of difficulties and conflicts.

Problematic and conflictual bonding in childhood is the main cause of partnership conflicts. That is why, in my opinion, most partnership difficulties are not solvable merely by better communication. A man can be as loving and concerned as he wants to be, but if his wife is rejecting and fighting her mother or her father through him, then he is unlikely to succeed. A woman can want to fulfil all her husband's wishes, but if he is acting out the rage he feels towards his mother, all her love will make no difference for him.

Case Study 12:

The unconscious search for the mother in the partner

Susan has already had many relationships with men. Currently she is in a relationship with a man considerably younger than herself who, in the opinion of her friends and acquaintances, is not suitable for her at all. After the initial phase of being in love, the relationship is currently full of conflicts, and yet Susan cannot leave. Although she puts a lot of value on her freedom and independence, she finally lets the man move into her small apartment. There is even more conflict. She becomes increasingly despairing.

In therapy, it becomes clear to her that she is repeating her relationship to her mother with this man. Unconsciously she had hoped that if she put her own needs on hold she would be able to achieve what she yearned for, namely, a secure and satisfying relationship. But she was likely to receive just as little from this man as she received from her mother. The other side of the coin is that the man could never receive from Susan what he did not receive from his mother. It is apparent from the sizeable age difference between him and Susan that he is likely to be looking for a substitute for his mother.

Of course, it is not always the case that a man and a woman as parents will continue living together and rearing their children together. Different religions, cultural systems and state laws have attempted, through legal provision, sanctions and support, to provide stable systems for the co-habitation of men and women, with care for the child in mind (Pawlowski 2001). Often social pressure and public morals have ensured that a couple who have produced a child do indeed marry, even if in their hearts neither wants to.

Often it is easier for men to live without their children than it is for women; nevertheless it is also true that many divorced men suffer from the absence of their children, particularly if the mother, due to her hurt and disappointment, fights with her former husband by not allowing the child to express his love for his father (Bäuerle and Strobel, 2001; Gardner, 2001; ten Hövel, 2003).

Bonding with one's Children

The wish to have children of one's own is basic to human psychological and emotional makeup, and most people see this as their greatest fulfilment. In the fulfilment of this, parents may arrange their entire lives around their children, being willing to accept the necessary restraints and sacrifices. Through having children, people become adults for the next generation.

Having a child however, does not solve the individual's

65

emotional problems – partnership problems remain, as do any problems with one's own parents. On the contrary, the arrival of children tends to bring all emotional conflict that has not yet been resolved, intensely to the surface. Having children, therefore, can be a great opportunity for one's own personal and emotional development, carrying with it also the risk of an emotional break down in the face of the unresolved problems.

At the bonding level, the parent-child relationship tends to be a repeat of the bonding experience of the parents to their own parents. Secure parental bonding with one's own parents is the best foundation for developing secure bonding to one's own child. All forms of insecure bonding to one's parents will de-stabilise the bonding process with the children. When parents try to be with their children in an entirely different way from the way in which they experienced being with their own parents, it may indeed be successful somehow. However there are limits to this at the deeper levels of bonding. If the nature of the relationship to one's own parents is not fully understood, any intentions not to repeat mistakes and shortcomings in the education of one's own children are unlikely to be successful.

Case Study 13:

"I thought I would do everything quite differently."

Mrs T. begins therapy because she is repeatedly overcome by panic attacks and anxiety. She seems to be dynamic and self-confident; she is always on the move with many things on the go including educating her daughter on her own. The relationship with the father of her daughter only lasted a couple of years.

In the course of the therapy, we get an indication of the origin of her panic attacks and anxiety states: as a small child, a neighbour sexually abused her.

Mrs T.'s behaviour changes markedly in the course of therapy. She becomes calmer, better balanced and more reflective. She can now see what is important to her and the ways in which she distracts herself, rushing into adventures that in the end do not help her. She also starts to see the burden she puts on her daughter by her restless lifestyle. Originally she had thought she was a progressive mother, one who could offer her daughter something different from what she had had at home, which had been emotional coldness, quarrelling and isolation. She now experiences her relationship to her daughter in a fresh way, relating on more solid foundations.

Order and Love

Love can only fully unfold within a certain "order", i.e. in an ordered system of bonding relationships. This ordered system includes specifically the difference between the types of bonding, for example, that parental love for a child, and sibling love between brothers and sisters, does not get confused with the love that occurs between a couple. No matter how much, for example, a mother and a son, a father and a daughter or a brother and a sister love one another, their relationship can never be a couple relationship without causing emotional disturbance in the system. Love alone cannot bring order to inappropriate bonding relationships.

On the other hand, a marriage and a family that is loveless is inhuman. For example to marry someone simply for prestige and power, without love, or to have children purely to meet social expectations is likely to result in lasting unhappiness. Additionally, parents who force marriage on their children are not expressing the love of parents for their children; rather they demonstrate the stubbornness of parents who regard their children as belongings that one can buy or sell. When social status and "family honour" count for more than parental love, this crudeness and lack of love is transmitted to the next generation.

Friendship Bonding

Why do children develop particularly close relationships to just one or two of their playmates? What ties us as adults to others to the extent that we call them "friends", or "best friends"? Apart from sympathies, preferences, hobbies and common interests the answer certainly lies in the unconscious patterns formed in our bonding relationships to our parents. The constellations method often shows that people with problems in their friendships have had difficult bonding relationships with their parents.

Adolescent cliques are not just a setting that supports the common adolescent quest to separate from parents. Sometimes the adolescent clique itself can become a substitute for the family, in an attempt to find what is absent in the actual home. Drugs like cannabis can function as a binding medium, joining emotionally deprived children into conspiratorial societies. Cannabis, as a result of its narcotic effect, can arouse symbiotic feelings, and then becomes preferable to the inaccessible mother or absent father. It is more easily available.

Case Study 14:

Cannabis or mother?

Michael (18 years old) is in year 11 at a grammar school. He has been smoking cannabis since he was 16. He is less and less motivated with regard to schoolwork; it is only his innately high intelligence that helps him to keep his head above water at school. He is completely oriented towards his gang and the hip-hop scene. His gang comprises four friends who share cannabis; all four come from unstable families.

When his mother throws him out of the home because of his drug use, he experiences the conflict. Should he stop smoking in order not to lose contact with his mother? In order not to risk his contact with his mother, even though tangled, he compromises. He pretends to his mother that he does not smoke anymore, and secretly carries on smoking with his friends.

Bonding Relationships mirrored in Employment and Professional Relationships

When I began to work with constellations in the context of work-related problems, the underlying patterns of the relationships at work quickly became apparent to me. Here the issues have to do with task orientation, clear hierarchies, appropriate recognition of achievements, positive ways of being accepted as a new member in an existing system of working relationships, and good ways of leaving those systems in the end. The issue of loyalty is different in a work situation, being entered into freely for a certain period of time. Working relationships are the most formalised of our relationships, and are the most regulated by the law. The process of emotional bonding here plays a relatively minor role, but the emotional component in work relationships is undeniable.

There obviously are difficulties in working relationships; for example, a previous supervisor is still held as present psychologically by his team, and so remains part of the system. The team might even be more loyal to him than they are to the new supervisor, who perhaps has different ideas concerning leadership and co-operation. As soon as these problems are recognised, they are relatively easy to resolve (Ruppert, 2001).

If, on the other hand, problems prove to be more persistent, when for example the relationship between a supervisor and a worker continually produces conflict, it is very likely that earlier personal bonding patterns from the family of origin are being evoked by the here-and-now work relationship. If for example, a worker sees in his supervisor his own father with whom he has remained in entangled conflict since childhood, perhaps because he felt deserted after his father separated from his mother, the difficulty at work can only be resolved when the father-son relationship is seen and resolved. Working relationships and their associated acute or persistent difficulties in my experience often reflect bonding conflicts in the original family systems of those involved.

At a seminar, a participant wanted to know why she undertook so many different types of work and always lost heart after a while. In her constellation each of the several types of activity she undertook proved to be attempts to re-enact one of the many problems both in her mother's and her father's family systems. Through her work situations, she was trying to resolve these problems – a mission that is impossible.

3.3 Psychological Health and Entanglements of the Soul

Characteristics of psychological health include:

- liking and valuing oneself,
- making good contact with others and being able to communicate,
- being confident and optimistic,
- enjoying life and being able to take pleasure in things,
- being intellectually agile, and
- being able to have alternative action plans (Fröschl, 2000).

When one thinks of life in terms of bonding processes, it works best if the person

- as a child in relation to the parents is able to feel small, safe and secure,
- as a man or woman has a sexual partner who is valued equally,
- is able to be with all his or her love the mother or father of their own children,
- is available for friends as an interested partner in play or conversation or as a reliable helper in situations of need,
- co-operates loyally with supervisors, workers and

colleagues and treats them with appropriate respect,
* finds his/her place within the social community in which she or he lives and feels like a member of that community.

However, on the contrary it often happens that:

* children feel superior to their parents, regarding *them* as the children they have to support,
* sexual partners are burdened with demands for symbiosis,
* children are misused as substitute parents or partners,
* friends become entangled in difficult partnership dynamics,
* work relationships are confused by sexual engagement,
* people have no connection with their cultural roots, and may completely reject the society in which they live.

The main source of emotional health for us as humans is contact with other humans, who are also the main cause of our emotional and psychological suffering. Essentially, it is only people who can cause emotional suffering for other people. We can cope with a lot in terms of stress (hunger, need, heavy work, adverse environmental and psychological conditions etc.), but we find it most difficult and painful to cope with bad relationships. In our relationships, we are challenged to learn to live with our fears, our anger, our feelings of guilt and shame and our love. Good interpersonal relationships are healing and bad ones make us ill. Relationships at the level of bonding form the most significant challenges to our health at the deepest emotional and psychological level of ourselves, because emotional and psychological bonding generates inter-dependency, our ability to share feelings such as joy and pain, to understand each other deeply. Emotional and psychological bonding serves as a source of love and strength; however, it can also bring grief and sorrow when that bonding has an underlying emotional "entanglement".

Entanglement in this sense means: "I cannot feel, think and decide independently of this person with whom I am entangled, because I am afraid that the relationship will otherwise come to an end and I am incapable of living without this relationship". Here the person experiences the bond to the other as a burden and a limitation, and is unable to feel free and happy in the relationship. At the same time entangled humans feel incapable of releasing themselves from the relationship. The moment they contemplate letting it go, they experience fear of abandonment and feelings of guilt. Conflicts that arise, and then accumulate in the entangled relationship, are essentially not resolvable. Having been pushed aside and suppressed beneath the everyday activity of life for as long as possible, they will always re-surface. These patterns of persistent conflict are extremely resilient and persistent.

People in entangled relationships experience themselves as incapable of action, and continue to wait and hope that the other will change so that they can then feel better. Partners in their relationships – parents, husbands, wives, children or work colleagues – however do not change. The only real option is to understand fully that the other can only make a decision to change in their own time. The person who tries to change another against their will always meets resistance, causing all their problematic feelings to reappear more intensely, exactly the feelings that they do not want to grapple with in the relationship. Entanglements bring up feelings that are disturbing and frightening, which one can spend one's life avoiding unsuccessfully.

If one tries to help an addict to break their addiction against their underlying will, one very quickly senses in oneself all the feelings that underlie the addiction, namely impotence, fear and rage. It is the same for those who have an addicted partner, and for children with addicted parents, or therapists with addicted patients. People who are not prepared to deal with the causes of their addiction are likely to draw others into their addiction.

The business of taking "behaviourally disturbed" children to doctors or therapists so that their symptoms are eliminated is also doomed to failure if the parents are not ready to look at their own situation. A child's "behavioural disturbances" are the mirror of the parents' psychological and emotional makeup, and if the parents are prepared to look into this mirror and find a better psychological and emotional understanding of themselves, this is generally the best help for the child.

All attempts to resolve "entanglements of the soul" without looking at their origin lead to further entanglements, or to new versions of the entanglement in a different form. Doctors, psychotherapists, social workers, teachers or magistrates can all become enmeshed in the extended entanglement processes, especially when members of these professions themselves have unresolved emotional and psychological issues. Entanglements always rely on reciprocity; if you do not take the bait, you don't end up wriggling on the end of an entanglement hook. If, for example, as a therapist you do not want certain feelings to arise in the patient, because you are afraid that these would be uncontrollable due to your own entanglement, you increasingly reduce the patient to a small child, and you become the over-protective mother or controlling father, with the patient remaining emotionally a child.

In an entangled relationship, no one is in their "right place". Parents have childish needs and look to the children to fulfil them; children try and "parent" their parents, and then try to replace their missing parents through friends and partners; partners then treat each other like children. Psychologically entangled therapists project their own needs onto their patients, and patients feel responsible for taking care of their therapists, trying to make sure that the therapist feels they are doing a good job.

The only way to resolve our entangled relationships is to look to ourselves and not to others. What is it in me that makes me susceptible to this particular entanglement? What are the origins in my background? This usually means facing the fears and pain from within our own system, frequently having their origins in the traumatic experiences of our family of origin.

4

Psychological Trauma

4.1 Introduction

That the human psyche can be traumatised and injured just as the human body can is not a completely new insight, but it has taken a long time for the idea to be widely accepted, and even now is still not well enough recognised in most societies. This is not simply to do with lack of knowledge or limited awareness; the causes in fact lie much deeper. The infliction of psychological and emotional hurt on others is so common that most of us do not want to see what is really going on. If we did, we would then have to acknowledge that war, for example, which quite deliberately produces death and physical wounding, also causes psychological and emotional injury to the survivors, including those who may not have been physically injured (Shaw 2002, 2003). And it is not just the victims of this violence who may be traumatised in war, but also many perpetrators and the civilian population. Those who advocate war would have to answer for the fact that they not only create psychological and emotional injuries in the here–and–now, but also for many generations to come. On a soul level, war has no real winners, only losers. Conflicts between humans can't really be solved by violence – this is one of the illusions resulting from trauma.

Similarly, when we acknowledge the existence and reality of psychological and emotional trauma, we can no longer ignore the amount of violence committed by human beings against each other in times of peace. Further disturbing realities follow: men brutally treated by other men, women abused by men and misused as prostitutes, children physically and emotionally abused by their parents, as well as the lifelong suffering from the trauma of child sexual abuse.

War and violence within the family are, more than any natural catastrophe or accident, primarily responsible for traumatisation (Herman, 2003). However, because of social resistance to such distasteful truths, and the inclination of people to repress painful knowledge, it took until the 1980s for the notion of 'trauma' to become appropriately acknowledged, particularly in scientific circles, as a cause of many psychological and emotional problems (Butollo, Hagl and Kruesmann, 1999).

4.2 A Definition of Trauma

The word 'trauma' means injury. It is used in this sense in the medical field to describe physical injuries which involve damage to bones or tissue (e.g. skull and brain trauma). In the psychological and emotional arena, one talks of a psychological injury when processes such as perception, feeling, thought, memory or imagination no longer function normally and are, either periodically or in the longer term, considerably limited in their function: for example, in the case of hypersensitivity and extreme wakefulness, when the smallest noise causes a person to jump with shock and sweat with anxiety, or if a person becomes obsessed by certain ideas or images, or his thoughts circle obsessively around a past event.

Gottfried Fischer and Peter Riedesser define the trauma experience in their teaching manual on psychotraumatology as

". . . the critical experience of the discrepancy between threatening factors in a situation and the individual's ability to cope,

75

accompanied by feelings of helplessness and of being at the mercy of people and events, which then cause a permanent shock to the perception of self and of the world" (Fischer and Riedesser, 1999).

Within this definition, several important points are outlined:

- A trauma is something relative; it is a relationship between the characteristics of a situation ("threatening") and those of a person ("individual coping mechanisms"). Only if the nature of the danger outweighs the individual's ability to cope does the "experience of discrepancy" occur and therefore become a traumatic situation. Thus, it is clear that the same situation could be traumatising for one person while another might experience it as only stressful or difficult. Age, experience, gender, self-awareness, or previous experience of trauma could all determine the difference.
- Trauma is concerned with something fundamental, the consequences affect us in the deepest part of our being, threatening what is vital to us, having repercussions throughout our lives. The consequences might be fatal or massively damaging to our health, or our very social existence might be under attack, our honour, our right to belong, our professional status.
- Trauma works primarily at the level of our emotions, the traumatic situation stirring up extreme feelings, bringing an extraordinary sensitivity that can have detrimental effects. The feelings of "helplessness" and "being at the mercy of someone" mentioned in the Fischer and Riedesser definition could be extended to include further related feelings such as "powerlessness", "loss of control" and "resignation/giving up".
- The experience of trauma has a lasting effect upon the body, mind and soul. While it is possible to move on from experiences of stress or worry, and be free of the accompanying symptoms when the stressful or worrying situation is over, the consequences of a traumatic experience never disappear completely.

- The consequences of traumatic experiences are far-reaching, affecting one's understanding of oneself – that is, the manner and way in which a person perceives and experiences him or herself – just as much as the perception of the world in which they live. After a traumatic experience, a person who previously might have been strong and self-reliant may feel permanently weakened and vulnerable. The world is no longer experienced as safe and secure, but has become life threatening.

Whether a particular event has a traumatic effect upon a person depends on their level of self-protection and self-support available in the particular situation, as well as the nature of the event itself. Feelings of loss of control and powerlessness may be minimized with the help of emotional, social, spiritual and practical self-supporting skills.

As can be seen from the points above, people who have been psychologically stable throughout their lives may be so completely overwhelmed by a traumatic situation, their psychological and emotional integrity so massively injured, that they develop symptoms of psychological disturbance. It is these people who will experience the complete disruption of their sense of self and of the world. "I would never have thought that something like this could happen to me."

4.3 Types of Trauma

There have been various attempts to classify trauma, the one often cited is that from Leonore Terr, who distinguished between two different types of trauma (Terr, 1991):

- **Type 1**: These are brief, sudden and unexpected events, characterised by acute danger to life and limb.
- **Type 2**: These are persistent and repetitive situations that overwhelm and are characterised by helplessness and powerlessness.

Examples of type 1 trauma include accidents (e.g. car or train crashes), criminal violence (e.g. rape or armed assault) and natural catastrophes of short duration (e.g. tornado, flood, avalanche).

Examples of type 2 trauma include torture, being a prisoner of war, sexual and physical abuse or experiences of being bullied.

While Type 1 experiences are short and one-off events, those of Type 2 may persist over many years, for example when a child in the family is continuously abused sexually by her father or persistently bullied by his classmates.

It is also useful to make a further distinction between people who live through the trauma themselves and those who are witnesses to the trauma of another person. Experience shows that witnessing a trauma can also be traumatising, for example for helpers and others present at the traumatizing situation (Stamm, 2003). If a person has to stand by and watch as others suffer or die, they will feel powerless and their experience of themselves and of the world may be seriously affected. Any emotional closeness to the victim of a trauma (for example another family member, partner or close friend) increases this effect. How can policemen, fire fighters or paramedics emerge from a catastrophe unaffected if they have to stand by helplessly while people die? How can a child maintain her psychological well-being if she has watched her parents being shot by soldiers or abducted before her eyes? How can soldiers maintain their sanity when they are required to 'clean up' a battlefield of bodies?

Case Study 15:

"How Les McCourt became a wreck"

Les McCourt, an English soldier fighting in the First Gulf War in 1991, was given the task of clearing up Highway No. 8, the route of the Iraqi troops' withdrawal from Kuwait which had been heavily bombed by the Americans. Part of the task included the disposal of bodies. "He sees himself as he hurries between the smoking metal wreckage, trying to wrap in any available rag what had once been pieces of humanity, for of course they had run out of body bags long since. They had not brought nearly enough, and so have to use anything that is available – a board, an old bed frame. So the mass grave in the desert fills and fills. In the end there are more than a thousand Iraqi dead. McCourt performs his work mechanically. His mind has shut off. Instead he has 'switched to automatic'. Only later do the symptoms of a post traumatic stress disorder appear: dulled feelings in relation to his wife, a sudden flood of emotions when he smells diesel or grilled meat at a barbecue on a pleasure boat, unrest, nightmares, tightening in his chest, nausea, a stomach ulcer, and finally a nervous breakdown with admission to hospital. Ultimately he was dismissed from the army due to unfitness for duty, followed by an exis-tence marked by visits to psychiatrists. "In August 1996 Les was discharged from the army. He felt used, abused, excluded and abandoned, or at least not supported in any way that would have been useful to him. Les attended his sessions with the psychiatrist. ... So he takes his tablets, three a day, to keep himself half on an even keel" (Excerpt from an article in the Süddeutsche Zeitung from 29/30th March 2003).

A further important distinction of types of trauma is whether they occur naturally or are created by people. Natural catastro-phes seem not to leave such deep and lasting wounds as the violence, ignorance and stupidity of humans. Human societies more often grow together in the event of a natural catastrophe; people help each other when overwhelmed and devastated by natural disasters. War and violence on the other hand destroy the already evolved empathetic structures of society, isolate the individual and result in people seeking support and protection within the sort of groups that will execute further acts of violence. Violence provokes new violence and sets in motion a chain reaction of traumatisation and re-traumatisation. Victims become perpetrators and create new victims. Bloody revenge provoked by the murder of family members, wars legitimised by previous wars, terrorisation that is justified by terror of the "enemy" – these are the chains of events that sadly define a significant part of the history of humans. And the perpetrators feel almost no guilt.

4.4 Experiencing and Treating Trauma

In the definition from Fischer and Riedesser above, some things, which are crucial to the understanding of the complexity of psychotrauma, are not yet defined enough, in particular the nature of the processes of the experience of trauma. In these processes, we have to deal with different time phases:

- immediate and direct psychological reaction to the traumatic situation ("peri-traumatic reactions") and
- short, medium or long-term psychological after effects of the traumatising experience ("post-traumatic reaction").

The first phase of a trauma situation is characterised by anxiety with an immediate heightening of all of the senses. This hypersensitivity ("hypervigilance") helps the person to see all the possibilities for escape from the threatening situation. This initial phase of trauma is also combined with a strong stress reaction which, through the excretion of various hormones (e.g. adrenalin and cortisol) massively increases the body's performance (e.g. through increased blood circulation) and mobilises all reserves of energy within the body. This phase of the trauma experience is concerned with attempts to save oneself and find a way out of the situation.

If these attempts are not successful the second phase begins with a shock reaction that abruptly interrupts the hypersensitivity of the sensory and motoric systems and the flood of emotions, thus averting the likelihood of sudden death due to over excitement (e.g. a heart attack) and the wasting of all the person's energy. This is followed by the deadening of the physical and emotional pain with the body's own pain killers (e.g. morphine). This stage of the traumatic experience is characterised by the so-called 'frozen/paralysed' reaction (Levine, 1998).

The Different Processes of Stress and Trauma

The difference between stress and trauma can be expressed thus: in a stressful situation one has the option of either fighting or fleeing ("fight or flight"), while in a trauma situation there is only one possibility– to become frozen or to split inwardly ("freeze or fragment"). The stress reaction leads to a mobilisation of the body's energy, while the trauma-emergency mechanism leads to a demobilisation and disconnection of energy, dulling the sensations. The stress reaction opens the psychological channels, whereas trauma closes them down.

There is only one way out of a traumatic situation during the first phase of the experience, and that is to interrupt our own experience by dissociating. Where persistent traumatisation is concerned, for example in situations of abuse or torture, fragmentation of the individual identity occurs more and more automatically. Only a certain portion of the total personality remains and endures the trauma, the other parts of the personality withdraw. This is the fragmentation process.

Thus there are four basic ways of inwardly dissociating and escaping from the trauma situation:

- blocking of perception: the person experiences themselves as if in a fog,
- freezing of the feelings: the person becomes numb, cold and emotionless,
- disembodied consciousness: the person's experience is as if they leave their body and the event is experienced as though from outside or above,
- splitting into sub-personalities (Huber, 1995; Herman 2003; Putnam, 2003).

Experiencing and coping with trauma initially are spontaneous psychosomatic processes, over which the conscious will of the traumatised person has only minimal influence. These processes are biologically rooted, emergency self-defence reactions that have presumably proved useful as survival mechanisms in the course of our evolution. Splitting and dissociative withdrawal from the trauma situation, however, can be learnt and consciously set in motion as a method of self-protection. People who have been victims of violence over an extended period describe their ability to split their personality as growing more and more rapidly.

4.5 The Post Trauma Consequences

The short-term consequences are that the traumatised person feels as though they are anaesthetised, feeling very little and continuing to carry out life's activities as normal. Thus, after a time it might seem as though the traumatic experience has had no lasting consequences, and in fact has been overcome. Outsiders, who have seen little or nothing of the traumatic event, might think that the event is past and resolved for the victim.

In reality, however, a physical and emotional conflict is taking place within the person, the aim of which is to guarantee that the traumatic experience is forgotten. The affected person tries to create distance between himself and the traumatic experience, unconsciously finding ways to prevent anything happening that might re-trigger the trauma which would send him back into the experience. Since the relevant perceptions, feelings and thoughts have been split off in the course of the traumatic experience, the emotional disturbance unleashed by the trauma is forced out of the conscious memory. The splitting off of the memories of the trauma leaves conscious awareness free to focus on survival, effectively banishing a portion of the individual's reality from consciousness (Ruppert, 2001).

However, even when memories of the trauma are split off

from our waking consciousness, they remain imprinted in the regions of the brain that are not conscious, and particularly in the cells of the body that are closely linked hormonally and via neural circuits with the midbrain and the brainstem. In the body as a whole, and in some particular parts of the body, the memory traces of the trauma remain. The traumatic experience with all its shocking imagery, sensations and feelings of horror ticks away like a time bomb, split off from conscious life but ready to explode at any moment. Thus, in a situation resembling the original trauma, the "defensive barrier" that keeps the trauma away from the consciously active brain may become too thin. If this happens the numbing of thoughts and feelings may be insufficient, the present situation experience becoming merged with the earlier trauma experience, and the regulatory mechanisms that manage the stability of the psyche and its functioning may go out of control again. Flashback images of the original situation ("intrusions") force themselves forward, flooding the consciousness.

Francine Shapiro, when talking about Vietnam veterans, described this process as follows : "Many veterans are not capable of crossing normal streets, they cannot go into shopping centres or visit sports centres because the crowds and the chaotic background noises activate old anxieties and release horrific flashbacks" (Shapiro and Forrest, 1998).

Post-traumatic Stress Disorder (P.T.S.D.)
(See Appendix 1)
The diagnosis of "Post-traumatic Stress Disorder" draws together typical trauma symptoms which may appear if trauma victims are not given timely and trauma-specific support.

> "Typical symptoms are repeated experiences of the trauma through intrusive memories (resonating memories and flashbacks) or in dreams, against a background of persistent feelings of numbness or emotional apathy, indifference towards other people, the feeling of being dissociated from one's surroundings, self-deprivation as well as avoidance of activities and situations that might revive memories of the trauma.

Commonly we may also find a fear of or avoidance of key words that might remind the sufferer of the original trauma. Less often, there may be a dramatic outbreak of anxiety, panic or aggression released by a sudden memory and intensive reliving of the trauma itself or the original reaction to it.

Normally a state of sympathetic hyperactivity ensues, with a sense of heightened vigilance, disproportionate fearfulness and sleeplessness. Anxiety and depression frequently appear in association with the afore-mentioned signs and symptoms, and thoughts of suicide are not uncommon. Drug consumption or disproportionate consumption of alcohol can also be complicating factors" (Dilling, Mombour and Schmidt, 1993).

Even when there is no obvious emotional link between a here-and-now incident and the original traumatic experience, and no obvious re-triggering, the traumatic experience nevertheless continues to have effects. People's perceptions, feelings, thoughts and actions are affected, even though they are not consciously aware of this process going on. The traumatic experience works like a filter through which all further experiences pass. Anxiety, anger, hopelessness and confusion, according to the nature of the trauma experienced, stamp themselves on the day-to-day experiences of life. Reality is distorted through the filter of the traumatic experience into a subjective actuality, but because this process happens unconsciously it is not available for self-reflection, and so traumatised people experience this filtered reality as the only possible truth. In reality it is only half of the truth.

Splitting of the personality (fragmentation)
At its most extreme, the processing of a traumatic experience takes the form of a splitting of the whole personal identity into fragmentary identities, resulting in multiple personae. The individual then has more than one identity, and these identities know little if anything of each other's existence. The traumatised person experiences himself as either in state A or state B. If he is in state A he knows nothing of state B and vice versa. Our 'I' consciousness is informed by an experience of

ourselves as whole and as an identity. Even though we are constantly changing in relation to our environment, we have the impression that we are still always the same person. Our psyche is not prepared for the possibility that this 'I' could suddenly cease to exist because multiple expressions of the 'I' have now arisen.

So totally do we perceive ourselves as having a continuous identity that, for people who are not well-versed in trauma theory, the phenomenon of a split personality is scarcely believable. Our consciousness mediates for us the illusion of a self-contained 'I' identity.

For this reason the phenomenon of "multiple personalities" or "dissociative identity disorder" (DSM IV 300.14) is often met with scepticism. It goes far beyond our essentially culturally determined concept of personality and subjectivity. Additionally, many psychotherapists who observe these sudden personality changes in their own patients overlook them completely until they have properly understood the real concept of trauma. I believe that the reality of this split identity provides an essential key to the understanding of psychic disturbance and the human soul. Even in the 1940s, Helen and John Watkins developed the theory of ego states based on the 'I' psychology of Paul Federn and on observations of patients. "An 'I' experience can be defined as an organised relationship and experience system, the elements of which are held together by a common principle and which is separated from other 'I' experiences through a more or less permeable boundary" (Watkins and Watkins, 2003).

The development of 'I' states in the course of a person's development is generally a normal process in that children have to learn to conduct themselves differently with different people and in different situations. They learn to take on distinct "roles" in relation to different situations, which are then freely available as 'I' states in the structure of their personalities. The boundaries between the individual 'I' states can be vague and the change from one to another can be partially conscious (e.g. "now I'll behave like a little child").

But essentially it is not in our full awareness.

In a traumatic experience however, extreme adjustment is demanded of an existing 'I' state. The experience is so abrupt and painful, that it can only be stored in an extra 'I' state. If it remained permanently in the 'I' consciousness of a person, that person could not survive. Therefore, in the inner psyche a boundary is put up between the traumatised 'I' state and the 'I' state that lives on after the traumatic situation. Frank Putnam systematically and comprehensively described the phenomenon of "dissociative identity disorder" following an experience of trauma. His book is, in my opinion, an essential text for all those who work with patients with trauma (Putnam, 2003). Putnam proceeds on the assumption that dissociation is a normal psychological process, allowing the individual to adapt to different demanding situations. This process only leads to the severity of a "personality disorder" under the influence of a traumatic experience. He lists the following as the most striking dissociative phenomena (Putnam, 2003):

- psychogenic amnesia: the sudden inability to remember important personal information,
- dissociative fugue: the sudden departure from home or the usual work place together with the inability to remember one's own past,
- de-personalisation disorder: where sufferers experience episodes in which they feel so unreal and alienated that they think they are in a dream, or have become a machine or are dead.

Which type of dissociation is observed and which effects are associated with the split-off 'I' states depend on the actual trauma situation.

The perpetrator in the victim
It is particularly important for an understanding of many of the consequences of trauma to know that, in a violent situation in which a victim is powerless before a perpetrator, the psychic

construct of the perpetrator duplicates itself in the victim. Why? Indeed it would normally be taken for granted that the victim would defend him or herself against the perpetrator and would do their best not to allow him or her any access to their inner self. It seems however, that there is a final attempt at survival that involves an identification with and an absorbing of the personality of the perpetrator. The personal 'I' is pushed aside and supplanted by the perpetrator 'I'. If the victim survives the violence, the perpetrator construct recedes into the background again, but remains as a split-off part of the personality.

Jan Philipp Reemtsma describes what he experienced in a kidnap situation. He refers to the part of his personality that experienced the trauma of the kidnap in the third person ("he"). "At one point he had the fantasy that the kidnapper should comfort him, touch him, lay his hands upon his shoulders. It is not easy for me to write this, it was not easy for him to admit to this wish... the desire for physical contact however oversteps the boundaries of submission. The power relationship is clear cut – it is not power sharing, but an extreme co-existence of the all powerful with the powerless, the one who is 'over-powered' wishes for the physical gifts of the dictator to be bestowed on him" (Reemtsma, 2002).

If a grown adult is so compelled to relinquish his or her personality in such a situation, how much less is a child able to withstand a perpetrator?

Addiction

In my opinion, experiences of trauma should be seen as the underlying causes for the many forms of addiction. Drugs, for example, are taken:

- to mask the traumatic experience and the feelings linked to it,
- to combat and/or suppress the symptoms of sleeplessness, anxiety and panic caused by the trauma,
- or to escape from the numbness and inner emptiness of a frozen trauma state.

87

Thus, drugs need to be able to anaesthetise just as much as to stimulate. Drugs are consumed both to dampen the physiological levels of stimulation, having a deadening effect (e.g. alcohol, marijuana, heroin, tranquilisers), or to stimulate the level of sensation (e.g. ecstasy, speed, cocaine). Cigarettes can have both effects; they calm and also make one more wakeful, consequently worldwide they are the number one drug and the primary cause of addiction. Other addictions, such as over-working, can also be a result of a traumatic experience: through continual occupation the re-emergence of traumatic feelings during periods of relaxation is avoided. Similarly, over-eating also suppresses feelings of loneliness and abandonment.

However, if we try to escape the after-effects of trauma through manipulation of brain chemistry in this way we get caught in the cycle of addiction, because in order to balance the influx of drugs the brain produces the exact antidotes so that, after only a very short time, a tolerance for the drug arises. Consequently the dosage must be raised, again provoking the escalated reaction in the brain chemistry and so on. Finally the addict has not only to fight the unchanged and unresolved problem of his or her trauma but also the physical, psychological and social results of his or her drug dependency. And addiction, in most cases, leads sooner or later to death.

The type of addiction often depends on the nature of the trauma. In Chapters 5 – 8 I give some brief comments on which particular forms of addiction may result from the four types of trauma. In addition, addiction is a major obstacle to therapy. A person who tries to manipulate his state of mind through addiction to substances or a particular behaviour is attempting to deny or disguise reality, and he will therefore have great difficulty in entrusting himself to the therapeutic process that confronts him with these realities and the traumatic experiences that lie behind them.

Suicidal tendencies

Choosing to end our psychological and emotional suffering through suicide involves similar avoidant motives. Probably for nearly everyone who has experienced a serious trauma, taking one's own life at some point occurs as a possible way out of one's anguish. In a moment it could all be over – the fear, the depression, the inner chaos and the bewilderment. Fricke, Schmidtke and Weinacker (1997) summon up statistics about suicide: At least 18% of drug fatalities can be seen as indicative of an underlying tendency towards suicide ("addiction as a step by step to suicide"). Many accidents are consciously or unconsciously staged suicides (e.g. traffic accidents). Approximately one in a thousand suicide attempts are 'successful'. The way in which suicidal tendencies are expressed has a gender specific background as already mentioned in chapter 1. While the number of suicide attempts by women is four times as high as for men, the number of 'successful' suicides by men is three times as high as for women. When a man decides to kill himself, he is usually successful.

Men tend to choose the more brutal methods (shooting, hanging), whereas women are more likely to overdose themselves with medication. It seems that men prefer to be perpetrators rather than victims when it comes to suicide; so for example they may call the police during a marital quarrel and then dramatically kill themselves as soon as the police arrive. Women are more likely to take the victimised role in suicide, they may overdose on sleeping tablets and wait to be saved at the last minute.

In my opinion, the different motives for, and forms of, suicide depend on the nature of the trauma experienced, and will be different for each of the four trauma types outlined below. The risk of suicide therefore can be differentiated in assessment, and then reacted to differently.

The persistent nature of trauma
It is very important in understanding trauma to know that
the sentence "Time heals all wounds" is not applicable.
Generally, during worrying or stressful situations, times of
peace and quiet are a great help, allowing the body, soul
and spirit to recuperate. However, the opposite is usually
true of trauma: the struggle to maintain psychological stability remains. The process of splitting and splitting off in order
to keep the trauma beyond the reach of conscious awareness
continually consumes psychological strength and energy,
exhausting the reserves. The inner psychological structure,
its adaptability and flexibility, can be increasingly lost by
time passing.

Even when the situation for the sufferer over time
outwardly normalises, the internal process of overcoming the
trauma does not move towards a peaceful conclusion. It can
even be that as time passes it deteriorates rather than improves,
and that it takes increasing amounts of energy to hold the
"damaged" personality in check, and to hold the whole
psychological system sufficiently stable. It is therefore not
surprising that many traumatised people also have to fight the
fantasy of ending this exhausting inner struggle against the
embedded traumatic memories through suicide.

While human nature provides emergency strategies for the
survival of trauma, it seems that the complete overcoming of
the trauma at the level of the soul is not within the scope of
natural self-healing.

Overcoming trauma is a many-layered process. As
Gottfried Fischer and Peter Riedesser discovered (1999), seen
in the long term, people with experiences of trauma vacillate
between:

- the attempt to deny the trauma, expel it completely from
  their life and give themselves over to the illusion that they
  can once again achieve control over their lives through
  specific ways of behaving ("trauma compensation
  pattern"); and

- the resignation to the fact that there is no hope of escaping the trauma consequences ("disillusionment pattern").

Through the fear of reactivating the memories of the traumatic experiences, many people avoid confronting the trauma, and so are constantly in flight from themselves. They try to distract themselves by caring for others (partners, children, patients...) and throwing themselves into busy activity. They may seek support for their inner fragility in political ideology or religious and spiritual practices, looking to external things for the sense of well-being that they can no longer find inside themselves. They frequently entangle their partners, children, friends or work colleagues in their trauma through this process.

Even in psychotherapy, many patients avoid the risk of venturing into the heart of their traumatic experience by looking for an explanation for their suffering in their immediate life situation. They cannot believe that an event that may be many years in the past, which they can hardly remember, could be the cause of their lack of psychological well-being in the present. Psychotherapists that are not conversant with the concept of trauma unfortunately will support them in this, perpetuating therapies that last over many years, and that can actually increase the trauma symptoms, not recognising that these symptoms are in fact the results of trauma. Consequently, cause-related therapy is not considered as an option and the possibilities of a therapeutic working through of the trauma remain unexplored.

The physical connection
A psychological trauma can be implicated in many physical symptoms and illnesses in different ways:

- The trauma gives rise not only to psychological and emotional damage, but also to physical damage. Example: if a woman is beaten and choked during a rape, her body will store the memory of the physical hurt.

91

- Psychological injury can be split off into the physical body; that is, the consciously perceived memory of the trauma remains only as bodily pain without a medical basis. For example: tightening of the chest because the loss of a loved one cannot be mourned.
- The traumatic experience creates an insoluble emotional conflict that takes up large amounts of energy, thereby weakening the normal harmonious interplay between body, mind and spirit, and so increasing the risk of the person having an accident or developing a chronic, physical illness (for example asthma, neuro-dermatitis or cancer).

Body, psyche and soul are self-organising and functioning systems. If a person is physically ill, they may not necessarily be psychologically ill and vice versa. Nor can the psychological health of a person be determined by their level of intelligence. Nonetheless, these systems must be co-ordinated within the individual and do affect each other. Thus, it can happen that the physical metabolism of the body may become impaired through feelings of depression. The hypothalamus, as an important command centre for human feelings, influences our sense of hunger and thirst through the hormonal system. The body's immune system exists in an active exchange of information with the hormone system and can fall out of synch when it is under persistent long-term stress. Often physical symptoms of illness are manifestations of a disturbance in the psyche, and these physical symptoms can therefore only disappear when the issues in the psyche are resolved.

There is much evidence to suggest that human beings are the product of a long history of evolution, in which many sub-systems have been united into a whole. These sub-systems pursue their own goals obeying their own inherent rules, and have to be integrated into the whole. Each system must be able to hold its own as a distinct entity in order to be functionally capable, and must also co-ordinate with other subsystems, neither following nor dominating. This means that metabolism, sexuality, perception, feeling, thought, imagination, memory, movement and action are relatively autonomic functioning systems within the human body, as well as exchange processes between people and their natural and social environment. So long as everything works together in a co-ordinated way we are psychologically and physically healthy.

The psychological functions are localised in a highly specialised way in the human nervous system, interwoven throughout the whole body while predominately concentrated in the brain. So the nervous system's task is to facilitate the development of the individual psychological functions and to ensure that they are co-ordinated.

Psychological health can be understood as present when the stream of energy and information between the relevant individual specialised elements flows freely back and forth. Perception is closely linked to feeling; feeling and thinking stay in communication; thought connects with action; memory influences perception and so on. In principle, there is no polarisation between heart and head, or feelings and cognition.

Conversely, psychological mis-development is brought about through influences which:

- hinder an age-appropriate development of psychological functions, or chronologically excessively delay this development
- interrupt the exchange of energy and information between the functioning elements or limit it to the minimum.

When these obstructive influences are so massive that they can no longer be balanced out by the whole system, the result will be psychological disorder. Thus, in the case of each individual person the same question must be put: how strong are the forces that ensure psychological and emotional stability and how strong are the forces that destabilise the whole system? In my opinion, it is primarily traumatic experiences that bring the psychologically functioning system and its complex inter-relationships and dynamics close to destruction.

The amygdala and the hippocampus

As in the case of stress reactions, brain researchers are finding increasingly specific processes and structures relating to traumatic experiences within the brain (van der Kolk, 2000; Bering, Fischer and Johansen, 2005). It currently seems possible to propose a small nerve concentration in the midbrain as being the essential control centre for trauma experiences. The amygdala clearly has the task of acting as a filter for dangerous experiences, drawing out from these experiences any information that might indicate danger and be life threatening. It stores these patterns of information, sending out corresponding alarm signals when it recognises a re-occurrence, so that an automatic and reflexive physical and emotional reaction is possible. However, under extreme stress the neurons of the amygdala fire so strongly that they interrupt any further delivery of information to other regions of the brain, for example the hippocampus, a nerve structure that also lies close to the amygdala. This, then, prevents the experience of the traumatic situation from being stored like other experiences, as a whole experience, episodically, biographically and in relation to the 'I'.

Because the hippocampus is also linked with the thalamus as well as both the cerebral cortices and the centre for speech, traumatic events are usually followed by an inability to express the experience through speech. A traumatic experience literally robs one of one's speech, it is an experience that is unspeakable. That is why people often only remember their traumatic experience in fragments. Retelling the trauma reveals the gaps and time lapses.

Case Study 16:

Fragments of memory

"A survivor could recall and relate the march of death west from Auschwitz to the next camp. He could describe the circumstances of that dreadful night, the frost and the

certain death for all those who fell behind. He had no doubt that he remembered everything, though he had never had the opportunity, or the audience, to retell the whole story. Shortly afterwards he was able to verify what he actually remembered as part of the 'media programming on the experiences of witnesses'. This showed that his memories were only specific, unrelated episodes and isolated fragments."
(Krystal and Farms, 2000)

When someone only partially remembers their childhood, or not all, there is an increased likelihood that during the forgotten time-period he underwent a traumatic experience. These memory gaps make it extremely difficult for traumatised people to act as credible witnesses in court. Judges, public prosecutors and lawyers need to be familiar with the effects of a traumatic experience on the person's ability to remember. A grounding in psychotraumatology would be useful for members of the legal and public prosecution professions.

Pharmacological experiments have succeeded in helping us to understand the phenomenon of "dissociation" that is typical of the traumatic event. Ketamine, a chemical that cuts off the activity of the arousal neurotransmitter 'glutamate' in the brain, when administered to test participants resulted in reports of a slowing down of sense of time, a loss of sense of identity ("depersonalisation"), and of reality ("derealisation"), and memory gaps ("amnesia") (Krystal amongst others 1994, quoted from Herman, 2003).

Thus we can see that, on the physiological level too, there is a qualitative difference between the stress and the trauma reaction. Both involve emergency mechanisms, however the stress reaction energises, while the trauma reaction paralyses. Stress makes one wide-awake, whereas trauma deadens one. The trauma reaction succeeds the stress reaction; it is the last resort when all else fails. Useful medical and physically oriented intervention can significantly further and support the healing process after traumatisation. However, they remain ineffective, if the relationship between the physical problem and the trauma itself is not recognised, whether knowingly or from ignorance, as in the following example:

> A patient described her feelings of complete defencelessness after a well-intentioned treatment by her chiropractor. She arrived at her next therapy session contemplating suicide. Her chiropractor had told her that nothing in her body was in the right place, and that he had "put everything to rights" again. But this process had deprived her of the physical construction that kept the memories of sexual abuse out of her conscious awareness.

Social aspects of trauma

The concept of trauma in my opinion cannot be reduced to merely an examination of biological or psychological phenomena; trauma always happens within a social context. There may be several people who are principally affected by an event, and a number of others who, although not directly injured psychologically, nonetheless may suffer gravely from the after-effects of trauma. We can imagine, for example, what might happen in a family when a soldier returns home, traumatised by the war. Small bonding systems like families can be pervasively traumatised by large occurrences such as wars, accidents and natural catastrophes, just as much as larger systems of people like villages, towns, peoples or nations.

Restricting the concept of trauma to those directly affected, as is done in the diagnosis of a Post Traumatic Stress Disorder, falls short not just in the understanding of trauma events, but also in the recognition of the possibility of doing something about it: "Psycho-social traumatisation implies injuries that cannot be countered purely on a psychotherapeutic level. The support package must also always have in mind the ability to influence the causes of the injury; for if political conditions are not explicitly considered the risk of any psychotherapeutic work being ineffective is great" (Heckl, 2003). Hence traumas are also social realities and they must therefore be considered in the light of both their social and political causes, conditions and consequences. The unconditional acknowledgement and acceptance of the reality of traumatisation would have an enormous impact on our social consciousness, and on our scientific, legal, health and social systems.

Influenced by the international interest in systemic constellations, I have had repeated opportunities to familiarise myself with situations in other countries, and because constellations can bring time periods from as long ago as 100 years into view, historical events that have traumatised whole countries collectively are portrayed in individual and family fates again and again. The Spanish civil war and the time of the Portuguese dictators have had just such traumatic after-effects on the lives of many individuals and families. In British families, the first and second world wars continue to have a powerful effect. In Germany, Russia and China one continues to find the traumatising effects of the dictatorships of Hitler, Stalin and Mao Tse Tung.

Too strong a focus on individualised trauma often does not help in understanding the symptomatology of some serious psychological illnesses. When considering a person who suffers psychologically he or she may not have experienced a trauma, but often is entangled in the trauma of their parents who may have suffered a traumatic event in war for example. Larger social events are often in the background of individual suffering even if they occurred generations back. Additionally there is the fact that traumatised people often receive little or no proper help from their social environment. In Case Study 17 a situation is described in which various reactions from the environment quite probably contributed to the consequences of the trauma becoming chronic for the woman rather than helping her to recover.

Case Study 17:

The consequences of a dog bite

Five years ago Mrs. M (aged 50) was on her way to work when, totally unexpectedly, she was badly bitten by a large dog on her right hip. During the experience, she was frightened that she would die, and suffered severely from shock. The physical wound was treated in the emergency outpatients department of a hospital, and after a couple of consultations with her doctor Mrs. M was referred to a psychiatrist because of her fear of dogs. Meanwhile she became extremely anxious, complained of nightmares and seriously disturbed sleep. She developed a powerful phobia of dogs which, in the course of time, and in spite of the drugs prescribed by her psychiatrist, worsened into panic attacks. These were accompanied by heart palpitations, shivering, sweating, constriction in the throat and shortness of breath. She also exhibited further symptoms of trauma such as constant anxiety, muscular tension, pressure in her head and dizziness, dry mouth and a feeling of helplessness. In the course of time she increasingly experienced symptoms of depression, exhaustion, loss of energy, an increasing sense of hopelessness and loss of the ability to enjoy life. She only occasionally left her house without being accompanied. She lived in constant fear that she would meet a dog.

The psychiatrist prescribed anti-depressants in addition to her other medicines. He advised her not to give up her work. By his hypothesis that her symptoms of fear and depression might indicate Parkinson's disease, which might later cause her blindness or lameness, he created even more anxiety and stress for her.

The medication did nothing to alleviate the condition for Mrs. M and after some time it became impossible for her to carry on with her work in the countryside where there were many unrestrained dogs. When she was confronted she could only avoid the possibility of attack by running to the nearest house or getting into her car. Two years after the original incident she was sacked because of her inability to do her job which plunged her further into depression. She was referred for three months' treatment in a psychosomatic clinic*, which stabilised her condition somewhat, and after a further three-months' stay in the clinic, one and a half years after the original event, she was finally able to give up one of her prescriptions.

A further cause of stress for Mrs. M was the long legal case that ensued, as neither the dog owner nor the insurance company wanted to pay damages. Using the argument that there was no "adequate causality" between the dog bite, her anxiety and the loss of her job, damages and compensation were withheld for some considerable time. Mrs. M's son suggested that "the dog owner was politically connected to several organisations in the town, and various things indicated some dishonest dealings in the whole business. Even our own lawyer is clearly implicated in the matter, a fact that he has never mentioned to us."

Although at the outset she had been supported by her husband, after five years he had become overwhelmed and resigned to the situation. Up to the day of the traumatic event Mrs. M had shown no psychological problems, nor had she ever taken drugs for such symptoms. She had never been fearful or depressed. She was socially well integrated and had raised two children. Relatives and friends described her up until the time of the incident as a very optimistic, amiable and hard working woman, who gladly undertook her job as a care assistant.

In cases such as this, a series of reactions from society and community contribute to a trauma becoming chronic:

- Medical interventions are undertaken without considering the possible traumatic background to physical injury.

* In Germany there are specialist clinics which focus on the psychosomatic process.

Orthopaedic, surgical or gynaecological treatments are followed through but the focus is purely on the diseased or injured part of the body, without regard for the emotional and psychological state of the patient.

- Existential anxiety would decrease if medical and social care systems took the fears of patients seriously and did not minimise or ignore them. The patient uses up precious energy repressing these fears that could be used for the healing process.

- Psychiatric interventions too frequently only use medication, omitting any enquiry into the traumatic causes of the symptoms, and without including any specifically trauma-oriented therapy in their interventions. Then, sometimes because the drug treatment is not successful, the traumatised patient may be belittled, made out to be unwilling to recover and return to work, or impossible to heal.

- Employees are sometimes forced to leave the workplace without being offered alternative situations within the organisation that they might be more able to cope with, their traumatic experience unacknowledged.

- Stays in treatment centres are recommended with non-specific interventions offered which only affect the secondary consequences of the trauma (e.g. the reactive depression) without focussing on and analysing the primary traumatic event (e.g. the life threatening occurrence).

- Demands for compensation and damages are rejected by insurance companies, leading to long-drawn out legal disputes in the courts. Neither the caseworkers in insurance companies nor participating solicitors and judges, are equipped with any basic understanding of psychotraumatology, so they judge cases according to a perception of the person as being in good psychological health, which is inadequate to an appropriate judgement of the consequences of trauma since traumatic events go beyond the normal level of experience.

The behaviour of a traumatised person is often misunderstood by the layperson, sometimes arousing annoyance, leading to the view that the person is malingering or a troublemaker. Judges, and even the lawyers of the injured party, may favour the injuring party, who because of his or her single-mindedness makes the stronger and 'healthier' impression. Traumatised people are often not in a good enough state to choose their lawyers with sufficient care, let alone confront them or terminate their services if it becomes clear that they are siding with the opposition.

Even close relatives such as parents, children and spouses may expect the traumatised person to return to normality within a relatively short space of time. With the best will in the world, they also find it hard to understand fully the psychological state of the traumatised person. According to their understanding of human health, time should heal all wounds, provided the sufferer has the will to heal. The fact that over time trauma goes deeper and deeper into the psyche, particularly when there is no immediate and competent help available, resulting in the traumatised person becoming increasingly sidelined or excluded, is scarcely known. Outsiders find it difficult to understand and accept that, without focused therapy, traumatised people themselves are unable to understand their trauma and its symptoms no matter how hard they try. Therefore, after a while, even close relatives may be unable to bear the suffering of the traumatised person, and may start to avoid her or persuade her to stop talking about her suffering and to feel ashamed of her inability to overcome the trauma.

4.6 The Transmission of Trauma Experiences over Generations

The effects of traumatic events are not limited to the actual victim, as we have seen, since a trauma takes place within and affects our relational systems, both public and intimate. However, that is not the end of it; trauma affects relational systems even when those originally traumatised are dead.

Sometimes the original event may be ten, twenty, fifty or even a hundred years in the past, but it can still affect those in the present, both psychologically and emotionally.

In order to understand this historical, and at times history-making, dimension of traumatic experience we must connect the theory of bonding with trauma theory. Through the medium of emotional and psychological bonding, traumatic experiences are passed from one generation to the next, so that children are drawn into and affected by the traumatic experiences of their parents. The changes in the person brought about by a traumatic event are extended to the children through the person's relationship as mother or father. It is through the psychological and emotional process of bonding, that the psychological wounds in a family are 'handed down' and inherited.

The trauma history does not even necessarily end with the second generation after the original experience. The children who have been psychologically affected by their parents will also pass some of this conditioning on to their children, again through the parent-child bonding process. And no matter how improbable it may sound, this is still not the end of the story. It is clear from my therapeutic work that even the great-grand-child may become entangled psychologically and emotionally in the traumatic experiences of his great grandparents. The entire sequence of generations can read like a succession of traumas in such cases.

As I hope to show comprehensively in the following section, this reflection on the trans-generational transmission of traumatic experiences in human relationship systems gives us a key to understanding many psychological symptoms of illnesses that otherwise often appear puzzling and inexplicable. That these observations are not fundamentally new has already been mentioned at the end of chapter two. There are many references in the psychotherapeutic literature to the possibility of the trans-generational transmission of traumatic experiences. The psychoanalyst Christa Schmidt made the discovery that some of the dreams of her patients could be understood much more logically if she did not relate the content of the dream solely to the personal unconscious. If one takes into consideration the possibility that the content of the dream stems from the experiences of the parents of the patient, completely new and more logical contexts of meaning are revealed.

Case Study 18:

A horrifying inheritance

"Many of my patients suffered from illnesses and psychological and emotional disorders which, in spite of years of medical and psychological intervention, seemed to be incurable. They were caught in what seemed to them to be inexplicable psychological and emotional conflicts and relationship disorders. They felt afraid and threatened. Some led their lives at times as though accompanied by an inner compulsion, actors in a role that was foreign to them. Several had the feeling that they had to spend their whole life in flight from something or imprisoned in a bunker. These phenomena were incomprehensible when referred to the actual life situations of the individual patients. Many of their dreams could not be explained by simply studying their individual biographies. Blitzkrieg, burning houses, collapsing walls, the frozen wastes of Siberia, shootings, rapes, plunder and persecution were sometimes the dream images of these patients, who had themselves not lived through the war and scarcely, if at all, discussed their parents' experiences of it. In many cases it was precisely this inexplicable aspect of the content of their dreams that uncovered the key to family secrets, led to a dialogue with their parents and finally to the disclosure of their parents' trauma. These had been unconsciously handed on to the children and, fascinatingly, have emerged in the real original experiences of the parents and the corresponding dreams" (Schmidt, 2004).

Carl Gustav Jung's ideas about a collective unconscious become more concrete and tangible in light of links between bonding theories and trauma theory. The acceptance of the notion that a patient's psychological conflict may not originate from their own experiences, but may indeed be inherited from their ancestors would fundamentally change our view and practice of psychotherapy. It would amount to a revolution in the different schools of psychiatric and psychotherapeutic thinking that currently assume the cause of illness as lying within the patient's own experience.

More and more scientists and therapists are starting to recognise a connection between trauma and bonding disorders. Professor Daniel Schecter from New York states: "Traumatised mothers with the symptoms of a post-traumatic stress disorder transmit their traumatic experience through constant interaction with their children on every level. The children react to the implicit communications of the mother and become an active, though inappropriate, participant in the mother's attempts to find meaning and peace in the face of destruction and physiological disintegration. The resulting interactions give rise to a variation on the theme of the original trauma. This echoes in the psyche of the mother and child and influences the child's development of emotional regulation" (Schecter, 2003).

Dr. Karl Heinz Brisch from Munich also elaborates in detail on the connection between experiences of trauma in parents and the development of bonding disorders in their children: when parents with experience of trauma "have a child, there is the risk that this child will have an increased probability of also developing a disorganised pattern of bonding. There is, meanwhile, a growing body of research evidence that implies a mechanism for the transmission of parental experience of trauma to the next generation. In interactions with their children traumatised parents behave in an aggressive, hostile manner, they make their children afraid or, because of their children, are afraid themselves" (Schuengel, 1999).

Many parents get into a state of powerlessness or helplessness when playing with or caring for their child. (George and Solomon, 1989) Because parents who are fearful or feel help-less cannot transmit the feeling of a 'secure, emotional haven' to their child, the child will not be able to have a constant, reliable experience of emotional security in their bonding process. The interaction with the mother or father, or in extreme cases with both parents, becomes for the child an unpredictable source of both anxiety and potential security at the same time. In any event, he never knows exactly what can be relied upon (Hesse and Main, 1999, 2002; Brisch, 2003). About 80% of children of traumatised parents show just such traumatised bonding patterns, outwardly expressed by contra-dictory motoric behaviour patterns and stereotypes, and trancelike states.

In my view, the methodology of family constellations contributes a great deal to this change in consciousness: that specific feelings can be inherited from our ancestors. In the book *Love's Hidden Symmetry* (Hellinger, Weber, Beaumont 1998), which made constellations work known to a wide read-ership, the text returns again and again to the subject of feelings, such as sadness or anger, that are 'taken over' by chil-dren or 'shifted' onto others in the family system. It is primarily through the inclusion of deceased relatives in constellations that the traumatic field is revealed, without Hellinger spelling it out in so many words. Traumatic indica-tors in a constellation are essentially interpreted as bonding indicators by Hellinger and many people who work according to his methods. Implicit in this however is the danger of short-circuited interpretations of the symptoms of illness, and a possible neglect of proven psychotherapeutic interventions in relation to traumatised patients. The phenomenon of trauma receives just as little attention from many counsellors and ther-apists who work with other methods. I am sure it will still take some time before this 'trauma blindness' (Riedesser, 2004) amongst all professional helpers and the general public is over-come.

4.7 Four Types of Trauma and their Core Emotional Conflicts

In the following chapters of this book, I will set out the four types of trauma that I have distinguished and attempt to illustrate the theory of the transgenerational transmission of traumatic experiences through relationships involving bonding.

It has become increasingly clear to me through practical work with patients, that *all* serious psychological illnesses have a psychological trauma at their root. Consequently, I have attempted to systematise further the concept of 'psychotrauma', already well-documented in the professional literature, and to render it accessible for practical application in the therapeutic setting. I make distinctions between psychological traumata according to their different causes. On a psychological and emotional level these traumata also entail different coping strategies and different symptoms of psychological injury. Each type of trauma accordingly also requires a special strategy for its therapeutic treatment.

I suggest the following classifications:

- existential trauma
- loss trauma
- bonding trauma
- bonding system trauma (trauma of a whole bonding system)

In my opinion this allows us to reduce the multiplicity of symptom models of psychological injury to a manageable number on the basis of underlying causes. It also enables us to clarify the link between traumatic events and the bonding process.

It seems to me that the essential aspect of psychological trauma is that it presents insoluble emotional conflicts. The experience of a trauma takes a person into a state in which, in the immediate aftermath, they are no longer able to function properly. No matter what the person feels or thinks or does he

cannot resolve the emotional conflict and finds himself helpless to improve his situation. This situation makes it more or
less impossible for the person to carry on his family and social
relationships appropriately. He unavoidably entangles others in
his own insoluble emotional conflicts, and finds himself more
easily enmeshed in the unresolved conflicts of others. In table
1 I have set out the respective core conflicts of the four trauma
types. They are thoroughly expanded upon in the following
chapters 5–8.

Table 1.

Type of Trauma	Trauma Situation	Central Feelings	Emotional Conflict
Existential Trauma (eg: accidents, rape)	Threat to one's mortality	Fear of death	To retreat and avoid or to stand firm
Loss Trauma (eg: sudden separation, death of a child)	The loss of a beloved person or an essential life status	Fear of abandonment	To let go and grieve or hold on to the past and what has been lost
Bonding Trauma (eg: rejection of the child by the mother)	The violation of the emotional bonding	Confusion of all emotions, disappointed love and helpless rage	To trust or mistrust people, or learning to love again
Trauma of the Bonding System (eg: infanticide, incest)	The perpetration of morally and ethically unjustifiable acts	Shame and guilt	To hide and conceal the issue or to take responsibility of guilt

Setting out trauma according to the type of conflict they
generate, allows us a different view of the various types of
trauma, and the difficulties of returning to a normal life after
a specific trauma experience become more easily recognisable.
When we look at the basic structure of such a conflict the
enormity of the task before the traumatised person wishing to
move beyond the trauma becomes clearer.

The implication for professional interaction with traumatised people and their family systems is that clarity as to the

type of insoluble conflict involved is essential. Only with this understanding can the helping professional find a positive outcome to the paradox for the patient or his dependents. The therapist is then able to resist distraction by the diversionary and avoidant strategies of the patient from the essential work on the core conflict.

5

Existential Trauma

5.1 Introduction

The most profound experience we can have is helplessly to face our own death, recognising the real mortal danger we are in, and be unable to do anything about it. I call these experiences 'existential traumas'. Existential traumas are always concerned with life and death, with being and non-being.

The following are examples of situations that are potentially life threatening and therefore likely to be traumatic:

- natural catastrophes (e.g. earthquakes, fires, floods, storms),
- serious accidents,
- terrorist attacks,
- the many dangers and threats to life resulting from war,
- violent assault, abduction, rape etc (Kramer, 2003),
- a diagnosis of a life-threatening illness (e.g. cancer, AIDS).

In situations of existential trauma our experience is that we no longer have control of our own life, not knowing if we will survive or what we can do to increase our chances of survival. The core emotional conflict stems from the fact that, despite the perceived danger of death, we cannot act and save our self through our own actions. We are essentially powerless to change the situation.

Naturally, fear of death is the overriding experience in situations of existential trauma. There may be accompanying feelings of guilt if we also have to watch as others die and we are powerless to help them. Soldiers, for example, who survived by chance while their comrades died, frequently report feeling guilty (Shaw, 2003). This may also be accompanied by feelings of shame, because of having been overwhelmed and humiliated by someone more powerful or because, during the traumatic situation, we lost control of our bladder or bowel muscles.

Panic Attacks and Anxiety

Panic attacks and anxiety seem to be mainly associated with trauma of existence. If we survive the actual traumatic event the shock reaction fades, and the immediate struggle to defend ourselves against the perceptions and feelings that threaten to overwhelm us becomes less. Usually after a certain lapse of time, we find that our consciousness is infiltrated by memories of the trauma experience (flashbacks). This usually occurs in situations that are in some way similar to the original situation, and which re-awaken the traumatic experience. All of the predictable processes and strategies described in the section on Psychological Trauma above (Chapter 4) will apply. This suggests that in an existential trauma part of the personality, that which experiences the trauma, stores it. After surviving the traumatic situation, this part of the personality is pushed into the unconscious, split off from the remaining structure of the personality, so that the person can carry on with their life. The split-off traumatised part continues its existence within the personality structure as a whole. It is alert to any danger signs that might re-trigger the traumatic experience, its purpose being to avoid any kind of re-experiencing of the anxiety and powerlessness of such a situation. In cases of existential trauma particularly it is likely that a part of the person would like to withdraw completely from any situation that might in any way be potentially dangerous. To that aspect of the person, only a place of complete withdrawal might feel sufficiently safe, where nothing unforeseen could happen. However, the attempt to avoid any anxiety gives rise to further anxiety, because the need to avoid provokes anxiety itself. When this split-off part senses danger, it sounds an alarm, which the person notices by a raised pulse, accelerated heartbeat, sweating, indigestion, and other symptoms that constitute a panic attack. (See Appendix 2 for a description of Panic Disorder from the DSM IV).

The experience of de-realisation (having no reference point for reality) and de-personalisation (not knowing who one is anymore) (ref. Appendix 2) fits in with the concept of the split in the personality. The part of the person that normally consciously perceives and experiences seems to have no apparent effective contact with the split off traumatised part, and so has no rational understanding of what is happening to them during a panic attack. During the attack, this split off part steps into the foreground, and the person experiences a re-traumatisation triggered by a current situation that is reminiscent of the original situation.

Claude Anshin Thomas was a survivor of the Vietnam War. The 'flashback' situation he describes directly relates to the original trauma: "It can happen that I am in a grocer's shop and take a tin of vegetables from the shelf and suddenly I am overwhelmed by fear that the tin contains a camouflaged explosive. Reason tells me that it isn't so but I spent a year in surroundings where it was so – and still today I am not able to fully process the depths of this experience" (Thomas, 2003).

It is particularly difficult to recognise the link between panic symptoms and traumas if the experience of the trauma situation has been completely erased from the consciousness, for example if the trauma occurred in very early childhood. However, if the event is known to the person, he will try to understand what happened, repeatedly re-playing it in his mind in the hope that there might have been a way out that he has overlooked. If he has the opportunity, he will repeatedly talk the situation through with others. People who were present during the actual situation are best for this, while priests and therapists may also be of help. However, this may not result in the trauma being fully processed. In addition reading books or watching violent films can't assist in overcoming the inner turmoil. In my opinion, it is only by working with someone who has sufficient experience in trauma work that the trauma-tised part of the personality can be released from the fear of death and be integrated.

The Longer-term Consequences

The long-term consequences of an existential trauma depend, amongst other things, on whether and how quickly the person is able to feel safe again. The overwhelming fear of death and danger can ultimately only be overcome if it is rapidly coun-teracted by a feeling of stability and safety. Protection from further experiences of attacks to one's life and health, for example by the police and justice system, is thus one of the most important factors in dealing with trauma. Unfortunately, however this protection is often denied, primarily where violence, for example in the family and out of the public eye, is concerned.

Case Study 19:

Defenceless and at the mercy of the neighbours

The consequences of the existential trauma of one of my patients struck me particularly. He was threatened with a gun and beaten unconscious by his neighbour. This patient, who prior to the incident had been a vibrant man, energeti-cally immersed in his life, after this trauma would break into a sweat at the mere mention of his neighbour's name. As his psychological and physical suffering worsened, he moved out of the family home to escape the daily meetings with his neighbour, which caused him great anxiety. However, this did not decrease the traumatic re-triggered reactions, which had already become chronic.

He became increasingly incapable of doing his job and a large part of his emotional and mental resources were occupied with attempting to suppress the persistent memories and flashbacks of the trauma. He suffered from stomach and kidney complaints in addition to repeated and sometimes serious accidents while working around the house. His entire family life, which had clearly been very happy prior to the trauma, suffered increasingly from the worsening consequences of his traumatisation. His children developed problems at school and were no longer achieving their targets.

What made the whole thing still more difficult, was the fact that the reality of the trauma and its effects were not acknowledged by either the civil or the criminal law courts. In my opinion, this denied him a level of social protection that he urgently needed in his situation. The legal judgement that was in favour of his neighbour, maintaining that he had not had a gun with him during the attack, confirmed my patient in his fear that he could not be safe with this man, who he feared was prepared to use violence and to kill. He was also frightened that the neighbour would find him at his new home and continue to pose a threat to him and his family. In fact he stated that he repeatedly saw the neighbour driving slowly and provocatively past his new home. The man seemed to revel in the fear that he provoked. He was like a hunter searching for his prey.

The fact that, for the patient there was a continuing danger after the original incident, made it significantly more difficult for him to make good use of his therapy.

Societal challenges and large scale existential trauma
The fact that existential trauma may be denied by society presents a challenge to the process of working through an existential trauma. In many cases the state has refused to acknowledge the trauma caused to soldiers by war. In the First World War soldiers who showed clear signs of trauma were punished as cowards or traitors in both Germany and Great Britain. A television documentary about American soldiers in the first Iraq war showed medical experts refusing to acknowledge that the physical and emotional illnesses of many of them were the result of trauma caused by war experiences (see also Case Study 15 above).

The situation is most favourable for victims of an existential trauma involving a large group or even a whole country, where the chances are good that the perpetrators of the trauma will be clearly identified as guilty. This has been the case with the victims of the 9/11 attack on the World Trade Centre in New York, who received a flood of offers of help alongside much medical, psychological and social support (Schecter, Coates and First, 2003).

The holocaust also shows the potential ambivalence of a society towards acknowledging the reality of a trauma, and the tendency to lie and shift social responsibility. The genocide of people of Jewish extraction and Judaic belief systematically practised by the National Socialists in Germany, brought millions of people into the situation of an existential trauma. On the one hand, it is a matter of great shame that, for a long time after the end of the war, people who survived the concentration camps were not acknowledged as trauma victims by the experts (see appendix 4). Whereas, on the other hand, it is clearly shown how much the acknowledgement of the concept of trauma is linked to a well-developed humanistic social consciousness. It is a question of political vision whether social resources are employed in ways that increase the level of traumatisation within a society, or in ways that heal prior trauma wounds, thereby working preventatively in relation to understanding the perpetrator-victim spiral.

Conflict acted out

Present situations can call forth old fears without the sufferer being aware of the context. If we recognise that the feelings outlined by patients are actually trauma symptoms it becomes significantly easier in many therapy situations to arrive at the kernel of the problem. If we stay with the superficial and focus on the triggering situation and not on the real causes there is in the main no real solution to the psychological conflict.

Case Study 20:

Panic at the thought of attending a wedding reception

Mr. P had been in therapy for a while and had progressed well. In one session however he described a curious panic that he experienced when he was invited to the wedding of his new girlfriend's brother. The more he considered whether he ought to go to the wedding the more he sank into despair. Ultimately he came to believe that all would be lost if he didn't go. Yet on the other hand he had the feeling that there was so much at home too that was not yet organised and that he absolutely must stay in order to get on with these tasks. Finally, he did indeed drive to the wedding, but was unable to enjoy the lavish occasion because inwardly he felt ill at ease.

I suggested that he enter into the feeling of panic and despair. He experienced it most clearly as a strong pressure on his chest. I helped him to deepen these symptoms through hypnotic support and to allow the accompanying images to surface. He saw himself as a little child of about four years old, who shrieks and romps and whose father tries to silence him. He re-experienced how his father threw himself bodily on top of him and pushed him down onto a settee. The moment came when he had to decide whether to stop shrieking or be crushed by his father and die. He sensed his completely powerless rage.

Tears streamed down his face, tears he never cried as a

child. On reflection he became aware how little he was able to articulate his needs except through shrieking and running away. To be unable to express his wishes, to feel threatened if he refused to do what was expected of him – this was the trigger that turned the wedding invitation into an existentially threatening situation. After the session it immediately occurred to him that he could have called the bride's family and checked out whether it would upset things if he didn't come.

Existential trauma and addiction
In order to suppress the extreme panic and anxiety of existential trauma, psycho-pharmaceuticals are the most frequently chosen addictive substances – that is, tranquillisers or sleeping tablets:

- Sleeping pills: Previously barbiturates, amongst other things, were prescribed to combat states of anxiety and disturbed sleep, but because of the high addictive potential of barbiturates and because overdose results in death, Benzodiazepine has replaced the barbiturate containing pills on the market. Benzodiazepine should only be taken for a maximum of six weeks, otherwise there is a danger of addiction. With sleeping agents that contain Benzodiazepine this danger arises after only two weeks continuous consumption. In order to get round the body's customisation to the drug, the dose must be increased, so that artificial sleep continues to be induced thereby increasing the addiction. This artificial sleep, however, lacks the deep sleep and dream phases that are of primary importance for psychological regeneration. When the sleeping tablets are stopped, the feelings of anxiety return, panic resurfaces and agitation and disturbed sleep increase. In addition, there are withdrawal symptoms, which increase the tendency to escalate the dose, increasing anxiety, leading to greater sleep disturbance and then requiring more medication.

• Tranquilisers: These dampen anxiety and feelings of grief, even making them disappear for a while. However they also suppress joyful feelings. Medically speaking they are only really useful – if at all – in acute circumstances, particularly serious emotional and psychological crisis, cases of massive anxiety, for example after a heart attack or heightened tension before an operation. The addictive motive for taking them, however, is often different as a medication-dependent woman briefly and succinctly puts it: "The tablets were my daily dose of hope. Then I had no anxiety about failing."

Often doctors prescribe such medication to patients for long periods. As long as the body plays along with it, i.e., if it works to an extent, prescription drug dependency can be lived as a socially tolerated, indeed even a socially demanded 'silent form of addiction'.

Alcohol dependency, as a means of suppressing anxiety is more notorious, with people drinking their anxiety away, at least from time to time, striving for some kind of acceptable social existence. There are gender differences as to the preferences for prescription drugs or alcohol. While two thirds of all cases of medication-dependency are women, the opposite is true of alcohol. Men are much more likely to be alcohol-dependent (Brachatzek, 1991; Deutsche Hauptstelle gegen die Suchtgefahren, 2004).

What underlies addiction as it relates to existential trauma, can only be properly dealt with when the sufferer is prepared and supported to confront the original traumatic situation. Claude Anshin Thomas outlines his addiction phase after trauma as follows: "I tried to run from my feelings, to get myself to safety... My running took on different forms. I ran by taking drugs; I ran by drinking; I ran by smoking; I ran by having sex; I ran by moving from place to place" (Thomas, 2003).

Existential trauma and suicide

People who have experienced an existential trauma are not a high risk in terms of a tendency to suicide. Nevertheless it should not be ruled out. War veterans have above average rates of suicide, and it seems that there is also the danger that, in their aggression they take others with them. They "punish" innocent people for what was done to them.

Suicide can also be "staged" unconsciously and appear to be an accident. For example, a patient who had experienced a massive existential trauma, climbed onto the roof of his house to repair the chimney wearing only sandals. He slid off the roof and fell into the garden. Miraculously he survived with a serious injury to his skull. As with the addictive reaction to trauma, suicidal tendencies can only really be disarmed by confronting the source of the anxiety.

In Search of a New World View

Existential traumas shake our belief in the safety of the world in which we live. We see death before our very eyes, and experience acutely our own helplessness. Addiction and suicide are attempts to escape this fear of death, signifying our surrender to this fear.

Other attempts to overcome the trauma may consist of attempting to counteract the experience of powerlessness with power, perhaps becoming obsessed with security, trying to foresee all possible dangers and taking every precaution against them. Some people attempt to become fighters or warmongers looking death straight in the eye and destroying everything that causes them fear. Shaw calls them "berserkers" (Shaw, 2002). On a large group level, for example in the case of a nation state, collective existential traumas have a similar effect: security and survival become the primary goal, and defending against threats from other groups leads to high-level rearmament and militarization. This, then, justifies the tendency to restrict life within the group by regulations about survival and security measures. The group then gathers around a powerful leader who can rule with a strong hand, and promises them protection against danger. From the outside, the group appears to be ready for war. Fear then drives all thought and action and makes people ready to kill.

Groups that live with this existential fear create belief systems for themselves about how their gods, their religion and their way of life are the only ones that can guarantee them safety from threat and danger. Wars are propagated as forms of self-defence, security and peacemaking. In the name of these ideas death, which everyone actually fears, then spreads. Traumas become, through traumas, not extinguished but augmented.

However when death, and our powerlessness in relation to it, is accepted as a condition of human existence, the experience of an existential trauma can lead to alternative ways of addressing the trauma: dealing with our anxieties, gratitude for survival, an understanding that life is too brief and precious to squander it on games of war and power. An existential trauma can thus lead to the recognition that we increase our own propensity for fear when we cause fear to others, and that, instead, we could increase our sense of safety by increasing the sense of safety of others – our 'enemies' and 'rivals'. When we protect our boundaries and are ready to defend them, we do not encourage others to cross them. Within every perpetrator, prepared for violence, there also lies hidden a part of the soul that longs not to be feared, but to be loved. Women who are frequently the victims of violence, long to love men rather than fear them.

5.2 Effects on the following Generation

Why do some people suddenly develop panic attacks quite unexpectedly? Why do some people fear travelling on the underground or being in closed rooms? Why do some no longer trust themselves in public places, feeling acute disabling anxiety?

Millions of people are tormented by such conditions every day of their lives, frequently being labelled with a diagnosis of 'claustrophobia' or 'agoraphobia', which are in the end only

Greek words describing the symptoms. It is a great diagnostic advance when a doctor or therapist accepts that anxieties that suddenly and strongly appear without any real here-and-now threat, might have their origins in a previously experienced traumatic situation. But if one goes even further, and considers the possibility that these fears might have been taken on from another person via the bonding process, then this gives rise to completely new possibilities for a better understanding of these states. New possibilities also arise for a specialised psychotherapy.

Case Study 21:

The trauma behind the trauma

After a car accident a woman began to get inexplicable attacks of anxiety, with images of horror, primarily that something dreadful could befall her husband or her little daughter. The accident seemed to have aroused a deeper layer of her soul, in which another trauma, long split off, lay dormant. When the woman's mother had been five months pregnant with her, her own father had met with an accident. His head had been crushed by a tractor wheel. The images and experiences from this gruesome accident, which her mother had witnessed, now flashed vividly within the mind of the patient; images of spilled blood and the experience of falling from a height, and of death. The patient experienced these images as extraordinarily real and feared that they foreshadowed something that would actually happen, causing her feelings of extreme anxiety about her husband and daughter. These fears, however, were actually the fears of her mother, traumatised by the experience of her husband's accident. By seeing this connection between her fears and the traumatic event in the process of a constellation, the patient could understand that she had taken on her mother's fears, and we could find a meaningful solution.

Such seemingly non-specific fears and feelings can come from even further back, as Case Study 22 shows.

Case Study 22:

Fear of the revenge of the king

A patient, who had been working in a freelance capacity for many years, began to get increasingly anxious about her future economic insecurity. Alongside her legitimate worries about generating new income, there seemed to be something unreal about her anxiety.

A constellation revealed the following connection between her actual fears and the tragic events that had happened in her family of origin. It clearly appeared from the constellation that her mother had been full of anxiety and unable to relate to her as a child at the bonding level. The mother's panic seemed to have overlaid all other feelings, while the representative of the patient initially sat in the corner feeling totally intimidated. During the course of the constellation it turned out, that the panic in the family came from generations before. The great grandfather of the patient, who had been an illegitimate son of a king and a commoner, had initiated a coup against his father, the king. As a result, the family of the great grandfather was subject to an ambush attack presumably initiated by the king. The grandmother of the patient, as a small child, had been present and had observed one of her sisters being killed during the attack.

During the constellation the panic within the family system dissipated when the representative for the great grandfather of the patient was acknowledged as the son of a king and thereby seemed to feel some peace. The representative of the mother also relaxed, her fears easing, and a reconciliation between mother and daughter was possible.

With persistent feelings of fear in cases of the transmitted effects of existential trauma, the solution for the patient lies in trusting themselves to embrace life, recognising that the earlier trauma situation is in the past and does not belong to them now. This counteracts the phenomenon of generalisation, whereby all situations become the specific original situation, which over time escalates anxiety. It is therefore important to understand existential trauma situations as one-off situations that are not repeated and that similar situations are avoidable if measures are taken.

5.3 Particular Issues of the Legacy of Existential Trauma

Holocaust survivors and the sufferings of their children
In Germany in the aftermath of the Second World War, psychotherapists eventually could not ignore the influence of traumatised parents on their children. The connection between the experiences of the survivors of the Nazi persecution and the psychological problems of their children was too obvious to ignore. "So little by little it was recognised that an extreme catastrophe like the holocaust had repercussions for the next generation" (Bohleber, 2000).

Various authors (Trossman, 1968; Grubrich-Simitis, 1979; Niederland, 1980; Moser, 1996) in studying these repercussions, have established that:

- traumatised parents transferred their anxieties to their children,
- the parents needed their children to comfort them, to get rid of their unbearable grief,
- they transferred their stored impulses to hate to their children,
- their loving feelings towards their children were paralysed,
- their insight into the needs of their children was inadequate.

They saw their children as substitutes for murdered members of their family, and required their children, through their lives, to restore family pride and heal the wounds.

As a result, the parent-child relationships in these cases were highly symbiotic, the children taking on the task of caring for the emotional and psychological stability of their parents, actively engaging themselves in the task of attempting to relieve their parents' suffering. Attempts by children to leave the family home often created a serious threat to the fragile family equilibrium, and re-awoke in parents their old fears of extermination, while the children felt guilty about leaving their parents to their fate.

Because many parents could not speak about their traumatic experiences, the children unconsciously picked up their parents' suffering and expanded it in their fantasies. Many unconsciously tried to make what had befallen their parents visible by acting out the trauma in their own lives; many were also angry with their parents for what they perceived as their weakness. In order to protect themselves from their parents' perceived weakness and pain, the children forced themselves to be fearless, even in the face of death. With all of the above, they in turn, terrified their own children, a process that could result in terror psychosis (Ruppert, 2002).

To summarise we can say: traumatised parents unconsciously transfer their experiences onto their children, who then identify themselves unconsciously with the fate of their parents. The child would then live with two conflicting realities: her own present day experience, and that of her parents from the past. "The result is an at least partial confusion of identity or the sense of a fragmented identity" (Bohleber, 2000). Case Study 23 describes in detail how sensitively children feel the fate of their parents, all the more so when it is not talked about. It also shows how the children can break under this strain.

Case Study 23:

The daughter of parents who survived Auschwitz

Kurt Gruenberg's description, in a special edition of the
German journal 'Psyche', of an example of the repercussions of the holocaust for second generation survivors,
leaves a strong impression. The woman he interviewed (he
called her 'Mika I.') was forty years old at the time. She
reported her experiences in her family of origin, in which
both her mother and father had been survivors of Auschwitz
and had remained in Germany after the war. The following,
which clearly moved her a great deal in the telling of it,
emerged in the interview:

- Harmony and unbearable tension co-existed in the family.
- Although the parents did not really get on they needed
  each other and couldn't part.
- Mika I. constantly experienced a mixture of compassion
  and sympathy for her parents. She senses the anguish of
  her mother for the many family members and friends who
  died.
- She experienced her father's choking attacks with him, as
  well as his lapses into childlike behaviour and his
  memory gaps after such attacks.
- Although she was her father's favourite daughter, he
  brutally and repeatedly beat her. She thinks that he
  inflicted on her the violence that he experienced in the
  concentration camp.
- In her view, her parents were 'too sensitive' to speak
  about the details of their experiences, but it was
  constantly present.
- All non-Jews were ultimately felt to be Nazis and therefore murderers of Jews, so non-Jewish friends of their
  daughter were shunned. Mika I. was beaten by her father
  after she met with a German boyfriend. She finally
  succumbed to the family rule that she should only marry

a person of Jewish extraction. Nevertheless after leaving home she accepted contact with the German world in which she lived, and by entering into relationships with non-Jews she tried to reconcile what seemed irreconcilable and to show that it is possible for Jew and German to live together. Basically she was constantly searching for a homeland and neither Germany nor Israel could be that homeland.

Shortly after the interview with Kurt Gruenberg Mika I. took her own life. The painful and sorrowful experiences of traumatised parents manifest themselves less in words than in individual phrases or gestures, in which the content of all their suffering is concentrated.

Case Study 24:

The image of a crying father

The author Kurt Gruenberg writes from personal experience and bewilderment: "I remember just such a gesture of my father's from my own childhood as we were watching a television programme that showed what the allied soldiers found when they liberated a German concentration camp. Up until then I had never seen my father cry. Now he welled up with tears. He bowed over in his armchair and covered his face with his hands. This made a strong impression on me as a ten-year-old boy. Even today I cannot forget the image. In that moment I sensed something of what had happened to him, had an idea of what was going on for him. My glance went to the four surviving photographs of his murdered siblings and his parents, that were placed in the same room" (Gruenberg, 2000).

Panic Attacks resulting from Memories of War

Bombardments, air raids and burning buildings echo in the sudden fears that crop up in the post war generation. Case Study 25 shows the results of an individual therapy with a young man who suffered from panic attacks. He held within himself his mother's panic having witnessed the death of her brother during an aerial attack,

Case Study 25:

Anxiety and hot flushes

A man of about twenty-five came to my practice, because he was constantly plagued by strong feelings of anxiety and hot flushes in his body. They occurred frequently at night and in socially stressful situations, such as during interviews. He experienced at these times an enormous pressure on his chest and profuse sweating.

In the initial interview he related the following: his mother's brother died in the Second World War during a bombing raid. He reported that before the event, for fear of the raids, his then twelve year old mother and her ten year old brother were sent away from Hamburg by their parents, to Würzburg. Shortly afterwards however Würzburg was also bombed. The patient's mother survived the bombing raid but had to watch while her little brother burned to death in a house hit by a bomb. The patient said: "My mother would speak to her friend about the event as though it happened only yesterday."

We did a constellation using cushions which showed the patient placed very close to his mother, while his father stood a way off to the side. The patient's parents had separated when he was eleven. The constellation revealed a dynamic that the patient confirmed in subsequent therapy sessions: his mother secretly wanted to follow her little brother to death – the patient described how she repeatedly

expressed suicidal intentions. She also unconsciously identified her son (the patient) with this brother ("she said that I
had inherited a lot from him.") In the constellation the
patient stood in front of his mother... he told me that he had
often thought of committing suicide. Up to this point in his
life he had not had a girlfriend, as he was strongly attached
to his mother. It was clear that through his early childhood
bonding with his mother he absorbed the terror she felt at
the time of her brother's death.

A resolution for this patient was then possible in several
steps:

- release from the entangled sphere of his mother and
  increased contact with his father;
- relieving the identification with the dead uncle;
- transformation of the experience of anxiety into the experience of pain and grief.

The last step was particularly important for the patient. Fear
of death continues until the death of a beloved person is
agreed to in the heart and the experience of pain is allowed.
In the sixth session the patient managed for the first time to
cry over the death of his uncle. His mother had been unable
to grieve for her brother because of her feelings of guilt that
she had survived and yet had been unable to help him.
Because of these guilt feelings, she could not accept the fate
of her brother and let him really die.

Because the patient was very motivated, this grief work
could be brought to a satisfying result for him within ten
sessions.

Existential traumas with their split-off feelings are transferred
from one generation to the next and as such are ticking time
bombs, which, given the opportunity, will go off. The number
of patients in doctor's surgeries who complained of feelings of

fear and anxiety after the September 11th 2001 terrorist attacks increased dramatically in the wake of the press reports. Events like September 11th can work as triggers that set off buried panic, like time bombs in the human psyche.

Case Study 26:

Panic anxiety because of a new boss

In the case of Mrs M, her panic attacks escalated wildly when she got a new boss. As a background to this the following could be reconstructed: The patient had a mother who, during the war, had to watch her mother, uncle and sister being shot in a low-flying enemy attack. Because Mrs M's new boss also seemed to have unresolved issues of terror which she tried to overcome by being compulsively controlling in her management work, an increasing entanglement grew between them. In their individual fears and vain attempts to overcome them, the situation escalated further for both of them. As the patient recognised this dynamic in the course of a constellation, she was able to free herself from this tangle and clarify her relationship with her mother as opposed to her boss. Little by little the relationship with her boss normalised itself.

6

Trauma of Loss

6.1 Introduction

As we have seen, an essential aspect of human existence is the process by which we make our bonded relationships; bonding between people happens through emotional experience, where the durability of the experience assures the permanence of the bond. Only when an emotional bond occurs between two or more people will they remain together and care for one another.

The strength of these feelings make it difficult for us to leave a bonded relationship, and it is only through a high degree of desensitisation that someone can leave another to whom they are bonded abruptly and with a clear conscience. Usually we are only able to leave those to whom we are strongly bonded by suffering extreme feelings such as anxiety, guilt and grief, and we will avoid such a separation for as long as possible. The stronger the emotional bond, the more anxious we will feel about the separation, and the greater the suffering if it actually happens.

6.2 Different Types of Loss Trauma

If a person suffers the loss of an essential and profound emotional and psychological bond without having desired it or being able to do anything about it, we can describe it as a trauma of loss or a "loss trauma". There are several situations that are likely to give rise to loss trauma, all of which are likely to be sudden and usually unexpected:

- sudden death of a parent when the child is young,
- sudden death of a child,
- sudden death of a sibling,
- sudden death of a loved partner,
- loss of a parent by separation or divorce,
- loss of parents by adoption, fostering or being taken into care,
- loss of a partner by infidelity, separation or divorce.

Trauma of loss can also be the experience of people who, through events such as war, are forced to leave their home, village, town, or country, suddenly becoming refugees. This kind of loss affected millions of people in the Second World War (Lehmann, 1993; Knopp, 2001).

The unexpected loss of a job can also be traumatic, particularly if it also means losing a long-standing membership of an institution or organisation, and the social status, position and material security that has been achieved (Berth, Albani, Stobel-Richter, Geyer and Braehler, 2004).

Loss of good health, for example through a serious physical illness such as cancer, or one's physical integrity, for example through an accident leading to a physical disability, may also be experienced as a trauma of loss. Sometimes the loss of a well-loved animal or pet, may equally cause a trauma of loss.

Not every loss produces trauma however. It depends on the specific circumstances already described in chapter four as to whether the loss generates worry, stress or trauma. The loss of a valuable item is normally only an emotional and psychological worry, perhaps producing a stress situation for example after the loss of a handbag, when credit cards must be cancelled and identification cards re-applied for etc. However this will not usually develop into a trauma.

In order to be categorised as "traumatic", a loss must place the sufferer in a situation of complete powerlessness and helplessness, and the thing lost must be the object of an intimate, vital, bonded relationship. With specific losses, such as the early loss of a parent or child, we can predict with a high degree of probability that the experience would fall into the category of trauma.

Some traumatic losses happen suddenly, such as with accidents for example, while others may be more gradual as in the drawn out illness and resulting death of a partner or child from cancer, AIDS or other incurable disease. These provide a period of preparation, but can still produce a persistent trauma situation.

Loss by prolonged absence of the mother
For newly born children physical contact with their mother is vital for their survival, and they will react to every separation with great anxiety. Prolonged absences of the mother are hard to bear, and the child will scream and cry until they have either re-established contact or they are exhausted. It is not until a child is about three years old that they can tolerate a prolonged absence of the mother without profound psychological and emotional suffering. At that age they are at a stage when they are able to understand the reasons why the mother cannot be there, and can be comforted with the knowledge and confidence that she will return within the foreseeable future.

For children under the age of three, a mother's absence lasting a few days or a week (for example if she has to go to hospital) can have a traumatic quality, which the child can only cope with by splitting off the feelings of anxiety, rage and despair. When the mother returns after a prolonged time, the child may not recognise her and the original trust between mother and child may have been seriously damaged. A bond that has been secure from the start may become an insecure-ambivalent attachment or even an insecure-avoidant attachment (Bowlby, 1998). The core feeling in the child's life may develop into anxiety, disappointment or hopelessness. In later relationships the child may become either exaggeratedly independent ("If no one else cares about me then I don't need anyone!") or exaggeratedly dependent and careful ("I have to take a great deal of care of other people and be there for them so that they don't leave me.").

Death of a mother in childbirth

The most serious of the loss traumas is the early loss of parents. The most extreme example of this for the child is when their mother dies while giving birth to them, not just because the mother is no longer there but because it is at the moment of birth, the moment at which life is passed on from mother to child. When the child becomes aware of this fact later in life, she may become seriously depressed from the idea that her mother died giving her life, that she was the cause of her mother's death. Children whose mothers died giving birth to them often avoid parenthood themselves. Many may seek stability for example in religion, perhaps entering a religious community or following a spiritual path. In the psyche of the person sexuality and motherhood become inextricably linked with death.

Themes of death and grief will be common in the life of someone who lost their parents early on, but they are likely to avoid the feelings; it is just too painful, so they frequently dismiss it and behave outwardly as though nothing important had happened. They cannot look towards their dead parent because they are afraid that they might then also have to die.

Loss of a parent of older children

The older a child is when she loses a parent, the harder it becomes for the child to openly express their grief. The essential phase of unrestrained grieving often doesn't happen especially when the

132

child cannot understand the reasons for the departure or death of her parent. This might be the case when for example the father has been killed in war, or suddenly disappears after a separation from her mother and is not seen again.

The child will try to protect herself from the emotional and psychological pain, additionally attempting to protect the remaining parent, by pushing away her feelings of grief, so interrupting the grieving process, causing this essential part of the child to be split off and hidden.

Case Study 27:

The suit of armour

A patient described her reaction to the sudden death of her father when she was eight years old as follows: "My father introduced me to nature and I was happy with him. I can't remember the first four years after his death. I don't know whether I grieved nor how much. I think I put on a suit of armour to protect myself from experiencing these distressing feelings. I think I thought that if I didn't I would also have to die."

In order to avoid contact with the traumatic feelings, children will often put *all* their feelings aside, both positive and negative. Instead, a controlling intellect develops with the most rational principles so as to avoid contact with the feelings of loss. As several patients have told me, they may even avoid reading the newspapers, watching television or going to the cinema so that they are not confronted with situations that might arouse the feelings. This means that life becomes either very superficial or an exhausting burden. Losing a parent impedes their ability to enjoy life, influencing their entire life, including, amongst other things, their choice of profession or work, e.g. they are more likely to choose a career that does not remind them of strong feelings, such as in engineering or technology.

The loss of parents through adoption
In many countries there is a minimum period before a child can be given up for adoption, and although this period may be short, it means that the baby will already have had a very intensive experience of their birth mother. Separating from the birth mother is therefore always a trauma of loss and as such, an experience of great impact. This is also true for older children. Adopted children not only lose their mother and father, but they also lose their membership of the system of their entire family of origin, both the mother's side and the father's. Additionally they may also lose bonded relationships with siblings.

When the fact of adoption is concealed from the child until they are older there is then likely to be a breakdown in the trusting relationship with the adoptive parents, which compounds the original experience of trauma. Every adopted child will ask themselves questions that undermine their self-esteem and sense of identity: Why did my mother give me away? Didn't she like me? Is there something wrong with me? Was I bad? What is wrong with me? Who was my father?

Loss by the separation of parents
The separation of parents is not as dramatic as the death of a parent, but even so can have a traumatic affect on the child. Whether the loss is of a parent who just leaves or is through a negotiated and visible process such as divorce, it is still likely to be very distressing for the child. Children will often conceal their feelings or express them through attention-seeking behaviour or physical illness. If one of the parents after the divorce or separation is manifestly pleased that the other parent is no longer present, the child becomes mistrusting of the environment as a safe place to express his feelings. Children always essentially want to have both parents; they would rather their parents didn't separate and they may act out to try and prevent the separation. They will never lose their attachment to the lost parent, even though they may have to adjust and outwardly attune them-

selves more towards the parent with whom they live after the separation.

Loss of one's child
There are various ways in which parents may lose their child:

- by fatal accident,
- by criminal incident (for example kidnapping),
- by fatal illness,
- by miscarriage,
- by abortion,
- by adoption or fostering.

It must be noted that in some of these situations, such as adoption, abortion and miscarriage, the father may be excluded from the effects of loss if he is not told of the existence of the child. When the child is the victim of a violent crime, impulses of revenge and retribution may add to a sense of powerlessness and feelings of guilt in the parents.

All of these events will develop in different ways according to type and circumstances. However, the longer the period of attachment between the parents and their child, the more dramatic is the loss. The early death of a first child has a particularly traumatic quality for a woman, and as a result children and death may become linked emotionally with each other for her. Each time she brings another child into the world, she may live with the persistent fear that she will lose this child too.

In the case of both a wanted or an unwanted termination the emotional attachment between the mother and child is already formed in the womb. Every woman will have an emotional relationship to the child she is carrying providing she herself is not already so traumatised that she is desensitised to herself and to the child, and controlled pregnancy terminations will normally produce feelings of guilt in both parents.

The same is true for adoption, not only for the child but also for the mother and possibly the father. Because most mothers are likely to feel ashamed of giving their child away, they may be unable to get help or support for themselves with processing the feelings involved. The loss of a child tears the emotional ties between parent and child and this provokes depression in the parents. The trauma of loss provokes the repression of feelings in connection to the lost child and, in addition, the parents may experience a pervasive difficulty in allowing feelings of love to flow freely towards others, because any such feelings will re-trigger the feelings connected with the loss. In trying to protect themselves from these painful feelings, they render themselves emotionally less available, or even completely unavailable, for the living children that they may have, and for their partner. They will function outwardly as a mother, a father, husband or wife, but they may never truly live in and experience their feelings.

The way that men and women deal with a loss trauma appears also to be different. While sexuality is often blocked in women that have lost a child, men tend to suppress their sadness by acting out sexually. This can cause extra troubles in the partnership of a couple that has lost a child.

Siblings also suffer trauma on the sudden death of a sister or brother, and their experience of their parents' feelings of powerlessness adds to their own emotional and psychological distress.

The death of a partner

While the bond with a partner is not as intense as the bond with a parent or a child, the death of a partner is also a loss trauma, particularly if the bonding relationship has grown over a long period of time. Even when a partner is physically no longer there, on a soul level he or she is often still there for the remaining partner. Some people continue to live as though the partner were still present, laying the table and making the bed for the absent partner, leaving their things undisturbed. The death of a partner can also evoke feelings of guilt or anger, according to the nature of the relationship and the circumstances of the death.

The remaining parent has a great influence on how the deceased parent remains present for the children. Sometimes the deceased parent is idealised and put on a pedestal, sometimes the memory is completely suppressed. In both cases the remaining partner and the children have severe difficulties in overcoming the loss trauma.

Separation from a partner

Partners between whom no emotional bond has grown have no problem in separating. However, if a bond has developed and a separation is desired, then there must be a clear dissolution of the bond before a new bond may be entered into. This dissolution is achieved only gradually and in phases. A partner who separates too quickly and rushes into a new relationship is neither able to release her- or himself from the old bond by a grieving process, nor to properly enter into a new relationship.

If we have learned to separate ourselves appropriately due to the successful separation from our own parents as part of becoming an adult, then we will find it easier to initiate and manage separation from another adult when a relationship has run its course. The person who is unable to separate appropriately from a partner, even though the relationship has run its course, deprives him or herself and the partner of the opportunity for psychological and emotional growth.

Trauma Reactions in Cases of Sudden Loss

In the case of the sudden death of a partner it is not possible for the survivor to prepare him or herself for the emotional loss; there is no substitute for the bond with the absent person. Suddenly the person towards whom so much feeling and thought has been directed no longer reacts. On a deep level, it is as if an essential part of oneself is now dead. Feelings, previously centred on the person who has died, flow abruptly into the void with nowhere to go. Even when the other still lives and the issue is a sudden and permanent separation from her or him, a part of the identity, on a soul level, is left hanging in the air. The feelings previously bound up with the other person can no longer develop further in any meaningful way. They become fixed as they are.

The immediate reaction to any sudden loss is shock. There is no warning and everything is thrown into question. Time stands still. Without the deceased or absent person one's whole life can seem meaningless. Feelings of anxiety set in – what shall I do alone in the world without the other? Feelings of anger direct themselves at the absent person – why did she desert me and leave me behind all alone? Guilt feelings emerge – what did I do wrong, to make her leave? Without the other person life seems meaningless, joyless, not worth living.

There are different models that separate the reaction to a loss trauma into distinct phases. John Bowlby tackles loss trauma comprehensively from the point of view of both adults and children in his groundbreaking work *Loss, Grief and Depression*, where he cites countless studies that explore the relationship of people with loss, primarily in cases of death (Bowlby, 1998).

He differentiated the following stages of reaction to loss:

- numbness,
- looking for the lost person,
- disorganisation and despair,
- reorganisation and turning to the future.

In addition, he found that, after a sudden loss, people will often live in the expectation that the absent or deceased person might return. Many people continue to speak to the deceased partner or child after the death and have inner dialogues with whatever image of the person they are able to keep hold of in their inner psyche.

Children will often avoid accepting that their parent is dead, while death itself terrifies them. As a result, they become overly anxious, clinging to what they have, and living with the continual fear that something dreadful might happen again. They have experienced the fact that adults can die suddenly, and consequently they are afraid to become adults themselves, believing, perhaps, that they too might suddenly die. It is therefore very important to help children to be able to live with the reality of death in such situations, without shutting down their own emotional and psychological developmental process.

Depression

With trauma of loss, it is likely that the process of dealing with the injury is incomplete, and that the personality splits, one part taking over the physiological and psychological memory of the loss and becoming dissociated, while another portion continues on in denial of those feelings that are connected with the trauma.

The part of the personality that carries the memory of the loss trauma lives in a state that we could describe as a chronic grief, or 'depression'. Loss that is experienced as anxiety or stress leads to depressive reactions that subside after six months at most, and after a few years are as good as no longer existing. Loss trauma however is, in my opinion, the cause of depression that gradually worsens and eventually becomes chronic (Appendix 3 gives a formal description of the symptoms of depression).

Consequently, as with existential trauma, we find in loss trauma different fragmentary or partial personalities, with distinct perceptions, memories and feelings. The un-traumatised part of the personality (the part that carries on with life) wants to live and be happy as though nothing had happened, while the traumatised part, in contrast, does whatever is needed to avoid situations that could re-stimulate the possibility of an experience of loss. Thus when the un-traumatised part seeks a friend or a partner, the traumatised part reacts with alarm: "Just don't get too close, too intimate, don't allow too many feelings" for the pain would be unendurable and unending if another emotional attachment were to be ruptured.

New relationships can only be entered into when strong feelings can be kept at bay.

Stages of grief

Is it possible to recover fully from a severe loss trauma? In some cases, probably not. However, it is possible to stop the process of further emotional and psychological pain. In letting go and moving on from the intense and painful state, the most important psychological process is the grieving process. Not expressing feelings of grief, even though the justification is still present, is unhealthy and has the effect of blocking all feelings. Grieving means allowing pain and tears, looking the anxiety of being left alone fully in the face. Grief begins when anger that the past and all that went with it is over ceases. Grief makes an end of reproach and feelings of disappointment. Grief offers the chance of readjustment and of acclimatising oneself to the changed reality. Grieving means letting go and saying goodbye. Grief means acknowledging and accepting the absolute. What is past cannot be brought back. Grief means withdrawing our own soul from the bond. Through healthy grieving, any feelings of guilt and shame are processed. Grieving frees the heart for new attachments. Grief can be consciously avoided: we decide we will not let the absent person out of our heart.

Case Study 28:

Avoiding grief

If we allow our grief, we may fear that it will overwhelm us, so we may suppress it. A patient put it this way: "I have an image in front of me all the time of my dead brother fully-clothed lying in an open grave. When I imagine myself accepting that my brother is really dead, and that someone will fill his grave, I feel cut off from all the love that flows between him and me. What should I do then? Where would I go with my love? Everything would be cold and meaningless."

Investigation reveals the following phases in the grief process of many people:

- A wish not to accept the loss, and withdrawal into isolation,
- Anger and rage about what has happened and jealousy of others who do not have to suffer this fate,
- Inward interrogation about whether the loss could have been avoided,
- Despondency and grief,
- Agreement with fate.

Only when the loss is accepted as a reality can the pain of grief be experienced and worked through, only then does an adaptation take place to the world without the absent person. Then the emotional energy can be gradually diverted from this loss process and invested in other bonding relationships (Worden, 1999).

Without social support or professional help, loss traumas are hard to overcome. In addition to a readiness to grieve, people who have suffered loss traumas need a community that helps them to enter into the grieving process rather than persist in an in-between state. Standing by and supporting the grieving person, and the rituals of grieving that go with this process, are important elements in every culture, thus facilitating the continuing life of those who have suffered the loss. A year of intensive grieving saves a lifetime of chronic sorrow.

Loss by suicide
It can be particularly difficult to allow grief for a person who has killed him or herself. Suicides often provoke feelings of guilt in the bereaved, and it is not uncommon for parents or partners to feel exposed to accusations of having perhaps driven the person to kill themselves through lack of love. Consequently, suicide is often thought of as shameful and kept secret from other people. Those left behind find it difficult to support the grieving person and only partially engage in the rituals of grieving.

Addiction in cases of loss trauma

In the initial stages of loss the desire to distract oneself from experiencing the pain is common, and as long as this strategy is limited to this first phase of traumatic reaction, it can be helpful. However, if this distraction becomes the only form of coping, it is likely to develop into an addiction.

Men commonly throw themselves energetically into their work or a new relationship, or may try and comfort themselves through excessive indulgence in alcohol and/or sexual activity. Women may also seek distraction through work. Inactivity, peace and quiet are feared most of all, because in that space the memories resurface. In some cases a solution is sought through the long-term taking of medication, in particular anti-depressive drugs. Only a confrontation of the trauma and the expression of the suppressed feelings in a full grieving process will resolve the addiction.

Suicidal inclination as part of the grieving process

People with severe depression are at greater risk of suicide, as a last act of self-determination in the face of a continual sense of hopelessness and meaninglessness. Many mothers who have lost a child say that they only stay alive for their living children. For themselves they would long since have given up, would gladly have gone to sleep without waking up. The easy availability of sleeping tablets is a factor that raises the likelihood of suicide for women experiencing a loss trauma. Women with small children may even fantasize including the remaining children in her suicidal act, and it is not difficult to understand how this fantasizing would affect these children.

Bert Hellinger has described this type of suicidal tendency in connection with trauma of loss as the dynamic of 'I will follow you into death'. In constellations work we frequently see how a client sets up his representative in such a way that they are looking out into an open space. We may suppose from this, with some degree of certainty that the representative looks towards someone who is lost or absent, for example has died in traumatic circumstances. In this sense, a desire to commit suicide is not actually the wish to die, but rather a deep wish to reconnect with the lost person. The psychoanalyst Juergen Kind (1996) named this 'the fusional form' of suicide, the wish to be reunited and 'merged' with the dead person, and by dying, this wish is achieved.

As a reaction to loss – for example when a partner leaves – some men in extreme cases may choose the ultimate aggressive 'solution': they murder their partner and may also kill their entire family. That this also destroys the perpetrator's own existence is seen as unavoidable. Suicidal tendencies and aggression, seen in this way, are immature ways of managing painful feelings. Reality as it is, is not accepted and the person would rather destroy that which he cannot accept than acknowledge it and perhaps thereby achieve some peace. People who mourn their loss fully have more chance of finding peace.

Searching for a new self-concept and world view
Loss trauma shakes our naïve belief in the boundlessness of life and the permanence of our bonding relationships. Acceptance of the finiteness of our and others' existence contributes to our process of maturation, and is particularly relevant in loss trauma. We can then recognise that others can only be with us for a time, and that in the end we will lose everything and everyone that we have. Being in touch with this pain liberates us. By contrast, if we try to hang on to everything, and do not acknowledge our losses, we become slaves to our own inability to grieve, and see only what is *not*, and not what actually *is*. Those who do this may live as though they too had died, along with everything else that is lost and dead. In fact, appreciating life as long as fate allows us, honours the dead, for they too would gladly have done this if they could.

6.3 Loss Trauma and its Effect on Subsequent Generations

The traumatic effect of loss is not confined solely to the person who directly experienced the loss, but is unintentionally transmitted to the following generation. Major existential traumas, such as the holocaust or other war experiences, were often not due solely to the effect of the experience of mortal danger to the individual themselves, but also to the effect on the individual of the experience of the deaths of their parents, children, relatives, and comrades. This process has been outlined in chapter 5.2 above in connection with the transmission of the traumatic experiences of existential trauma. The experiences of loss trauma can be similarly transmitted.

A mother's brother who died in the war, the missing brother of a grandmother, the grandfather who never returned from a foreign country, the killed fiancée – all these people remain firmly in the deeper consciousness of the family. The children born later sense the pain in the soul of their mother, particularly when she is in the grip of her feelings for the dead or missing person. Children are sometimes named after deceased loved ones; it is easy to imagine what a mother might feel when she holds her child that bears the same name as her beloved dead brother, or the fiancée who never returned from the war.

Depressed parents – depressed children
The child of a mother caught in a trauma of loss becomes 'accustomed' to the fact that intimacy and loving contact with her mother is linked with feelings of heaviness and sadness. A silent heaviness becomes the central feeling for the child, and the predominant emotional link between her and her mother, and any intimacy with others is always linked with this sadness for the child. The mother provides no comfort or support because she is looking for these things for herself. When she picks up her child, she connects with the distress within herself; she sees the liveliness of the child and feels her own sadness. She senses that she can no longer be so alive because of her experience of loss. She tries to comfort herself through her child and at the same time knows that this will not work. The child understands that she cannot get any joy in life; when she tries to get close to her mother, she feels her mother's

sadness. If she stays by herself she feels lonely. She learns not to expect help from her mother and that she cannot help her mother in return. She believes that she has to hide her liveliness from her mother for fear it will sadden her. Consequently, in later life the child will unconsciously seek in a partner that same air of sadness that she found in her mother. The child sees no chance of realising the joy and zest of life in an intimate relationship.

Hyperactivity in children

Restless and hyperactive children who, even when very intelligent, don't seem able to concentrate in school, may be affected by a parental loss trauma, for example a parent whose father or mother died when they were a child. The child senses their parent's pain and sadness without understanding it. They sense at an unconscious level the unresolved trauma of their parent, and sometimes this pressure is eased by their restlessness. Treatment with medication may suppress the symptoms but makes no difference to the origins of the behaviour, and neither does well intentioned educational support. The strength of the inner experience is too overwhelming, being an expression of the defensive position of the traumatised parent: to confront the effects of the pain of the trauma of my mother/father is too much, the fear is that I would be driven close to the edge.

Loss of siblings

Children who have a sibling who loses their life in sudden tragic circumstances carry a special burden. They not only lose their sibling, but often also lose emotional access to their parents, in particular to their mother. Because they feel the suffering of their parents they think that they can no longer ask for anything for themselves, nor risk any disagreement or confrontation. They become silent and withdrawn. A patient whose sister had lost her life in an accident on the way to school before she was even born, grew up in her dead sister's bedroom and, as an outward expression of her inner loneliness, developed compulsive nail biting

145

and hair tearing. Because any outward stimulation was lacking in the gloomy atmosphere of the family home, she occupied herself in this stereotypical way. Her parents only saw the dead child when they looked at her, and so she never felt seen for herself. People who have lived with such a fate often feel as though their parents looked right through them.

The fear of losing a child themselves can also become a permanent stress for the surviving children in adulthood. The following example shows what may be concealed behind the over-protective behaviour of a mother.

Case Study 29:

Over protectiveness

A patient suffered with compulsive anxiety about her small daughter. She had to watch over her constantly and check that nothing happened to her. She explained that she had, as a three year old, watched as her younger brother drowned in her parents' swimming pool. This trauma caused her mother to withdraw into herself and become emotionally unavailable for her daughter who in turn experienced her mother as inaccessible. As a child, the patient also felt guilty because she had witnessed her brother's fall into the water, and she believed that her mother no longer loved her because of this.

A constellation showed that the patient's child also sensed the pain of her grandmother (the patient's mother) over the death of the boy, and that she felt a need to bring the grandmother back into life. At the same time, in order to protect herself from her grandmother's pain she had developed a tendency to retreat into a fantasy world of fairytales.

A resolution of this three generational entanglement in a constellation required support for the representative of the patient's mother so that she could face her pain over the accidental death of her son. Thereafter a clarification of the relationship between the patient's mother and the patient was possible. Only then could the problem of the patient be resolved, in that she could relax her compulsive need to watch over her daughter.

Identification in constellations

In the context of loss trauma the theme of 'identification' frequently arises. The child may become identified unconsciously with someone in the family who perhaps died tragically young or was painfully missed by a parent. The child may slip unconsciously into this close identification with the missing person in order to reach their mother who is unable to relate emotionally to her child. The child's unconscious maxim is: "my mother sees and loves me only when I am more like the person she misses".

Another, similar, process often recognised in family constellations is the identification of the oldest child with an earlier partner of either the mother or father. This may indicate that one, or maybe even both, of the parents has not yet been able to free themselves from this earlier intimate relationship. The loss of this earlier partner may have occurred through a separation (e.g. broken engagement) or through death (e.g. an accident).

As a subject of discussion in marital relationships, an earlier partner, or a previous, unresolved emotional bond with an ex-partner, is often taboo. The experience of the loss of an earlier partner, when painful and traumatic, is split off at a soul level and suppressed, and the feelings bound up with this event may lead an uncontrolled life of their own.

The first child of the subsequent relationship may then represent in some way this previous loved person, feeling the most intense emotions of this unresolved bond. Too great an intimacy then may develop with the particular parent involved, who may in turn transfer his or her unresolved feelings for the missed person onto the child, at the same time creating a distance from the other parent. The child cannot be in his own place as just a child of both parents. The child senses the unconscious expectation to comfort the parent, whom he experiences as sad, and supplies him or her with an excessive amount of love, trying to compensate for the love that has been lost. Such children immerse themselves in the unfulfilled longings and needs of the parent, attempting to make him or her happy. They also sense that their parents are unable to come together emotionally, living instead parallel but separate lives. This makes the children even more unhappy. Some children, whose mothers are still very deeply connected to a previous lover, imagine that their father may not even be their real father.

In families where one of the parents is entangled in such a loss trauma, children may easily develop into a "mother's boy" or a "father's girl", even as adults unable to disengage themselves from their parent. They feel like prisoners within the parent-child relationship, and because they cannot free themselves they may also develop a secret anger and hatred for the respective parent.

Case Study 30:

A mother's boy

Wilfred Wieck describes with great openness in his autobiography his symbiosis with his depressed mother: "It was my task as a son to save my mother. She burdened me with this. Both of us had fallen into the trap, from which she could not free us. But she was the only one. The woman to whom I owed my life ... on whom I was totally dependent. She was the first wife in my life. I will speak openly about my mother. I don't want to accuse her. Today I sometimes get dizzy when I imagine her plight, her pain, her boundless loneliness, her agonising death. These ideas distress and disturb me. Then I think of how rarely she was happy. Because of her lack of boundaries I was mostly too close to my mother. I wouldn't insist, as Hesse did, that my mother understood me better than anyone else. ... I see too clearly her pitiable dependence on my father, the melancholy way she coped with life, constantly expecting hostility. Little good lay in her spoiling me above everyone" (Wieck, 1992). Also: "My father was not patriarchal and yet was a man typical of patriarchal culture, a powerless fellow, who was also not very thoughtful about us children. He was more patient with my sister but I was never sure of his affection. He didn't open up to anything beyond his uncultured technical world as an engineer. In such a drab and empty office atmosphere there was no conversation because the only real relationship was to objects and machines ... It is clear, that the unemancipated wife of a man who was so limited was understandably unsatisfied in many respects" (Wieck, 1992).

The child, who is thus symbiotically linked with the parent of the opposite sex, is not able to be a child, nor an adult in relationship. The child's sexuality is evoked early on by the identification, and at the same time must be denied. Because of this symbiotic identification it is often not possible for the child to establish enough of a relationship with the same sex parent to establish their own full sexual identity. Usually in fact, the same sex parent is extremely devalued. So a boy may develop an inner attitude that is more feminine and a girl a more masculine one. The boy, for example, imagines himself as a better husband for his mother than his father, knowing better than his father does, and imagines himself better able to satisfy his mother. This empathising with the parent is experienced as a deep love, but at the same time has to guard against sexual desires and fantasies. So love is seen as a 'pure' state, a kind of symbiosis and inner merging without coming physically closer as man and wife. In the case of daughters who are bonded with their entangled fathers against their mothers, the danger of sexual abuse is high.

Severe depression
As a final word on the theme of trans-generational transmission of feelings stemming from loss trauma, in Case Study 31 (below) I describe my work with a patient whose mother had

been given up for adoption at the age of one year. This case shows that a condition, which according to psychiatric classification corresponds to severe depression, can improve if the real cause is found and the original trauma is properly seen. All other forms of treatment, particularly medication, are incapable of arriving at this result. More often, they result in the transmitted trauma feelings being unresolved at a deep level and thereby becoming chronic.

Case Study 31:

A sea of tears

The situation at the start of therapy: Daniel S. is forty-three years old. He no longer sees any meaning in his life. His wife, with whom he has a small daughter, separated from him two years ago, and he now has his own flat. Nevertheless, in the last few weeks he stayed with his wife, who occasionally cares for him as though he were still a child. He feels completely helpless, full of fear and incapable of living. Everything looks grey to him and he feels as though he sits in "a sea of tears".

He and his wife were married seven years ago. This was initially a very happy time for them, they understood each other well and the relationship was sexually satisfying. With the birth of their daughter he had realised the focus of all his desires: his own family, people who belonged to him and could not leave him.

Then it seemed to him that his wife began only to care about the daughter. Arguments between them became more and more frequent because his wife wanted to make everything perfect for their daughter, and would not let him be involved in her upbringing. He felt as though he was an intruder, a spare part, excluded and lonelier than ever. After the separation, he suffered because he was once again living alone and was seldom able to be with his daughter.

To the question as to whether he had ever had to struggle

with feelings of abandonment and loneliness before, Daniel explained that, when he was about twenty, he had gone on a trip to Australia. In the course of this trip he increasingly fell into a state of hopelessness and isolation. Nonetheless he had had the feeling that he must at all costs make the trip. After his return he became very depressed and initially began individual therapy and later also couples therapy, which made a few things clear to him but ultimately did not really resolve his problem.

On the subject of his childhood and adolescence, he said that he suffered greatly from his father's harshness and had been in competition with his older brother. He described his mother as a thoughtful woman with whom he currently could no longer feel any emotional intimacy. She was very religious and would really have liked to enter a nunnery. For her the subject of sex was forbidden.

During his school days he received acknowledgement exclusively for good reports and sporting achievement. Outside school he was always a loner and never found a group of friends. In the course of time he became ever more withdrawn and did not develop any self confidence. In relation to girls, he was, as a youth, very shy, girls appeared out of reach to him. That his attractive wife liked him was a source of pride and happiness to him.

In answer to the question as to whether there were any special incidents in his family of origin, he explained that his parents had met in the middle of the 1950s and had married quickly because his mother had wanted to get away from home. Of his father's family, he knew that his grandfather had been very strict and that his grandmother had had a stillborn child.

He was aware that his mother had been put into foster care at the age of one and had then been adopted by her foster parents. In answer to the question as to why his mother had been put into foster care he said that his mother's mother had died shortly after her birth and he assumed that her father could not raise the child. The mother had first learnt that her parents were not her biological parents when she was fourteen, and she then refused to have any contact with her biological father.

In answer to a question about a goal for his therapy, Daniel began to weep intensely and said that he would like to get out of the deep black hole in which he felt he was. He would like to be free of inner despair and anxiety about his life, and to be able to sleep properly at night and concentrate on his work during the day. Primarily he would like to have the feeling of being important to and loved by another person, otherwise nothing had any meaning.

The course of the therapy: the fact that Daniel's mother had lost her own mother was the key to his therapy. His mother had been traumatised by the loss of her mother, and in the bonding process with Daniel she was therefore essentially unavailable to the baby. In several constellations, it became clear that the representative for the mother behaved as though she were absent, orientated more towards death than to life. Her husband and children experienced her as unreachable. Therefore Daniel was in an extremely ambivalent situation: he wanted to experience his mother, her love and warmth, but at the same time, intimacy with her was tied up with the experience of being pulled into the abyss of her fear and pain.

The solution to the conflict lay in Daniel acknowledging both these needs within himself: the child's need within him for the love of his mother, and the need of the older child to distance himself from his mother and her suffering, preventing him from growing up and becoming an adult. In a constellation it was possible for Daniel and the representative for his mother to embrace each other, while in his individual work he practised differentiating between himself and his mother and her symbiotic needs.

In the constellation, the deep well of depression that separated Daniel from his mother could be made clear. As Daniel saw in the constellation how impossible it was for his mother, and what she needed in order to look at her own mother, he developed significantly more understanding of her.

This step made it possible for Daniel to investigate the truth by making enquiries at the relevant records office. He found that his mother's mother had not in fact died in childbirth, but had given birth in a home and had offered her daughter up for adoption. Daniel's symptoms of depression, that in fact were his mothers feeling of abandonment, fitted significantly better with a situation in which a child was forsaken by her parents than one in which a child's mother died early. For example Daniel's mother had never said anything about the whereabouts of her mother's grave.

Daniel's commentary on the progress of his therapy: "My experience before therapy was that I had no foothold, I belonged nowhere and I experienced intimacy only at the price of sacrificing myself. However this did not fit with my illusion that my mother would always be there for me. The most important step was for me to recognise that my depressive feelings about life were strongly linked to my mother's early history."

7

Bonding Trauma

7.1 Introduction

It is a basic human need to develop secure and supportive emotional attachments, without which we feel existentially threatened and helpless. For a child, the attachment to his parents is essential to his survival, which explains why it has such a momentous and catastrophic effect on the psyche of the child if this need for a secure and stable attachment cannot be satisfied by the very people towards whom this need is directed – his parents.

There are parents who systematically neglect, reject, hate, beat, and sometimes even murder their children. These parents make their children the object of their own physical and emotional needs and project onto them their own need for love, fears they have not managed to overcome and feelings of hate. Thus the worst that could possibly happen to a child does in fact happen: a traumatisation of his attachment need, i.e., a bonding trauma. How does such a development come about?

7.2 Development of Bonding Trauma

The Emotionally Inaccessible Mother

The key to understanding this process lies in the logic of the trauma. Traumatic experiences can lead to people being incapable of forming proper emotional attachments; they can form relationships as such, but not attachments. When such a person then becomes a parent, their need to protect themselves from any confrontation with their own split off traumatic emotions renders them incapable of having loving feelings towards their own children. As a result of the emotional numbing caused by their own trauma, they cannot experience any positive feelings towards their child. The needed deep connection between a child and his mother just doesn't 'click', as if key and lock don't fit. To use another metaphor, the wall onto which the child could attach its emotional rope has no hooks. It is smooth and sealed off.

In this way, mothers in turn become the cause of their own child's bonding trauma. The child's need for love, warmth and emotional security is starved; he is seeking something that is not available to him, because of the emotional vacuum in the parent that even the sight of their child cannot fill.

If any emotional exchange does take place between mother and child, this comprises the split-off trauma feelings which the mother, despite all efforts at suppression and repression, cannot control or keep to herself. The child that is ready for attachment then becomes flooded by the deep feelings of fear, rage, shame and depression of the mother. Yet the child loves his mother as all children do, and clings to her with all his feelings. Instead of love and affection the child thus takes into himself the emotional chaos of his mother's trauma.

When a traumatised mother is not able to open her heart to her child, life with the child becomes a continuous source of stress for the mother. The child lives with the implied reproach that he has ruined his mother's life; every little thing causes friction. The child is always in the wrong and there can be no possibility of reconciliation, because the only way this could happen would be if the mother dealt with her repressed trauma. The child cannot do anything because he understands even less than his mother does her inability to show genuine feelings. His survival strategy has to be to withdraw into himself resulting in his living in a fantasy world with his loneliness. On the other hand he is inevitably and unavoidably attached to his mother and maintains his need to love her and be loved by her. Not to be loved by his mother becomes an unbearable emotional conflict for the rejected child and he will fight with all possible means against this rejection. He tries as hard as he can to feel himself into the chaotic soul of his mother and tries to do everything right for her, in an attempt to be spared her rejection, aggression and disregard. At the same time he will flee from his mother's attempts to seek solace and act out her symbiotic needs through him. In the end whatever the child does he is incapable of getting his mother to love him, for her soul has been too severely wounded. Love is a feeling that she would only be able to feel if she lived through the traumatic pain that destroyed the longing for love in her.

For the child, the feeling of an internal void, the impossibility of making contact with another person, becomes the central experience of his life. He continually seeks the intimate contact with others that he did not experience with his mother, always disappointed and left living out his internal loneliness perhaps through the spheres of art, religion or nature.

Flight from the Father

When the child cannot form an attachment to his mother, he will turn instinctively to his father and try to get from him the love, security and warmth he cannot get from his mother. Sometimes this works and the child's attachment to his father can replace the failed attachment with the mother enough to keep him from despair and emotional chaos. However, attachment with the father can never fully replace attachment with the mother. For a woman the later consequences of such an emotional development become evident in her adult relationships and then in her attachment behaviour towards her own children (see Case Study 10). Women who suffer from bonding trauma frequently choose as partners men who have also suffered bonding trauma, which then means that a child of this union who turns to his father because his attachment with his mother failed, has little chance of finding love and safety with his father, and is quite likely to become enmeshed in his father's trauma.

7.3 Particular Issues to do with Bonding Trauma

Sexual Abuse

Rejection and emotional neglect of a child by the mother often co-exists with forms of sexual abuse. It is not by chance that sexual abuse is the consequence of a bonding trauma in a family.

Sexual abuse comes in various guises: observing the naked child (voyeurism); forcing the child to watch pornographic pictures or films with the adult; displaying one's genitals to the child (exhibitionism); tongue kissing; touching genitalia; masturbating in front of the child or forcing the child to masturbate; oral, anal or vaginal penetration of the child's body. Sexual abuse is based partly on seduction and persuasion using the child's need for physical closeness and tenderness, and partly on threats and violence if the child tries to refuse to fulfil the perpetrator's demands. Sexual abuse is not usually a single act or "mistake" by the perpetrator who is unable to control his "drives", but a consciously planned and deliberately executed situation, sometimes lasting for years until the perpetrator loses interest in the child. For this to be possible, the perpetrator needs to live near the child. Consequently they are more likely to be a relative of the child rather than a complete stranger.

Sexual abuse occurs more frequently than is normally

made known publicly and possibly even more than professionals in the field think. Andreas Kloiber recently presented a study on sexual abuse of boys and considers it possible that every fourth girl and every tenth boy has been a victim of an adult's sexual advances at some time in their life (Kloiber, 2002). In current research into violence against women in Germany the authors conclude that "13% of the women interviewed, i.e. almost every seventh woman, reported that since the age of sixteen they had experienced forms of sexual violence that would be legally classed as forced sexual acts. 40% of the women interviewed had experienced physical or sexual violence since the age of sixteen" (Müller, Schröttle, Glammeier und Oppenheimer, 2004).

There have been various attempts to define sexual abuse. Often aspects of sexuality and power are highlighted: "sexual abuse begins where adults or young people significantly older than the child establish a physical proximity to children in order to satisfy their own needs for intimacy, sexual pleasure and power" (Kastner, 2000).

Within the framework of a concept of a multi-generational psychotraumatology I suggest the following definition for sexual abuse within the family: sexual abuse is the consequence of the traumatic entanglement of a child in a traumatised family attachment system. This definition stresses both the traumatising aspect of sexual abuse and the aspect of entangled attachments causing and caused by the abuse.

Consequences for Sexually Abused Children

Sexual abuse obviously has significant emotional consequences for the child. This is especially true if the abuse takes place in the immediate or extended family. Gottfried Fischer and Peter Riedesser categorise the consequences of sexual abuse under four points (Fischer and Riedesser, 1999):

- Traumatisation of the child in relation to its sexuality can lead to the following: mistaken ideas about sexuality and

morality, disgust with sexuality, shamelessness and lack
of boundaries, compulsive sexual behaviour, promiscuity,
prostitution and sexualisation of all relationships;
- Stigmatisation and blaming of the child leads to feelings
of guilt and shame, damaged self-esteem, the feeling of
being crazy, the feeling of estrangement from others, self
isolation, self-harming behaviour, delinquency and drug
use;
- The experience of being powerless can lead to: splitting,
dissociative amnesia, nightmares, phobias, eating and
sleep disorders, school problems, truancy, aggressive
behaviour and somatisation of emotional conflicts;
- Betrayal of a child's trust leads to: depression, extreme
dependency, anger, enmity, incapacity to evaluate others,
early marriage caused by the unsatisfied wish for an
intact and healthy family.

Sexual abuse by a close relative represents one of the worst
experiences of trauma, with extensive consequences for a
child's whole life. The earlier in its life a child experiences
sexual abuse, the more intensive the sexual contact, the more
extreme the violence, the nearer/closer the relative and the
more intense the attachment between perpetrator and child, the
more concealed and serious are the consequences for the child.
There is scarcely any event that harms girls and boys more
than sexual abuse and sexual violence.

The traumatic consequences of sexual abuse are particularly extensive because they are committed, and denied,
predominantly by the people whom the child loves and trusts.
Thus the child becomes confused in its feelings and its internal
ethical-moral orientation. In situations of sexual abuse the
child experiences completely contradictory feelings and
thoughts:

- I am preferred – I am being used
- I'm getting special attention – I am being abused
- I am valued – I am being humiliated

- I am the centre of attention – I am isolated
- I want to scream – I must stay silent.
- I want to defend myself – I am colluding
- I am big and responsible – I am small and helpless
- I am transfigured – I am tainted
- I need protection – I must protect others
- I must preserve – I want to destroy
- I am experiencing pleasure – I am experiencing disgust

The sexual abuse of a child connects to the abuse of her need for affection, love, warmth, security and her ability for childish empathy. Consequently the child cannot discover her own identity. She can't locate where she belongs in the family, she doesn't know whether she is a child or an adult. She doesn't know what to do and what not to do, what is right or wrong. She can no longer tell the difference between truth and lies and thus can no longer distinguish between what is illusion and imagination and what is reality.

The Perpetrator

Child and adolescent abusers are almost always adult men and male adolescents. Abuse of boys is usually committed by men. There is comparatively little information in the public arena about women who abuse their sons or daughters, but it does happen. Abusive women –mothers, grandmothers or sisters – usually have been abused as children themselves, so that they have no sensitivity for the child's boundaries of shame, and will consciously sexually excite and stimulate the child or express their needs through the child.

Male perpetrators usually come from a child's immediate environment: fathers, stepfathers, brothers, uncles, grandfathers, and neighbours with access to the family, teachers, priests, educators and so on. They develop elaborate strategies to approach the child, "grooming" him or her, ensuring a long-term compliance that prevents the child from revealing the abuse to others, and so succeeding in making the child feel bad, worthless and guilty.

Case Study 32

Is it my own fault?

Laura, whom we previously met in Case Study 1, describes her situation and the symptoms of suffering that followed being a sexually abused child:

"All my life I have been over-anxious and easily startled, driven by restlessness and pursued by nightmares every night. Headaches and backaches have been my constant companions. I have suffered from recurrent depression and reached a point where I simply could not feel anything any more. I constantly doubted whether I could trust my own feelings, and often I could not properly sense what I was feeling.

"My memories often simply disappeared. When I had an argument, a short time after I couldn't remember what it had been about. I lived in constant fear of making mistakes in everyday life, in my job and my relationships.

"I often had problems concentrating, and then my vision blurred and everything seemed fuzzy. Sometimes my own screams woke me up at night. I often woke up in a terrible panic, not daring to breathe or to move. I just froze. I always felt responsible for everything and guilty about everything.

"Often I idealised my father and condemned my mother, but I even felt guilty about doing this. I always felt very lonely and longed for a happy relationship. I often fell into a deep hole, crying for days and not being able to leave my flat."

Perpetrators will as a rule feel innocent and not plagued by scruples. The perpetrator feels safe in entangled relationships with partners and family, breaking through one boundary of shame after another. Anita Heiliger analysed 29 court cases and found the following examples of various perpetrator strategies:

- *Strategies of perpetrators in approaching their victims:* often the abuse is initially incorporated into playful acts. The sexual games are presented to the child as completely normal. The child's perception becomes twisted and warped and they are persuaded out of their true feelings. The perpetrator puts himself into the role of educator and relies on the obedience of the child.
- *Strategies to secure access to the child:* the child's resistance to the sexual acts is slowly worn away. The perpetrator provokes understanding and pity in the child for his needs for sexual fulfilment. He achieves this through begging and other persuasive means, thereby provoking feelings of guilt in the child. He makes the child feel important by making her his favourite and treating her as such. He gives money and presents. He favours her over her siblings at the same time increasingly giving the impression that it is quite normal for him to satisfy his sexual needs through the child. When the softer methods of persuasion, seduction and bribery don't work, he resorts to harder means to demonstrate his authority and power. Outwardly he hides himself behind a façade of morality and decency, and presents himself as an example of integrity and responsibility. He swears the child to secrecy and increasingly isolates her. He tries to break up any mother/child relationship driving a wedge of mistrust between them.
- *Perpetrator strategies after the discovery of abuse:* if suspicion of abuse begins to arise, the abuser accuses the child of being a notorious liar or of being sick. He presents himself as the victim of unjustified accusations and will enact the caring father, uncle or teacher. He starts to threaten therapists, social workers and the authorities and employ lawyers to intimidate and silence them. A case of sexual abuse that has been revealed is made light of and

the child is made out to be the driving force. Facts are twisted and the abuser makes out that he was seduced by the child.

- *Perpetrator strategies after convictions:* even after court convictions abusers seldom accept responsibility for what has happened. Few show any willingness to accept the perspective of the victim, instead presenting arguments to exonerate themselves: they were under the influence of alcohol when it happened; no violence was used; life circumstances were bad; they had low self-esteem; they were afraid of adult women and inhibited in their presence; the child herself wanted to play the sex games.
- Some abusers try to fill their inner emptiness, depression or lack of satisfaction in their lives with addictive acting out of their sexuality. Some abusers enjoy torturing other human beings, becoming aroused by their fear. This kind of sadistic perpetrator would not stop at murdering a child. Usually it can be assumed that as a child this kind of person has himself been a victim of sexual exploitation and humiliation.

Accomplices and bystanders

There are also those who share responsibility for the emergence and escalation of sexual abuse, as well as bystanders who know the abuser and secretly, or sometimes openly, deny his acts, or tolerate them, and do not help get the child out of the situation. Mothers in particular play a significant role here.

Children point to abuse by the way they behave. They start to cry if they have to go to bed at night; they get stomach ache; they use sexual terms; they either refuse to eat or stuff themselves with food; they neglect hygiene and neglect their rooms. If mothers do not pay attention to these warning signals, but instead treat the child as disobedient or even as mentally disturbed, the child will lose trust not only in their mother but also in their own perception and experience. They will try to adjust their experience and perceptions to accord with those of their mother. Consequently they fall into an ever increasing internal chaos of feelings and thoughts. They will desperately try to find ways of protecting themselves through magical ideas and thinking, flights into fantasy, and will sense the plight of other children without being able to express their own.

Case Study 33

Good-for-nothing

Laura has never experienced help from her mother: "As a child I often longed for my mother or someone to be there for me and protect me. Every night I was afraid of falling asleep. When I was very little my parents felt threatened by these fears and punished me for them and sometimes hit me. They said I was terrorising them by not wanting to sleep.

"I learned that if I showed my fears, I was punished. So I tried to keep my fears secret, and withdrew more and more into my fantasy world. As far as I can remember, I hardly had any dolls, so I took all my cuddly toys to bed with me. They were to protect me and I protected them. There was an almost compulsive order to the way I arranged the animals. It was a ritual to protect me. When my parents went out, I had another ritual: I repeated certain words quietly and compulsively to myself and that helped me to hide my fear.

"I could never do things right as far as my mother was concerned. She was not able to love me; she always prophesied that I would end up the same way as my father's step-brother: as a good-for-nothing in the gutter. She said I was just as megalomaniacal, bad and evil as my paternal grandmother.

"As an adolescent I always felt ugly and unlovable. I thought: I hope nobody notices what I'm really like: useless. I escaped into my dreamworld. There were for me two worlds that existed side by side. The real world, in which I was unhappy and where there was a lot of fear, and the world of my daydreams. I could wander for hours through my dreamworld. I stayed awake for ages at night and created a fairy tale world for myself. I always longed for a fairy prince and at the same time I was frightened of one. As an adolescent I wanted to have a perfect family with children whom I would protect. As a schoolgirl I did some work experience in a children's hospital and wrote my essay about child abuse in the family."

Mothers are particularly liable to tolerate abuse of their children (not noticing it, denying it, not hindering or stopping it) if:

- they themselves have suffered from a bonding trauma in their relationship with their own mother;
- they have suffered sexual abuse, splitting this experience off within themselves so becoming emotionally insensitive to their child's feelings;
- they have been entangled in the abusive dynamics of their family of origin, and their own mother or one of their sisters has been sexually abused;
- their own mothers have passed on to them their trauma emotions, making them emotionally numbed;
- they have a rejecting attitude to sexuality in general or to their partner in particular, which might have been caused by their own experiences of abuse;
- they are afraid of the consequences should the abuse be discovered, for example, they fear divorce because they might lose financial security, or they fear public shame if their husband has to go to prison.

The Blind Love of the Child

In the eternal hope of attracting the love of their parents children become entangled in the sexual abuse, hoping that if they are obedient and comply there might be less conflict between their parents. Some feel sorry for their depressed and weak

165

father and think he will feel better by using them. Daughters may reproach their mothers secretly, or openly, for not sexually satisfying their fathers thus causing rows and conflict. In her role as the "surrogate partner" the child becomes a rival to her mother and there is even a tendency for abused daughters to defend their fathers, because in contrast to their emotionally blocked and unavailable mother he has at least shown them some feeling and warmth. I have seen cases in which a child clings to her abusive father with her whole being because she has only ever known coldness and rejection from her mother, whilst in the intimate physical contact with her father she at least has experienced feelings of closeness and warmth.

The siblings of an abused child also become entangled in the unhealthy dynamic of sexual abuse in the family. In their own way they are also entangled emotionally with their inaccessible parents, and have to conspire in the family secret of abuse of one of their siblings through denial. Some may pity the abused child whilst others are envious of her because she seems to be the favourite.

A Society that Looks Away

Sexually abused boys and girls go to playschool, primary and secondary schools, later to university or to work. They know that society has a strong tendency to deny, repress, play down or make a taboo of discussion of sexual abuse. Perpetrators are protected from accusations, accomplices are not confronted with suspicion, children are stigmatised as having behavioural difficulties. Sexual abuse is seldom brought to court, even more rarely does it lead to convictions, and even then relatively mild sentences are often given. There are influential counter-movements which publicly oppose disseminating education about sexual abuse and which engage scientific support for their campaign, one of their aims being to undermine the credibility of child witness statements (e.g. the "false-memory" movement).

Those who might potentially be there to help an abused

child, such as teachers, police, lawyers, social workers, psychologists or doctors, could themselves be in danger of becoming entangled in the confused family systems. Helpers often feel overwhelmed, helpless and impotent when confronted with the phenomenon of sexual abuse. The subject of sexual abuse is sometimes ignored in psychotherapy, even unequivocal symptoms pointing to sexual abuse being missed or ignored by therapists.

There is also another section of society which is not of much help to the sexually abused child. These people or groups tend towards righteous anger without being sufficiently aware of the complicated emotional dynamics of sexual abuse. Many people condemn fathers and mothers out of hand, over-identify with the victims and demand injudicious revenge against the abusers. They are sometimes supported in this attitude by a press bent on sensationalism. However, this leads to a reinforced tendency for families to conceal sexual abuse all the more, in order not to be exposed to public contempt.

Borderline Personality Disorder

In bonding trauma we find that the affected children, and later adults, display symptomatic reactions which psychiatric diagnosis would classify as personality disorders. In particular the diagnosis of Borderline Personality Disorder is being increasingly applied in psychiatry (Kreisman and Straus, 2005). The list of symptoms presents extreme fears to be at the core of the traumatic event, particularly fear of annihilation, abandonment and separation.

The *Statistical and Diagnostic Manual of Mental Disorders* (DSM IV) names the following as criteria for Borderline Personality Disorder:

1. frantic efforts to avoid real or imagined abandonment
2. a pattern of unstable and intense interpersonal relationships characterized by alternating between extremes of idealization and devaluation

3. lasting identity disturbance: markedly and persistent unstable self-image or sense of self
4. impulsivity in at least two areas that are potentially self-damaging (e.g. spending, sex, substance abuse, reckless driving, binge eating)
5. self-harming activity
6. recurrent suicidal behaviour, gestures or threats, or self-mutilating behaviour
7. affective instability due to a marked reactivity of mood
8. chronic feelings of emptiness
9. inappropriate, intense anger or difficulty controlling anger
10. transient, stress related paranoia or severe dissociative symptoms

I cannot imagine that these kinds of symptoms could emerge in a person without them having personally experienced trauma or being deeply entangled in their mother's trauma as an infant. I consider theories that propose such symptoms as being attributable to organic or genetically influenced brain disorders to be unrealistic and artificial conjecture. In my experience the extreme symptoms in a Borderline Personality Disorder as presented in therapeutic work are entirely the result of a combination of bonding trauma and sexual abuse.

Ritual Abuse

Children who are subjected to ritual abuse and violence by being sold by their parents to paedophiles, or given to secret societies that practise ritual violence, experience a dramatic increase in trauma symptoms. We do not know how often this happens, as the perpetrators are careful to cover their tracks. Camouflaged – sometimes even in institutions which purport to protect children – and undisturbed by police or the law, these groups are organised like a mafia abusing children in the cruellest ways. In black masses and satanic cult behaviours, children are given drugs and raped, buried alive in coffins, forced to consume urine and excrement or to kill other small children. What is practiced in these circles is so perverse and crazy that it goes beyond any normal imagination (Huber, 1995 and 2003a; Froehlich, 1996).

Such sadistic people are usually organised in lodges, secret societies or brotherhoods, and have sworn to serve "evil" as the opposing principle to "good", which they do not believe exists. It seems likely that they are themselves traumatised which they handle by projection: their own trauma will be healed through the traumatising of others. As powerful, mystical and secretive as these various "Satan's priests" and "Grand Masters" present themselves, the cause for their deeds is in itself banal: they are emotionally dissociated, without roots or any sense of connection. They attempt to overcome their fears through a perverse world-view and by combating any emotional weakness in themselves. They cannot allow the experience of their own pain due to lack of love or emotional support from their parents which remains buried deep within them. They are themselves children who have experienced bonding trauma.

Digression 3: The traumatic source of National-Socialist ideology in Germany

National-Socialist ideology was based on the framing of empathic feelings as weakness and a determination to eliminate them. As can be seen from Adolf Hitler's biography, Hitler himself was not an internally integrated and mature person. On the contrary, having no paternal support in childhood, he became fixated on his mother, who was likely to be trapped in her own trauma of loss after the sudden death of her first three children. She was anxious and weak and Hitler was ashamed and disgusted by his ancestry. His father's mother was a maid and his father's father was unknown. His mother was both a niece of his father and his third wife (Binion, 1978; Ruppert, 2002). Hitler denied his own family background but required others to disclose their family tree up to four generations back.

After his mother's death he drifted about in Vienna and Munich until he found a role for himself in the First World War. When Germany lost the war he was thrown back on his own resources to maintain his existence, and could only deal with Germany's loss by committing himself to a world view of saving Germany. His aim was to redress the balance for the defeat in the First World War, which many Germans had experienced as a disgrace and humiliation. He imagined himself as "the greatest leader of all time" and unfortunately, since at the time many people in Germany were just as uncertain, anxious and full of self-doubt as he was, and wanted to forget the national shame of their defeat by building a new and strong Germany, for a while to the German people he became just this.

The systematic destruction of the "weak", as exemplified by disabled or mentally ill people, experiments on human beings and the breeding of humans for slavery, were not the ancillary activities of a reactionary state ideology in their national programme of combating "sub-humans", but, from a psychological point of view, their very core, which Hitler embodied in his own person. Hitler wanted to overcome the weakness within himself by destroying it in his environment. Observation of Hitler the human being reveals the banality of his inflated power ideology: a human being who cannot manage the feelings of trauma that he has taken from his mother attachment, and who, with no paternal support, seeks his salvation in the denial of these emotions which engender panic and fear in him. He takes refuge in abstract ideas and principles that despise human beings. He inflates himself, making himself large and powerful, because internally he experiences himself as small and insignificant. He seeks support in a society outside his family, which can never be large enough to compensate for his absent feeling of belonging to his family of origin. He wants to be both father and mother to this new society, to be its absolute creative principle.

Other Personality Disorders

Children who have not suffered trauma themselves, but whose mothers suffered trauma, can develop various forms of personality disorder depending on the different conditions of their childhood development (relationship with their father, position in relation to their siblings whether eldest, youngest etc., their own temperament, social environment or social class):

- *Histrionic Personality Disorder*: must be the centre of attention; sexually seductive and provocative behaviour; superficiality; exaggerated impressionistic language style; theatricality and self-dramatisation; easily influenced; takes relationships to be closer than they actually are (DSM IV 301.5).
- *Narcissistic Personality Disorder*: has a grandiose sense of self-importance, e.g., fantasies of unlimited success, power, brilliance, beauty, or ideal love; believes that he or she is unique; requires excessive admiration; has a sense of entitlement; is interpersonally exploitative, i.e., takes advantage of others to achieve his or her own ends; lacks empathy: is envious of others; exhibits arrogant and haughty behaviour.
- *Antisocial Personality Disorder*: failure to conform to lawful behaviours and norms; deceitfulness; irritability and aggressiveness; disregard for others; lack of remorse.

Because girls are more often victims of bonding trauma in their families than boys, they are also more likely to develop borderline symptoms. If they have not been sexually abused and are thereby orientated strongly towards their father or a surrogate father, they will tend to develop a histrionic personality structure.

Men who have not experienced sexual abuse tend to develop symptoms of bonding trauma if they grow up in an environment where neglect, brutality and violence are a part of everyday life, if they are hit frequently by their parents in childhood, or if they experience their parents as powerless victims of social conditions, as for example, in cases of children whose parents belong to a social fringe group such as immigrants and guest workers in a foreign country. For descendants of immigrants the norms of the guest country are no guideline for their own conscience (Ruppert, 2001). A conscience that respects norms and values can only develop in an atmosphere of love between the child and their mother and father and a feeling of belonging to a family. In a trauma situation this is not available.

A narcissistic personality structure can develop in a child within a family that on the surface seems to be normal. Many biographers of Hitler are surprised when they establish that Hitler grew up in a modest but sheltered family environment. They fail to see that Hitler's mother was severely traumatised by the death of her three children before his birth, and even if she had not been emotionally influenced by these events, she must have been traumatised before then and thus incapable of forming healthy attachments.

Adolf Hitler fulfils all criteria named above of a narcissistic personality structure. In the fullness of his power he staged what the child had discovered lurking behind the emotional void in his mother's psyche – mass death. This mass death, horror and terror that he spread compulsively around him was, in my opinion, an attempt to establish some sort of contact with his mother. Just as his mother was unable to integrate her reactions to the trauma of the death of her three children, so Hitler was also deeply impacted, and at the same time left devoid of emotion at the spectacle of death. In my opinion, it is only thus that he could stage and observe the death of millions as a spectator devoid of fear, rage, pain or pity. Additionally, because he could not understand himself or anyone else, he was driven to change the world, and he thus entangled millions of people in the personal fate of his own severe bonding trauma. It is also likely that his most loyal followers were, like him, incapable of looking at, or refused to look at, the darker sides of their souls, their own pain, desperation and fear. Whoever feels the abyss in his own soul is likely to avoid self-reflection and may become instead a propagandist of an ideology, projecting onto others what he cannot endure in himself. Thus, the Jews became a screen on which the National Socialists could project their worst features, attributes and excesses.

Mobbing and Bullying

Bonding trauma for children or adults can also underlie mobbing situations at school and at work. Although relationships between pupils and their teachers, or employees and their superiors do not have the emotional intensity of that between parents and children or between couples, nevertheless there is even so a high level of mutual dependency, and strong feelings of solidarity and loyalty develop between pupils and work colleagues (Ruppert, 2001). People who learn together in any institution or organisation must be able to respect each other. If this is violated through scandal, slander, deliberate disadvantage, physical or mental violence, then the victims of these mobbing attacks can develop significant emotional wounds through their experience of powerlessness in preserving their personal dignity.

If the person being mobbed cannot leave the system he is in, which is often the case, he feels trapped and helpless (Grueünwald and Hille, 2003; Kolodej, 2003). Whatever he does is turned back on him: if he engages with his work, his behaviour is criticised and devalued, if he does nothing, then it is interpreted as a refusal to work. The consequences are often symptoms of psychosomatic illness and mental disorders such as acute fear and depression. Additionally professional mobbing can easily destroy a person's private life so that this no longer serves as a refuge and source of renewal.

7.4 Consequences of Bonding Trauma

Addiction

The feeling of an internal void is the central symptom in bonding trauma. The drugs that are used in such cases may seem to fill this void at least for a time. They must be powerful in order to stimulate insensitivity and overcome the painful emotional experience. Usually antidotes against these powerful drugs need to be taken to avoid a collapse of the biochemical regulation mechanisms in the body and brain. The resulting frequently thoughtless consumption of multiple drugs is an addictive feature in people with a background of bonding trauma. Substance and non-substance addictions such as to computers, sex, shopping or addictive relationship behaviours are all to be found in varied combinations in people with bonding trauma.

In particular, experiences of violence in close relationships encourage the consumption of hard drugs. The authors of the study on violence against women in Germany quoted above established that: "on the one hand there is high consumption of alcohol and medication, and especially a very much higher consumption of tobacco by women who have experienced physical or mental violence and sexual molestation" (Müller, Schröttle, Glammeier und Oppenheimer, 2004). Bonding traumas in my experience can result in the hardest kinds of addiction. Heavy heroin addiction expresses most clearly what is happening in the inner world of the addict: he feels like a nobody that is kept alive only by the next shot of heroin. Everything is risked just to escape for a few moments from the chaos of feelings or the frozen wastelands of his inner life.

"I am not loved and I cannot be loved by anyone. The only thing that warms me a little is heroin" – that is the childlike message of severe drug addiction. This attitude is so firmly anchored in many addicts that even state institutions capitulate and relinquish believing in the idea of any possible abstinence. Substitution programmes are initiated with measurable, though on the whole only moderate, success (Raschke 1994). Drug addicts accept death, since they cannot see any other way out of their emotional chaos and inner emptiness. Unless they confront and deal with their painful experiences of bonding trauma, in my view they cannot escape from their addiction. Addiction therapies must show them how to face their emotional wounds without dying of worry and desperation. Only then can addiction therapies be successful.

Suicidal Ideation in Bonding Trauma

As already indicated, people with bonding trauma often flirt with death, which does not seem very different from their life, perhaps even seeming like a release compared with their internal emptiness and loneliness. Some cannot take their life seriously. They constantly put themselves at risk with drug use, unsafe sex, driving under the influence of drugs and other risky behaviours. Because their own life seems worthless and they have no empathy for other people, they have little hesitation in pulling other people with them into their abyss and even death. If abuse and violence are added to the initial bonding trauma, then the coldness and sadism of the perpetrator who abuses and hits the child will come to form a part of the child's fragmented psyche. The child itself will develop sadistic and murderous impulses, which he will then direct against himself and others. These self-destructive impulses can be understood as the memory of the wounds that others have inflicted on him and that he now directs towards himself as auto-aggression. Life forms into a chain of physical and emotional pain, further experiences of pain and catastrophic relationships. And even so, it is surprising how strong the will to survive can be even in someone in such a constant state of suicidal ideation.

Case Study 34:

Lifelong suicidal thoughts

Let us allow Laura to speak again: "As a teenager and young woman I often suffered from migraines and terrible period pains. I felt ill and my circulation was weak. My mother just kept telling me to pull myself together. Throughout my childhood I had thoughts of suicide. As a teenager I longed to have a relationship, and yet I was afraid of relationships. Just before I started my first proper relationship when I was 23, I was raped by a casual acquaintance. My relationships with men were always disastrous. I never had any feeling for my body. At 28 I had depression and was given anti-depressants by my G.P.

"I moved out of my parent's home when I was 20, and at that time my bad relationship with my parents, especially with my mother, had escalated. After that I came into contact with drugs, but managed to get out of that environment myself after a short while and several experiences. I really wanted to study psychology after leaving school, but I was afraid that I was not normal enough for this.

"When I was 30 I met the man who was to be the father of my children and soon after became pregnant with my oldest son. I knew even during the pregnancy that this relationship was doomed to fail. I experienced a lot of pressure, control, contempt and emotional violence in this relationship. After my second child died during childbirth, I was so weakened that I simply submitted to my fate. Only after the third child did I manage to separate from him. All this time I was terrified that my husband would do something to my children. Nightmares which I had had all my life now become unbearable.

"Suicidal thoughts wouldn't go away. I only didn't do it out of fear and concern for my children. These thoughts followed me all day, every day, and throughout each pregnancy. My life was constant stress. This constant stress followed through in my working life as well, which was marked by short lightning careers and catastrophic crashes."

As suicidal ideation in these cases is almost part of the normality of their lives, some people develop an extraordinary capacity to survive the most dangerous situations. There is little prospect of healing this kind of suicidal ideation through compulsory hospitalisation in psychiatric wards or through enforced medication. Taking their disappointments and their woundedness seriously, and looking at the causes is, in my opinion, the only way to gain access to these patients and perhaps keep them from carrying out their suicidal intentions.

The Search for a New Self-Concept and World View

Bonding trauma is characterised by disappointment in the need for love, security, protection and acceptance. The people you have to rely on most, your parents, are not there for you and some parents abuse the child's dependency, tearing down the child's boundaries and offloading their own traumas into the child. Understandably, an existential philosophy develops out of this that is founded on mistrust with no scruples or boundaries, because there is no family conscience to teach the child to differentiate between good and bad. Flight into promiscuity or prostitution, breaking the law and criminality ensue, as do hating everyone and possibly withdrawal into complete isolation. People with experiences of bonding trauma are vulnerable to groups and organisations that worship violence, and political and religious fanaticism. Men who have experienced severe bonding trauma carry within themselves the potential to murder. They may act out their own unbearable pain time and time again, but it is never resolved.

However, the experience of a bonding trauma can also teach one to experience love as something precious. Even the love of parents for their children is not a given. It is something very special. This special nature of love is replicated in many other relationships, whether these are with people, with animals or with nature. Whoever has experienced bonding trauma and does not want to succumb to addiction or fall into a kind of permanent aggression and suicidal ideation must draw energy and strength from many positive sources to keep him or her alive and fill his or her inner void. She must learn to become aware of herself and discover who she is before she can open her boundaries to others. Only in a loving relationship to herself can she find what she originally hoped for from her parents. Perhaps this inward attention and healing will finally even soften the hearts of her parents within her own soul. For the love of the parents towards their child is present in every case; it just needs to be freed from the prison of trauma.

7.5 The Effects of Bonding Trauma on Subsequent Generations

What effect does a traumatic mother attachment and a disturbed father attachment have on the following generations?

Bonding traumas are by definition multi-generational, because the mother's trauma affects her ability to bond with her child, resulting in a bonding trauma for the child, which may later manifest as a personality disorder, in turn affecting the child's ability as an adult to bond with their child. From there it is easy to see how emotional chaos originating in the mother's trauma will continue into subsequent generations. Neglected, emotionally and sexual abused girls often get pregnant as teenagers – either out of ignorance of how to protect themselves from unwanted pregnancy, or because they believe that this will be a way to forget their traumatic experiences with their parents as quickly as possible. These adolescents try to create an intact family for themselves, hoping that the birth of a baby will heal their own traumatic emotional wounds. The reality is, of course, that they become overburdened by the needs of their child. Some of these mothers are unable to give up their addiction to cigarettes, alcohol or heroin for the safety of the child during their pregnancy and, without help from social services and intensive care, many of the children would waste away through neglect, possibly even starving to death. These adolescent mothers repeat with their child what they experienced from their own parents: misuse of the child for their own symbiotic needs, inability to give love and not having a place in life. Michaela Metzdorf has described in detail such a family situation over several generations (Metzdorf, 2001).

Women who have suffered bonding trauma either seek men – often modelled on their fathers – whom they can keep at a distance because they too are caught up in their own bonding trauma, or who are brutal and inconsiderate and to whom they look for protection. They fail to notice when their own daughters are, in turn, sexually abused, if not by their fathers, by a teacher, a youth leader or sometimes even by a priest (Schmideder, 2002).

The mothers who have suffered bonding trauma are unaware of what their sons and daughters feel and experience because they themselves do not feel properly. They cannot distinguish between appropriate and inappropriate physical intimacy and distance, and they cannot give their children a clear sense of their own body, or for social loving or sexual relationships. Some are constantly worried about their children, but often they are unable to give them any emotional sustenance. They cannot incorporate the experiences of their own childhood into the up bringing of their children, because this would be too painful and so they keep this part of themselves locked away. The tortured child inside the adult is not allowed to show itself or to speak, it has to stay hidden and quiet. They cannot admit to the grief and pain of their emotional wounding by their parents. They are afraid that they would not be able to bear it, and so unconsciously pass on their unresolved fears and depression to their children. Through anxiety, like small children, they cling on to their own children at the same time that, in their emotionless state, they reject their children.

The child's problems start at birth when they cannot take nourishment from their mother, and at the same time are flooded by the chaotic feelings, terror and depression of their mother. They will replicate the experiences and feelings of their mother without having been traumatised themselves. They find it difficult to take in food, are often ill, become restless and later find it hard to concentrate at school.

Case Study 35:

Full of existential fear right from birth

Laura: "My first son was very poorly after he was born. He could hardly keep any food down, and was constantly sick and screaming with pain. At first I spent days and nights carrying him around in the hospital and then at home. I cut myself off from the outside world. Physically and emotionally I was feeling worse and worse. After 8 months we finally made it. Through a strict diet I was able to breastfeed my child without him getting tummy aches.

"After the death of my second child I fell into deep depression. I felt guilty and had constant suicidal thoughts. I clung to my first son like I was a small child. Without him I would not have taken a single step outside the flat. I could only sleep at night if he was in my bed beside me. I only managed to come out of this hole in my third pregnancy."

The children of these traumatised mothers try hard to understand this mysterious being who is their mother, wanting to help her in her distress. Consequently, they open themselves up even more to the mother's emotional instability. In their dreams and fantasies they may experience sequences of their mother's trauma including images of violence and explicit sexual content. The helpless children are constantly exposed to this contrasting fluctuation between emotional flooding and icy coldness. Later on in life they tend to seek out partners who are as equally split as their mothers.

Sex Addiction, Prostitution and Sadomasochism

When, as a result of her experiences of sexual abuse, a mother is confused and unable to differentiate between love and sexuality, this confusion affects her relationship with her child. She is unable to notice when physical contact erotises her child and arouses it sexually. In physical contact with the child she occasionally reverts back into her own childhood experiences. Her split-off feelings, from when she experienced sexual abuse, may come up again when she looks at and touches her own child.

Particularly sons may get into terrible emotional confusion when they experience the split-off emotions and sexual abuse experiences of their mother. Sorting out the boundary between them and their mother's body, which is difficult at best, becomes increasingly problematic. The longed-for intimacy with their mother is confused with sexual impulses that they are unable to understand or sort out.

This situation is reinforced when the relationship between the parents is also confused, for example when the mother, as a result of her experiences of abuse, chooses a man who will not be a danger to her, in that he cannot tolerate intimacy. If he does try to get close she will place the child between herself and the man, the child serving to satisfy her needs for closeness and intimacy with safety. Without being consciously aware of it, she "feeds" the child with sexual impulses, thereby flooding the child. At the same time, she is afraid of sex and makes it a forbidden subject. She is particularly fearful of the sexuality of her son as he grows up, and for the son it becomes an increasingly confusing situation which he cannot solve. His need for intimacy with his mother is unconsciously sexualised by her at the same time as she rejects his sexuality.

The son then does not learn good boundaries for physical contact and confuses intimacy with eroticism. As he grows up he may even experience his mother as expecting him to satisfy her sexually, and is horrified to imagine that his mother might even want to sleep with him, being unable to eradicate such images from his head. By puberty this emotional confusion can lead to psychotic episodes.

The abuse of the mother as a child is, as a rule in my experience, the cause of sexual addiction in the son. An addictive attitude to sex only ends when a connection is made with the mother's own experience of abuse, perhaps when she is able to work through it in therapy (Ruppert, 2002).

Children love their parents even when their parents are unable to love themselves. Even when parents are ashamed of themselves and reject and despise themselves, their children still try to win through to their hearts. In one striking constellation I had the opportunity to experience how the love of a child can help its mother to find her way back to loving and respecting herself.

Case Study 36:

The search for the mother in the red light district

Rudolf took part in a constellations workshop to try and understand why he had been drawn to hanging around red light districts over the previous three years, and why he had left his wife and child, although he loved them.

In the constellation a scenario developed in which his mother seemed to have been sexually abused and humiliated by several men. She could no longer tolerate intimacy with any man or with her own son. She did not believe herself worthy of being loved.

In the constellation, when Rudolf told the representative who stood in for his mother that he found her lovable in spite of everything that might have happened to her, the representative for his mother could not at first believe him. Then her defensive attitude began slowly to disappear, and she felt deep pain. For the first time the representative reported being able to recognised the suffering and love of her son, and in the end they embraced warmly.

Rape

Wars have served as justification for the rape of the enemies' women. Such excesses of rape affect generation after generation, hindering good relationships between men and women long after a war has finished. The women may, for example, develop fear of the manhood and sexuality of their own sons.

Case Study 37:

Fear of her own son

Thomas is attracted to women with whom he can feel pain and sorrow. He loves the woman deeply even though she may reject him. He is furious with women who in his opinion fool around with their sexuality superficially and frivolously. He despairs that these women may reject him, although he is prepared to do anything for them.

Unconsciously he is repeating the pattern of his mother attachment. On the one hand his mother enticed him, but the path to reach her was blocked. But by what? His mother to all appearances has never been subjected to sexual abuse herself.

The answer to the puzzle lay in the fate of his grandmother. During the war she had been raped by several men and consequently split off this emotional experience. She could neither laugh nor cry any more. She found some comfort in her daughter and succeeded in allowing herself to feel some emotion in this context. Thomas' mother in bonding with his grandmother had taken these split off emotions into herself and so was unable to allow her own son close to her. She related to him superficially and held him at a distance. Thomas was a man and therefore threatening, like the men who had raped his grandmother.

A mother's rejection of her sexuality was also the reason for the sadomasochism of another patient. This patient had always tried to win approval from his mother through high achievement at school and at work. This led to professional success, although he was unable to enjoy this success or be happy about it. He had taken on the trauma of his mother's sexual experiences from which she had suffered all her life. Only in sadomasochistic relationships was he able to act out his desperate love for his mother along with his helpless rage against her.

Bulimia

Bulimia is the unbridled, greedy bolting down of large amounts of food indiscriminately, followed by self-induced vomiting. Attacks of ravenous appetite can occur several times a week or several times a day. The short-lived feeling of relief that vomiting brings is followed by a phase of dejection and feelings of guilt. About 3% of women between the ages of 18 and 35 display these symptoms (Laessle, 1994).

If one considers this from the point of view of trauma and attachment, then bulimia may be a direct consequence of sexual abuse in the family. On the one hand the child hungers ravenously for love and affection which is not available, constantly and addictively attempting to satisfy this hunger by bolting down huge amounts of food. On the other she rejects incestuous closeness and sexualised physical contact, which she finds disgusting. The food she has so greedily swallowed has to be vomited up again. To put it metaphorically: the emotional nutrition received by the child from a mother who has been sexually abused is unpalatable, the child cannot digest it. The child cannot bear the traumatised mix of feelings she experiences in her mother that are connected with disgust about physical contact, at the same time longing for maternal intimacy. On the emotional level the only thing available from the mother is something that makes the child feel unwell. And so she must distance herself from her mother, achieving this by

defiant and aggressive behaviour. This behaviour then repeatedly reverts to despair and resignation.

The physical closeness of the child with her need for love
also reminds the mother of the sexual abuse she experienced,
and so intimacy with the child becomes unbearable for her too,
so she blocks any closeness by cutting off her feelings.
Externally she functions well as wife and mother, while internally she wants to flee.

The father/husband in this dynamic tends to play the role
of an extra who cannot make contact with either his wife or his
daughter. He does not understand what is happening. Usually
he is also someone who has difficulty in allowing his own
emotional pain any expression, so externally he organises and
runs a well-ordered family life, and fantasises that one day,
through material prosperity he may be able to soften the hearts
of his wife and children.

An important aspect of bulimia is that it is played out in
secret, indicating that bulimia is a way of protecting a secret in
the family. Outwardly everything is supposed to look decent
and perfect and no-one is supposed to notice what has really
been going on in the family.

Case Study 38:

"I need you both".

Ingrid is bulimic. Outwardly she appears bossy and confident, internally her despair is clearly present. She still lives
at her parental home, isolated in her room. Home life
consists of one row after another. Her mother has been
struggling for years to separate from Ingrid's father. She
despises him as weak, but can't move away.

Ingrid's constellation reveals the following: bulimia is the
symptom that protects her from closeness, by feeling unwell
and nauseous. The symptom belongs to both mother and
daughter in that they both experience intimacy as dangerous,
and that is why they block their feelings through the bulimia

whenever the father approaches them. Ingrid cannot tolerate closeness with her mother either. So no-one can approach anyone in this family. The father, rejected by his wife, in despair tries to seek intimacy with his daughter, and this holds the danger of incest. This is also why Ingrid cannot bear to have him close. She flees from him and, like her mother, despises him as a weak man. She fantasises about being rescued by a strong boyfriend.

The roots of this entanglement seemed to lie in Ingrid's mother's line. Both Ingrid's mother and grandmother had been sexually abused by Ingrid's great grandfather. The great grandmother seems to have known about this. Ingrid's mother's personality is split insofar as she seeks closeness to her grandfather on the one hand, whilst on the other she despises him and all men as weaklings.

In the constellation the solution occurred when the abuse was openly addressed as abuse and no longer tolerated as "normal" in the mother's family of origin. In order that the great grandfather's compulsive need to commit sexual violations could be stilled, the representative of the great grandfather needed to be able to feel his own pain. The actual great grandfather had acted out his pain by abusing his daughter and granddaughter. For the grandmother it was important to express her suppressed rage towards her father and this was possible in the constellation. Gradually the representatives for Ingrid's mother and grandmother were able to approach each other. The mother's representative now recognised that she had been unfair towards her husband. He had never stood a chance with her. The father's representative was able to access his own feelings and became aware of his great sense of loneliness. Ingrid and her father's representative had an emotional exchange about this which enabled Ingrid and her father's representative to come closer to each other. Eventually they were in each other's arms, in tears. Finally Ingrid said to her parents' representatives: "I love and need you both as my parents. I will leave you to deal with whatever still needs to be sorted out between you."

Compulsive Behaviours

Compulsive behaviours – hand-washing, showering for hours and frequent changing of clothes – for a child or adolescent can also have some connection with sexual abuse of his or her mother. Women who have been raped often display this kind of behaviour – trying to wash away the traces of the rape. They want to be clean and pure again, but of course washing doesn't remove the internal feeling of having been defiled.

In emotional intimacy with a mother who was raped, the child may take on her feelings of defilement. As several examples have shown me, the mother completely splits off the memory of the sexual violence, and when the split off feelings come to the surface in therapy, the patient then displays the most intensive feelings of disgust. The rape event may even originate a generation further back, and thus the hidden consequences are transmitted by the grandmother through the mother to the grandchild.

As will be shown, eating and other compulsive disorders are often not just the consequence of a bonding trauma combined with sexual violations. Because they have a strong delusional component they can also be symptomatic reactions to a bonding system trauma. What I understand as a bonding system trauma and how it can affect generation after generation will be explained in the following chapter.

8

Bonding System Trauma

8.1 Introduction: Keeping or Revealing Family Secrets

Major crimes committed by human beings against each other cause the deepest psychological and traumatic wounds: crimes such as murder, manslaughter, robbery and rape. It is complex enough when such deeds are committed outside of the family, for example, if a husband or father goes to war and he kills or maybe is involved in rape. Or perhaps as a professional such as a lawyer, doctor or scientist he plays some role in executions or performs experiments on humans as happened in some of the concentration camps during the second world war. Or, if a wife or mother, she works as a warden in a concentration camp. The deeds committed in these kinds of circumstances happen outside of the family and not against family members, and yet since all perpetrators of such acts come from a family, perhaps even have children of their own, the crimes affect the whole family bonding system.

Crimes such as murder, extreme violence or inappropriate sexuality committed *within* the family bonding system cause the most devastating effects. These acts include matricide, fratricide, patricide, infanticide and sexual intercourse with one's own children or siblings and will project the whole family system into a state of emotional trauma and chaos. Such events are impossible for the family to integrate emotionally and psychologically, and have to become hidden and secret. How can a family deal with events such as these? What if the sexual intercourse of a parent with their child or a brother with his sister results in the birth of a child? Where do all the feelings of guilt and shame go if a child born from incest is "disposed of"?

These are events that are so impossible to deal with on any level that they pull the whole family bonding system into an abyss of secrecy and cover up. In my view, the murder or manslaughter of a family member, or incest resulting in the birth of a child are trauma situations of a very particular kind. Several people in the family will know about the deed, and while such deeds should lead to the dissolution of the family bonding system, specifically to a separation between husband and wife or parents and children, often the opposite happens. The family closes around the secret, it is denied, repressed, hidden. Specific situations that occur might include:

- The murder of a father, mother or sibling that is camouflaged as an accident,
- A child born with a disability is secretly killed,
- A child born from incest is killed or camouflaged as a late birth, given up for adoption or put into a home,
- Children resulting from incestuous relationships are aborted even in very late stages of pregnancy,
- A child born from a father-daughter incest is attributed to another man and its real father is never named.

8.2 Trauma of the Whole Bonding System

I have chosen the term "bonding system trauma" for situations of this kind in order to make it clear that the whole system of bonded relationships, specifically the family bonding system, is traumatised by these kinds of events. The effects of these events in a family system very likely cannot be resolved for several generations.

Digression 4: Regicide as bonding system trauma

The idea of defining a separate category for trauma of whole bonding systems can also be applied to non-family relationship systems, specifically to groups of people who are connected through relationships of loyalty. For example, regicide would be an analogous example within a system of a nation-state. King Ludwig II of Bavaria (1845 – 1886) was addicted to building castles and investing all the Bavarian state money in art, and was as a result officially declared mad, legally incompetent and deposed as king. Nowadays Ludwig II would probably have been diagnosed as having a narcissistic personality disorder. His unexplained death on 13 July 1886 is still disturbing for some citizens of Bavaria today, because many doubt that it was suicide as was officially declared, and believe that Ludwig II was probably murdered by order of the Bavarian state leadership. Within the Bavarian psyche this king has still not been laid to rest (Reißer, 2002).

Employment relationship systems may also be influenced by murder or robbery and become trapped in a bonding system trauma. During the Nazi period, Jewish businessmen were disenfranchised of their businesses, houses and land, and were put to work as forced labour. These abusive actions then became a burden for the new owners of the businesses in that success for the new company is based on robbery, murder and lies, and honest communication within the company and between the company and the outside world is impossible (Ruppert 2001). Psychiatric institutions and hospitals participated in the murder of the mentally ill during the time of National Socialism, and I believe that these institutions will not be able to find closure unless these crimes are faced, recognised and mourned with clarity. Inhumanity that is not acknowledged tends to be repeated.

Crimes Committed Outside the Family

There are differences between the effect on a family bonding system of crimes committed within the family bonding system and crimes committed against someone who does not belong to the family system. Whatever one person does will always have an effect to some extent on everyone else in the family system. So, for example, it can become a psychological burden for the family system if a father committed or participated in a murder, or if a mother took part in criminal experiments on human beings whilst working as a nurse, as was often the case in Germany before and during the Second World War (Bar-On, 2003). Such crimes are usually kept secret and to understand the consequences we need to know how such deeds come into the family. For example if stolen goods are bequeathed to children, this inheritance can become a burden of guilt or shame to the children. Or if a woman took part in Heinrich Himmler's "Lebensborn" programme, was coupled with an SS-man and gave birth to a child which was subsequently handed over to foster parents, then this deed will affect her relationship with any further children she might have. Psychotherapists in Germany often see the effects of these events in the fates of the grandchildren and great-grandchildren. In many other countries the cruelties of slavery for example, the exploitation and terror this induced, are likely to burden not just the children, but the grandchildren and even the great-grandchildren unconsciously, and, depending on the individual case, lead to seemingly unexplained feelings of shame and fear, ideological inflexibility, unconscious attempts to put things right and lives of suffering (Lebert and Lebert, 2002; Welzer, Moller, Tschuggnall, 2002). However, as a rule crimes committed outside the family produce less confusion and emotional splitting than wrongs committed within the family. The specific effect of these crimes needs to be explored carefully in each individual case. In many cases crimes outside the family are combined with violence within the family.

Case Study 39:

"Grandfather, you are mad"

Norbert came to a constellations seminar because his relationships with women always went wrong. He is a good-looking, sensitive, intelligent and friendly man in a secure job. However, in relationships with women he becomes childlike. As a result his partners soon lose interest in him.

In his constellation it became clear that his bonded connection with his mother was impaired. His mother seemed like a small child, unable to access her own mother who it seemed from the behaviour of the representatives in the constellation, it was likely had been sexually abused by her father. The representative for Norbert's mother also seemed terrified of her father and it seemed that the cause of this fear was that her father had been active as a doctor in the Third Reich in Germany during the war. As a small child she had noticed how Jewish children in her neighbourhood suddenly disappeared.

The solution for Norbert lay in speaking out about the sexual abuse and in confronting the abuser as represented in the constellation. It turned out to be one of the few times that I have experienced in a constellation where a culprit as represented does actually feel remorse for his deed, and this enabled the representatives for the grandmother and her father to approach each other. This in turn allowed some contact between the representatives for the grandmother and her daughter, Norbert's mother, who was then able to connect to the representative for her husband (Norbert's father) and address the issue of his having experienced her as absent, and so cheated of her love. However, the representative of Norbert's grandfather continued to find excuses and justify his crimes as a Nazi doctor whenever he was confronted in the constellation. Norbert was finally able to tell the representative for his grandfather, "Grandfather, you are mad and you nearly made my mother and me mad with fear." Norbert was able to access his feelings and approach the representative of his mother with love.

Guilt . . .

In principle the solution to feelings of guilt is remorse for the deed, apology and restitution as far as this is possible. For this to happen the deed has to be admitted and responsibility taken for it, and this process cannot begin unless the deed has been revealed. Some perpetrators, who are not completely emotionally desensitised, try to deal with their guilt in secret. They may subject themselves to punishments and forms of self-sacrificial atonement, or they may choose a path of exaggerated piety, appearing saintly.

. . . and Shame

Usually shame plagues the perpetrator even more than guilt and fear of punishment. To be ashamed means that one no longer wishes to be the person one actually is, a desire to vanish, to not exist. Shame is also the fear of social contempt, fear of being annihilated, banished from the community, the terror of the loss of one's right to belong and as such is very close to a fear of death. It is the fear of social death.

The French psychoanalyst Serge Tisseron wrote a monograph on the phenomenon of shame (Tisseron, 2000) in which he makes clear that shame is also a feeling that can be catching. If someone is ashamed, those observing feel uneasy, and they would like to end the shaming scene as quickly as possible. In Tisseron's view the only appropriate way to overcome feelings of shame lies in finding something positive in the feeling of shame itself. ". . . the striving of an individual . . . to reclaim his own identity which will give him the right to a place in the community" (ibid.).

A person who does not admit to his deeds may tend to retreat into intellectualisation or abstraction fearing that if he were to allow himself to express his feelings he would disintegrate. For this reason, some fathers, unable to admit to things they did during a war and who want to maintain their image as men of honour to their families, may become dogmatic and insensitive towards their family and their community, their retreat into intellectualising being a defence against facing the abyss of their feelings. Additionally, a child, sensing his parents' feelings of guilt, responsibility and shame, will try to protect the parent from these feelings, and may also dissociate and intellectualise as a way of keeping him and them away from their difficult feelings. So if a daughter, for example, tries to reveal the truth of the sexual abuse that she is suffering, then one of her sisters or brothers may help the parents to suppress this truth by declaring her crazy and a denigrator of the family.

Secrecy and Collusion

The experience of shame guarantees the turning of socially unacceptable and embarrassing deeds into secrets. And it is not only the perpetrator who holds the secrets through shame, but also those who may know or suspect, who looked away in order not to be confronted with their own feelings of shame, thereby colluding with the secret. Through this collusion of secrecy the participants become dependent upon each other and the deed continues its lively existence. An event does not disappear just because people look away or do not speak about it: like a dark cloud it hangs over people even as they try to hide it. As Serge Tisseron discovered, one cannot really keep a secret: ". . . it makes itself noticeable in a certain tone of voice, in certain gestures, in the use of incongruent or unusual words and even in the objects with which the bearer of the secret surrounds himself. Depending on the circumstances and personality structure the 'seeping through' of secrets expresses itself either as 'scream' or as 'whisper'. But it always affects the way that someone who is hiding something behaves with his relatives, friends, work colleagues and children" (Tisseron, 2000).

Tisseron draws our attention to the particular effects of secrets within a family when he continues: "Friends and casual acquaintances, however, have no reason to allow themselves to be influenced by the secret which they may suspect in the other. However, those who have a strong emotional bonding to the other are in danger of being severely harmed" (ibid.).

The child who is mis-fathered
One category of family secret is when a mother knows that the recognised father of her child is not the biological father. For example perhaps the mother had an affair that was one of the few moments of happiness in her life and a child is born. Or a child is born from rape or incest. This kind of secret may have difficult consequences for the child. Relationships in the family may not seem clear, and family members may not feel in their rightful 'place' in the bonding system, and children can sense this. They know at the deep level of bonding the secrets within the psyche of their mother and so are likely to become more and more entangled and confused in the relational and emotional disorder of the family.

Case Study 40:

Love and Fatherhood

Martin is plagued by insecurity, from time to time slipping into paranoid and deluded psychotic states. He remembers his childhood as a constant series of rows between his mother and father. He has long suspected that his alcoholic father is not his real father, but doesn't know for sure. However, there is a story in his family about a man who shot himself in a forest glade near Martin's home town that seems to be in some way important to him.

In a constellation that included representatives for Martin, his mother and his father, when a representative for the man who shot himself was placed, it seemed that the representative for Martin's mother felt very drawn to this man. The representative reported feeling love for him, as if he was the only bit of light in her life. It seemed to make sense to Martin, who felt able to absorb this possible moment of love and happiness between his mother and her lover. While he cannot know, it seems possible to him that this may have been his father. It also made sense to him of the conflict between his father and mother, but he decided he could hold the image that he may have been conceived as a child of a moment of love.

Homosexuality as a forbidden subject
Secrets and taboos are culturally imprinted. Even the proscription against killing children and old people or the taboo of incest have not been universally prevalent in human societies. Up to two or three generations ago, even in the so-called modern European countries, illegitimate children, unmarried mothers and homosexual leanings were embarrassing in the extreme and subject to social contempt. Even today homosexuality is still one of the most difficult subjects to air in a family attachment system since it brings up feelings of guilt and shame. Some fathers experience their homosexual son as such a great source of shame that they break off all contact with their child. For these reasons homosexuality can become a forbidden subject and a family secret.

Nowadays gays and lesbians are, in some western countries, increasingly active in bringing homosexuality out of this forbidden zone. This then helps others to admit to their own sexuality, at the very least to themselves in therapy. To openly admit to one's own homosexuality for many is an important move to avoid sinking into depression.

The disclosure of homosexuality can play an important part in therapy when another family secret is somehow connected with it. A further entanglement can ensue when, for example, a person senses that he is homosexual, but marries and has children to comply with the norm and keeps his homosexuality secret from his partner and the children. The emotional bondings get confused through this.

Case Study 41:

The homosexual father

Christian (30 years old) feels very confused at times, and he has frequently been under psychiatric care because of this, having been taking medication for many years. Christian converted from Christianity to Judaism to try and find some useful truth and support from religion. In his behaviour he presents as an engaging young man who is somehow burdened. When he was 16 his mother told him that the man she was married to was not his real father, and this was something that he remembered already having heard from his mother's mother when he was only six. He has never met his biological father and his mother had hinted that his real father had homosexual tendencies.

During a constellation the likely reasons for his inner confusion became apparent: the constellation showed his actual father as having survived a mass execution of Jews in the National Socialist era, later having had a homosexual relationship with a German. The mother of Christian's mother had known about this Jewish fate of his father. Christian's mother also seemed to have known that Christian's father had lived in a stable homosexual relationship and that a marriage with him was not possible.

Through these disclosed revelations Christian awoke from his illusory world. He could now see both the suffering of his biological Jewish father as well as experience his love for him.

Several months later Christian wrote in a letter: "I am astonishingly well . . . I see the two men who stood with me at the end of the constellation as my biological father and my stepfather. Cool, isn't it?"

Secret guilt: a road to insanity
People who are guilty and feel unable to speak out from fear and shame are likely to be emotionally very vulnerable. The

integrity of their sense of self is threatened: they are caught between the part of themselves that has to keep the secret and the part that longs to unburden themselves and be free from the constant pressure of their conscience. Being thus torn between these two poles causes a split in the personality that may well in extreme cases result in psychosis or schizophrenia.

Part of the process seems to be that the mid-point between these two poles of "secrecy" and "revelation" is likely to make a person apathetic and unable to make decisions or take action, which in turn leads to difficulty in thinking, feeling and physical movement, even resulting in the psychiatric condition of "catatonia".

When nearer the pole of secrecy they become suspicious of everything and everyone, becoming paranoid. It is as if he or she imagines those who they think may suspect as shining torches around inside their head where they hide their thoughts about the deed. To appear as unsuspicious as possible, the following are some of the strategies that might be developed:

- They make out they have no problems in their life. Their childhood was good, their parents were honourable people, their marriage is fine. Nothing particular or remarkable ever happened.
- They are uncommunicative, taking the view that one should not talk about certain things.
- They may ignore or act as if they had not heard certain questions.
- They may distract themselves by changing the subject or busying themselves with something else.
- They may faint or use other avoidant tactics.
- They may be threatening and aggressive.
- They may philosophise, intellectualise and steer conversations in a different direction.

Behind these behaviours is a terror of emotional turmoil from which there seems no escape, making their attempts at avoidance vehement and determined. If the deed becomes known they will make crude attempts to justify their actions by defining them as normal. For example, in paedophilia cases perpetrators will often attempt to justify their behaviour by saying that children enjoy it or that the child was seductive. The longer the perpetrator lives with his secret, the deeper the split in his personality becomes. Indeed, some perpetrators may in the end convince themselves with one side of their personality that the deed never happened at all, or that someone else did it.

At the other polarity they long to disclose the deed, hoping for redemption from their feelings of guilt and shame. Any disclosure usually begins with hints and allusions, for example when all the associated photographs have been taken out of the family album, one remains which shows a picture of the man who is the real father of the child rather than the man one thinks is his father. Or there is one photo that shows the grand-father in Nazi uniform, although there was never any talk in the family of what that grandfather actually did in the war. There is an object (a picture, a book, a knife, a watch), which always seems to be lying around the home for no reason, but which seems to come along in every house-move or which seems to cause a row if someone wants to throw it away or put it in another place.

Case Study 42:

The picture of the gypsy

One client said that there was a picture of a gypsy dressed in red in her parents' house which seemed to have the function of symbolising a secret, drawing attention to the fact that the mother had had a lover before her marriage who had been a gypsy and who had later been killed by the Nazis.

Secrets can also be contained in ghost stories.

Case Study 43:

The ghost in the cellar

Susanne never felt at ease in the company of her mother. Even when being together was more joyful, a moment would come when she felt she had to get away from her mother or she would feel ill and extremely fearful and anxious throughout her body.

During a constellation Susanne suddenly remembered something her mother used to say: "My mother once told me about a man who had been a supplier to her parents' business when she was a little child. Since this man died my mother said that she had felt he haunted the house and that she could hear his steps in the cellar." After Susanne had given her unconscious permission to disclose everything so that she could understand her fears and anxiety, suddenly the following connection occurred to her with a great clarity: her mother had been sexually abused by this supplier for a long time and one day she had poisoned him.

This spontaneous thought led to an enormous shiver throughout Susanne's body and subsequently to a feeling of great relief for her. After a while she reported feeling peaceful and deeply relaxed. She said: "I feel as though something is draining away from me."

Hope for release from the burden of holding the secret may involve looking for a person to tell. The ritual of confession in the church offers a way of disclosing secrets to a priest who is vowed to silence and can give ritual absolution for the "sin". It is possible that an exaggerated involvement with religion might be motivated by a wish to reveal and the hope of receiving absolution from the church for a deed that one believes would not be forgiven by one's fellow human beings.

People who do not have access to religion sometimes find

the equivalent in a psychotherapist who they feel they can trust with their secret. Psychotherapists of course, while respecting confidentiality, are not able to give the client absolution, but just being able to talk and not feel judged, feeling accepted can provide its own kind of release and absolution. This is obviously why clients will test their therapist very carefully to make sure that they can trust them with their secrets. Finding their way to a therapist is often the last option, taken when all other means to deal with the tension between secrecy and disclosure have failed. Flight into illness, psychiatric care or dementia is often a preferred unconscious choice. Secrets are often taken into the grave, or only disclosed on the death-bed.

Dementia in old age
Senile dementia may be not just an organic illness. It is likely that as physical strength declines, emotional conflicts more easily surface, the urge to find expression overcoming the failing physical strength. Older people who become increasingly overwhelmed by efforts to contain their internal splitting can become unpredictable and lose their equanimity more and more easily and frequently. The unresolved conflicts of their life urge for expression. Children who are prepared to listen attentively to what their confused elderly parents are saying may get hints about what has happened and been kept secret in the family.

8.3 The Effects of Bonding System Trauma on Subsequent Generations

Perpetrators keep quiet primarily to protect themselves, while accomplices keep quiet in the hope of not losing their family, out of a deep sense of loyalty to their family and fear for themselves, their children and their grandchildren. The victims often stay quiet out of shame. Some family members collude with the secrecy because they have been drawn into the secret as partners, siblings, friends, doctors or priests and think they might still salvage something and help to balance out the wrong with good. However, in my experience this only encumbers subsequent generations with an un-talked of burden, and many children, grandchildren and great grandchildren may suffer emotionally as a result.

The effect on the child
What effect does it have on the child when parents live with the burden of a secret? Serge Tisseron has discovered the following from observing his clients: the child will try to understand the internal split of her parents. Why does her mother behave so strangely when confronted with certain people, or names, or objects? Why does her expression change? Why does she get fidgety and anxious? Why is she suddenly so cold, rejecting or aggressive? Have I, the child, done something wrong? Can I trust my mother or is she lying to me?

According to Tisseron, growing up in this kind of atmosphere has the following likely consequences for the child: "If the secret events at the start are 'unspeakable' for those who experienced them, then they become 'unnameable' for the second generation. That is, they are not accessible for verbal description, the content is unknown, one just senses and questions their existence. In the second generation specific learning difficulties may appear, together with mild personality impairments as a result" (Tisseron, 2000).

I have many times made similar observations with my own clients. Paradoxically, it seems as if the second generation can deal with a family secret somewhat better than the third. In my experience, it is often so that the hidden event only becomes troublesome, or "appears", after the birth of the child of the next generation. If a mother has a child after the event, in other words when the trauma is already deeply embedded within her, the mother's emotional turmoil flows directly into her child in the bonding process, and so creates emotional turmoil in the child. The child of this child (third generation), i.e. of a woman who bonded with a mother who holds a shameful trauma secret, is very vulnerable indeed to emotional entanglement. This child experiences in his bonding connection with his mother as he searches for emotional security, his mother's turmoil. Or, from the perspective of the mother, any contact with her child arouses all the feelings that she experienced in her relationship with her mother which she unconsciously absorbed. The less successful the emotional contact between a mother and her child in the present, the more vehemently the unresolved family past pushes to the fore. One client formulated it as follows: "My mother is not present for me. She is transparent, and everything that lies behind her floods towards me." This particular client found herself in an intensive emotional bonding through her mother with both her great grandfathers, who had both been involved in murders.

Schizophrenia in Later Generations

"Schizophrenic disorders are generally marked by fundamental and characteristic disorders in thinking and perception as well as inadequate or flattened affect" (Dilling, Mombour and Schmidt, 1993). People who are diagnosed as schizophrenic are in my experience neither unintelligent nor unemotional, nor do they have an incurable disorder in their perception or thinking. I have seen that schizophrenia is a state in which a person can neither use his intellectual capacity to the full nor trust his feelings. His thoughts are brought into question by his feelings and his feelings by his thoughts. There is no agreement between the two and any clarity quickly disappears as everything seems to go round in circles. It is not perception and thinking per se that is disordered, but whatever the perception and thoughts refer to that is completely confusing.

This irreconcilable contradiction between thinking and feeling can be explained if one understands the mutual blocking of thinking and feeling that occurs against the background of an unknown secret in the family and the ensuing bonding confusion. The polar tension in the system between the urge to keep secret and the urge to reveal causes the person in the later generation, who knows nothing of the actual event, to mistrust the messages of his parents and grandparents and so mistrust his own thinking and feeling. This is schizophrenia.

Case Study 44:

Hero or criminal?

In what follows I describe in rather general terms a situation that I have experienced in clients in several variations. The jobs and genders are more or less interchangeable. When, for example, a grandfather was in the war, this can be seen as an honourable achievement in the family, perhaps because he was a doctor and treated the wounded. However, if this grandfather also participated in actions which contradict the Hippocratic Oath or are even crimes, which happens not infrequently in war, then his son, who might himself have chosen the profession of doctor, has a problem. If the son wants to model himself on his father, then he must not know about any of the negative things his father has done as a doctor. However, he will sense that something is not quite right about his father's heroism because he can feel the subliminal fear and shame whenever it is talked about. At the same time, he does not want to destroy the positive image he has of his father. At some point he stops thinking about it, and at the same time he will also stop feeling because unconsciously he will deaden the feelings.

This schizoid attitude is then passed on to his son as in the unspoken message "My father was an honourable man, but we mustn't ask the detail of what he really did." The father does not allow himself to be pinned down either regarding the truth about the facts, or about the clarity of his emotional judgment. His son, who doesn't even know how his father's schizoid thinking in connection with his own father all hangs together, becomes confused and possibly even crazy. Emotionally, he can find no common ground with his father that makes sense, nor do the intellectual games between them give him any satisfaction in the long run. He is starved emotionally as he is kept at arm's length by his father. He senses that something is not right, but doesn't know what.

Psychoses and Delusions in Later Generations

Currently there are many who contest the psychiatric line that "psychoses" are primarily physical and genetically inherited illnesses. Stravos Mentzos belongs to this group. For him not only "neuroses" but also "psychoses" are a form of expression of emotional conflicts, which need to be understood (Mentzos, 2000).

Like Serge Tisseron, I assume that "psychoses" can develop when all the images that have to do with original trauma, images of rape, seduction, murder, of blood and dead bodies, stench of corpses or screams for help, emerge into the consciousness of a person who comes later, and has not himself experienced any of these things. Flashback images of traumatic events seem common not only for the person who suffered a trauma but can also occur within the minds of their children.

Perhaps triggered by a current conflict, all that has been absorbed from the previous generations through the bonding process now emerges into consciousness. Since, in the triggered situation, the deadening that so far succeeded in keeping the traumatic residue out of consciousness no longer works, these images and feelings suddenly become so real and present that they are experienced as something one has gone through oneself. The affected person suddenly finds himself in the midst of an event that took place decades ago and to someone else. He does not know what it is about, he just senses the oppressive feelings and thoughts of the original holder of the secret: fear of discovery, guilt and shame. Alternatively, it could be the experience of overwhelming love, passionate or brutal sexuality that originated in an incestuous or other forbidden love or sexual relationship. A person in a psychotic state experiences the original trauma in the present as if it had happened to him, and in trying to understand and make sense of it he mixes it up with impressions and events from his own life. In this way, the confusion in the mind becomes greater and greater, and everything is no longer understandable.

In my opinion and from experiences with clients, psychoses are flashbacks of traumatic feelings from past generations. The person experiences overwhelming feelings without knowing the relevant events which would give meaning to the experience. He tries to find a solution to a problem which he cannot really define; he looks for a way to escape the threatening experience or to understand its meaning. In his psychotic state he experiences what the perpetrator experienced: terror of discovery and a need to escape. He also has the option of doing what the perpetrator couldn't do, could only dream of as a solution: finding a space to talk, to admit to his guilt. He will look for forgiveness and redemption and at the same time may think that he himself is God, who can put everything right. He is terribly afraid of being condemned, of being taken by the police or of going to hell. In a psychotic episode he can also simultaneously experience being like the victim (Ruppert, 2002).

Delusions are a final attempt to resolve hopeless internal emotional conflict situations. When the reality of the experiences and responsibility for them can no longer be defended against by splitting and suppression, then reality itself must be denied. The real world then seems an illusion and everyone else – "not me" – lives in this illusion.

The Schizophrenic Carrier of the Systemic Trauma

As bizarre and crazy as the behaviour of psychotics and schizophrenics might seem, they do have meaning and have a basis of truth. It is possible to understand the meaning if one can see the displacement of events in time and space in the triggered experiences. The unresolved traumatic events with which parents, grandparents or even great grandparents were entangled as well as the resulting emotional conflicts continue on, being re-stimulated and staged anew in the confused experience, thinking and speech of a descendent. They appear in his personality split, in his hallucinations and delusions. He is the carrier of the system's symptoms. He absorbs the splits between the perpetrator and the victim within the family into his very soul, and attempts at a deeply unconscious level to hold them in order to hold the integrity of and to belong to the family. He splits his own identity in order to be able to accept the lies and distortions as reality and truth. He has a deep unconscious love for the perpetrator in the family and at the same time fears him. He weeps at this deep level for the victims and yet scorns them for their weakness. In this way children become mirrors of the emotional splitting of their (grand)mother or (grand)father. If they don't succeed in this attempt at reconciling the lies with the truth, they look for guilt and blame in themselves and gradually become increasingly confused and in the end crazy.

"Psychoses" are phases of high emotional confusion, which sometimes flare up for a short time and sometimes last several weeks. They are often followed by a state in which the person affected cannot understand or sort out the experiences he has gone through in his psychotic state. He does not know whether he has dreamt all of this or whether what he has experienced is reality. He can no longer distinguish between his real I-state and what comes to him as hallucinatory invasions from the traumas of the past. He continues to feel trapped in his thoughts and reflections and just goes around in circles becoming more and more schizophrenic. Moreover, since he is no longer able to be well adjusted as a consequence of these inner conflicts, society requires him to recognise that he is ill. Because he cannot do this, psychiatrists assume their clients' lack insight into their illness. Discussions regarding conventional insight and understanding into their illness do not help the client, since they are experienced as intellectual power games, which is exactly what he recognises from within his own family: intellectualising without ever building an emotional relationship. The client would be helped more if the helping professions, including psychiatrists, had the insight that behind every schizophrenia there are events which have to come to light for the origins of the psychotic feelings to be understood. Insanity only develops when reality is denied, and it is only the truth that can heal delusions. In my opinion, insanity has its cause not in the psyche itself, or even in the genes of the client, but in events that happen in the family. If psychiatrists were to adopt this perspective they would be able to let go of the need to control and suppress psychotic episodes and schizophrenic behaviour as the only means to deal with this type of mental illness.

The Perpetuation of Insanity

Family events to which a psychosis draws attention may be connected to social and political events. Social insanity is related to family insanity (Ruppert, 2002). That the "Lebensborn" programme (see Digression below) was one of the many insane actions of the Nazis is reflected in the development of the "Lebensborn" children, in their children and in the following generation. Damaged mother-child relationships, the non-existence of father-bonding and the secret substitution of the biological mother with an adoptive mother form the basis for fear and confused feelings in these children. When they in turn became parents they passed on the trauma experiences to the next generation.

Digression 5: The "Lebensborn" Project

The "Lebensborn" Project, founded in 1935, was organised by Heinrich Himmler. In co-operation with the Race and Settlement Office of the SS, its aim was to ensure racially pure and genetically healthy descendants for the SS. Hitler's plan for the destruction of non-Aryan life was to be flanked by the breeding of pure-race Aryans (Lilienthal, 2003).

Aryan women, impregnated by Aryan men, were to be cared for throughout their pregnancy until the child could be passed on to a chosen family (Engelmann, 1983). Nine "Lebensborn" homes came into being within the Reich, and after war had broken out others were set up in the occupied countries (e.g. in Norway).

These "Lebensborn" homes were situated in palatial settings and reported only to the SS leadership. "Thus they were able to issue birth certificates for children born... and fill them out in such a way that there was no indication of extra-marital or illegitimate birth. The mothers could choose whether to keep the children and bring them up themselves or whether to let "Lebensborn" adopt them; the vast majority ceded the children to the SS, for most of the pregnant women were racially pure but under-aged, who had kept their pregnancy secret from their families, and many of them were trainee nurses. The fathers, who were required to prove their racial suitability, were almost all members of the SS" (Engelmann, 1983). A good thousand young girls became pregnant following Nazi propaganda for motherhood. Many of them were themselves taken in by the Lebensborn homes. It was mainly girls working and living as trainee nurses in the homes who became pregnant. Towards the end of the war all the "Lebensborn" documents were destroyed by the SS.

The "Lebensborn" project had as its core intent the repudiation of emotional bonding between wife and husband, and between mother and father and child. Feelings were no longer to play any role in the upbringing of children. The children were, as early as possible, to learn to live without feelings for their biological parents and to orientate themselves solely to national socialist upbringing.

Let's come back briefly to Laura's story. The reason why Laura's mother had not protected Laura from sexual abuse by her father lay in her own confusion. Laura's mother was a child that was given up for adoption to the Lebensborn project. This probably happened because, whilst her father had had Jewish ancestors, her mother was a passionate fan of National Socialism to the day she died. This explained why Laura's mother felt that she had no parents, and Laura felt that she was not really her mother's child. As a child in her home environment, Laura behaved as if she were a stranger there, as someone who did not belong and was not in the right place. Laura felt as her mother had felt when she was a child. Moreover, her mother tried to adopt a child in spite of not being able to cope with her own child. These attempts to adopt make sense against the background of her own origins and of herself being adopted. This example shows how a mother's experiences can cause confusion in her child. She interprets the child's behaviour in a way which is confusing for the child. The child is termed as "ungrateful" although she longs for nothing more than closeness to her mother. It doesn't matter how the child behaves, the mother will always interpret her behaviour in a way that has nothing to do with the child's thinking and feeling, but which in fact mirrors her own difficult fate.

Case Study 45:

An Ungrateful Child

Laura writes: "I never felt as if I belonged to my family, I often thought that I was adopted. For me going to grammar school was like a release. I have more memories from that point on, though there are also big holes. The new school was a long way from home and it was a girls' grammar school – something I was very happy about. I was always very withdrawn, often alone and had no friends. I was extremely afraid of being amongst strangers. The journey to school in the morning made me very nervous, I was afraid of getting on the wrong train or missing my stop. I had the feeling that everyone was staring at me. I felt terribly sick and longed for the earth to swallow me up. I kept thinking that people knew something about me, but I didn't know what it could be. And yet I was happy to be going to this school. It seemed like a safe harbour, perhaps because it was so far from home.

"When I was 10 my parents wanted to adopt two girls, twins. From time to time we visited them in the orphanage. I think they were about my age. The girls spent their holidays with us. I think this went on for about two years. My mother always gave me to understand that the two girls were better than me and above all more grateful than me. The only reason the adoption didn't go through in the end was because the girls' mother withdrew her consent."

Eva, whom we mentioned in Case Study 2, also has a mother who was in the "Lebensborn" Project. This insight came about through several constellations in various therapy groups, which eventually helped Eva out of her confusion. The incongruities in Eva's mother's life story could then seem to make sense. Eva could understand why her love for her mother seemed blocked, why her mother felt rejected, and why this feeling of rejection became the central bonding experience between her and her mother. This also seemed to explain why love could not have free expression between Eva and her own daughter and why in turn this daughter had put Eva's granddaughter into care, thus rejecting her own child. Here we have three generations of rejected daughters.

After this had been revealed, Eva's feelings began to flow more easily in the right direction. I asked Eva to present her own view of this, which became quite a long story. I have included some important passages here.

Case Study 46:

Rejected children

"Schizophrenia – my diagnosis. As good as incurable I was told by psychiatrists, clinics, doctors; lifelong medication, which would not guarantee freedom from episodes. The only way to get some relief was to avoid dangerous situations, recognise early warning signals and go straight to the clinic. Learn to deal with the illness. That was the situation when I first became ill fourteen years ago. I felt completely insecure, I didn't understand myself any more. That was until two years ago, when I first came into contact with family constellations.

"I had had a long journey behind me in the twelve years prior to that, with three psychotic episodes, the last one being life-threatening for me. Somehow I worked and worked on myself to be able to live free of medication, at least in the periods between episodes. Lifelong medication – no, – I didn't want to accept that. Medication (Haldol) that shrunk my emotional world, the intensity that I like so much about myself. They packed me in cotton wool and during the worst times managed to do it in a way that I couldn't even move properly. I was like a robot, incapable of holding a knife and fork. I had blisters on the soles of my feet because I couldn't lift my legs up enough.

"Self-experience, therapy after therapy, over 300 hours of psychoanalysis, all that helped me to get to know myself and avoid dangerous situations. For twelve years I tried to somehow manage to deal with my illness. There was no thought of a cure. Dealing with the illness – that's as far as I got, and working through my childhood in analysis, especially clarifying to some extent the difficult relationship with my father.

"Then another episode occurred, a third, serious episode, which was life-threatening and which almost led me to despair. I had worked so hard on myself, facilitated and supported by therapists, how could it be that episodes of that magnitude still occurred, I asked myself. Should I come to terms with the illness after all? Were the doctors right – was it incurable?

"In the meantime I had heard a lot about 'family constellations' and read two books. I had respect for the method, but also felt fear. Courage flickered up from time to time and I attempted to do a constellation myself. But no facilitator dared to come within reach of my soul.

"That was until a friend who is a facilitator gave me the book 'Verwirrte Seelen' [Ruppert, 2002], and told me about a specialist for psychosis. A hope seeded that I might be able to get to the root, to the cause of my illness, and perhaps even be cured and become healthy. So I dared to try it after observing the author of the book at work in his group. I booked in for a constellation. And he dared, courageously and confidently, to take on my soul.

"In my first constellation I could identify the point of healing. I felt it clearly and it brought me hope, strength and confidence. To my surprise, and far removed from what I had previously assumed, the problem lay in my mother's history. She had always rejected me as a child. I was able to recognise that my vulnerability was rooted in this. Episodes always happened when I was rejected in a relationship, or was left or had to leave a relationship. The doctors had advised me at the time never to get into a serious relationship again. Not even to fall in love again. A superficial life, nothing deep: shallow and safe, that would be better for me. Recognising the moments of danger, the problematic situation, that was important, as I had learned in therapy. But only now, in the constellation, was I able to recognise the root of the evil and face it, experience it, and understand it.

"But there was also shock and much pain – my beloved mum, the only one with whom I had a deep relationship, even though she had repeatedly rejected me. Fear and panic flared up and a new crisis which proved to be part of my healing process, I recognise that now all the more clearly.

There were fears. I began to realise things for myself, and repeatedly faced the fact that my mother really did love me, even though she kept rejecting me. And then I looked at my own relationship with my daughter, where I had deeply reproached myself for rejecting her repeatedly. For other reasons. And constantly questioning myself, I examined my own feelings for my daughter. I began to understand that sometimes mothers have to reject their daughters – for whatever reason. And that this in no sense means that mothers do not love their daughters.

"Understanding and recognising why I often had such split feelings towards my daughter. And recognising and resolving my reproaches towards my daughter, who gave up my beloved grandchild for adoption. That is all my family history, and seen from this angle and under all these circumstances, it was actually fairly normal. It could not really have developed any other way. After all, she also was just following a tradition. I began to understand, accept. Everything makes sense, even though it's very painful. I began to understand why, in light of these past events, my only way of dealing with the sheer pain of it all was to take flight into psychosis.

"A second constellation followed – the next step towards health. Here I was able to look back even further into my mother's history. The whole thing was like a puzzle, one piece fitted into another. My mother's story went back to Lebensborn. I was able to see her own inner strife and confusion there in this constellation. And I was able to understand better and better. No wonder that she kept rejecting me. In her circumstances and in view of her personal history. Conceived and brought up to be something special – until the war was over. Then rejected again by her mother. Living in the face of a lie. It was inevitable that in reality it is she who is confused.

"Love can flow again, from me to my mother, tender love, in understanding and knowledge – for I can no longer talk to her about it. I think that would all be too terrible for her. I began to understand why I actually always had to assume a mother role towards her. Why I took her in my arms and not the other way round, as it should really have been.

"A process of clarifying, again and again, talking for hours, further situations in my life were released. Thinking about how I can go on ... memories suddenly surfaced. Results came out of the second constellation. Sometimes I felt like Sherlock Holmes. On the trail, like a detective; this second constellation motivated me to go on researching, to clarify and gain insight. I began to attempt very carefully and gently to create some sort of order in my family; to put things on the right track, sometimes only in a roundabout sort of way, on no account to hurt anyone and afraid, too, of course, of losing them.

"Some circumstances arose quite spontaneously. My sister suddenly moved back to Germany, and we are finding our way to a wonderful sisterly relationship. I am the elder ..."

Franziska Klöckner, a student of mine, documented Eva's case in detail in her diploma dissertation (Klöckner, 2005). Ironically, after her evident cure, Eva's psychiatrist said she had probably never really had schizophrenia as by definition schizophrenia is not curable. That is another way of protecting oneself from confrontation with reality, by means of paradoxical theoretical constructs, which is not so dissimilar to delusional thinking.

Mania and Schizoaffective Psychosis

In addition to paranoid-hallucinatory psychoses, which in my opinion have their origins in the fear of the original perpetrator, there is another diagnostic group in psychiatry, the "schizo-affective psychoses". The symptoms include depressive periods alternating at times with manic phases (Keßler, 1997).

In my view mania can be understood as the energy of love

which is suppressed because it is combined with erotic and sexual feelings and therefore forbidden, for example between a father and daughter, a mother and son, or brother and sister. If people go beyond the boundaries and taboos of sexuality that forbid incestuous or extramarital love affairs then they feel for a moment overwhelmed with pleasure and after that deeply ashamed and guilty. Incestuous love energy for children can be immense, overwhelming and boundless once it has been set free. Of course, the existence of such forbidden love is officially denied and split off within the psyche, so cannot be processed in the soul of the people involved or within the whole family. For example even if the mother does not talk about her forbidden extramarital love, the child knows it in her soul.

These unresolved psychic energies of course can also be transferred from one generation to the next via the bonding processes. In a child's manic episodes, the suppressed truth of her mother's experiences can break through, overwhelming the child and throwing her into emotional turmoil. As one consequence, the child has immense difficulties later in being able to trust in her relationships, and there is always likely to be an air of seduction around her. Such "forbidden love" may become more appealing than ordinary love, but of course is socially unacceptable. Trying to have a conventional relationship will be elusive as long as the desire for the excitement of the forbidden love is not relinquished. Children who discover in their mothers' soul the "happiness" of forbidden love think that this is true happiness, and they become incapable of having a "normal" partnership in their own relationships.

Case Study 47:

Overwhelming sexuality

Birgit came to therapy for two reasons: firstly, she wanted to understand why her younger brother became psychotic and remained seriously confused. Secondly she longed for a good relationship for herself. She contributed to the break-up of her own marriage by initiating rows with her husband over petty issues for so long that in the end he walked out. After that she had many relationships that she found exciting, but that seemed always doomed not to become steady partnerships.

In several constellations her internal personality structure clearly showed that there was a very small child within her that was terribly lonely and frozen emotionally having no contact with any other living being. In the constellations the representative for the mother always seemed very distant and unreachable. Two further sub-personalities within Birgit appeared, one as a cheeky, self-motivated, nature-loving girl and the other as a laughing, easily seduced adolescent.

What emerged for Birgit in one of the constellations was the possibility of an incestuous but seemingly very loving bond between her grandfather and her mother. The representative for Birgit's mother in this constellation experienced overwhelming feelings of sexual energy streaming through and around her.

Birgit said she was personally very familiar with the feelings described by the representative for her mother, and that it now made sense to her as to why her mother had idealised this grandfather and her grandparents' home, which she enjoyed going to because her own parents were often fighting at home.

Anorexia and Obesity

Anorexia may not only be a child's way of protesting against sexual abuse as mentioned before. Some types of anorexia are combined with the patient's readiness to die. It clearly is a delusional state since the person's self-perception is that she is overweight, even though she has actually starved herself down to skin and bone. She cannot eat even when she is completely emaciated and staring death in the face. How can we understand this delusion? It seems that, when an eating disorder goes as far as starvation, there must be deeper issues and secrets behind such obviously disordered behaviour. A bonding trauma for a child can be embedded in the bonding system trauma of her mother's line.

If we think causally, a trauma that could mirror the symptoms of this physically fading away and disappearing, is the disappearance of a child within the family, with the consequence that the living child may hunger at her mother's breast because another perhaps dead and secret child draws the mother's attention away.

Case Study 48:

Just like a doll

Claudia, an anorexic, extremely frail looking woman of twenty, came to a constellations group with her mother. Her constellation helped to surface the following picture: Claudia's great grandmother had grieved for a child that she had disposed of because it was the result of a forbidden relationship. Absorbed by this trauma she was unable to make any sort of physical contact with her later child, Claudia's grandmother. She treated her like a doll, made her pretty and imagined that she could see the deceased child in the living child. Claudia's grandmother then passed on these bonding experiences to Claudia's mother. Claudia's mother then revealed that her mother had also lost a child that died shortly after birth which compounded the trauma of loss.

Claudia's mother seemed to have only been able to connect with her mother through this dead sibling and was bound to it through her suffering. Therefore, she was unavailable for her own daughter, she could establish no loving contact with her that wasn't ruined by grief.

In the constellation, when all the dead children were placed and the grief was experienced by the client, her mother and their representatives, a huge wave of energy flowed through them all, and the possibility of an emotional bond between mothers and daughters began to form. Claudia and her mother found their way to each other in the company of the representatives of the female ancestors and the dead children. There seemed to be a great emotional release for Claudia and her mother, as if a valve that had been switched off for a very long time had suddenly been turned on again.

Claudia got in touch with me a month after the constellation saying "I am getting better altogether, and the positive effects are visible in the whole family. Thank you ..."

I ran a seminar specifically on the subject of eating disorders in July 2005 where most of the participants were heavily overweight, to the extent that sometimes they could not move without help. In all cases the same dynamics seemed to underlie the obesity: babies and small children had disappeared in the family system; they were either left to die or had been killed intentionally. In contrast to work with anorexics however, the overweight clients seemed to have pitched their will to survive against the unconscious emotional pressure to dissolve, and protected themselves by overeating with the resulting obesity. The excess weight can then be seen as a protection against going crazy or committing suicide.

The deeper causes of eating disorders make it clear why training anorexics in good nutrition doesn't make any sense. Diets don't work for obese patients and achieving a lower weight will be replaced by other addictions that deny reality (e.g. alcoholism).

Obsessive Compulsive Disorder

Even if the number of cases with which I have worked is too small to make a generally valid statement, nevertheless a hypothesis can be made about obsessive compulsive behaviour that, on the surface, we can see it as a means of controlling internal chaos. But what are the roots of such a chaos? As long as the obsessive behaviour is clearly irrational and does not make sense in the face of the evidence of reality, in my opinion it is likely that something is hidden or kept secret at the deeper level. It could be the case that the original trauma that this behaviour indicates is some kind of family secret. In the following case study the patient's counting compulsion seemed to be linked to the question as to whether one of the children had gone missing.

Case Study 49:

Is somebody missing?

A woman who suffered from a counting compulsion came to a seminar together with her therapist. The client only had the compulsion when she was at home, and it was expressed in her compulsively counting and recounting especially items of washing. Additionally throwing anything away that was no longer useful to her was combined with mortal fear thus leading to an accumulation of rubbish in her flat. This prevented her from being able to deal with a forthcoming move to another flat, so she had sought therapeutic help.

In her constellation the representative for her mother's mother displayed the strange behaviour of counting and re-counting her children, officially six, and kept getting muddled in her counting. The representatives for the children were particularly afraid of one of their siblings. The representative for this child wanted on the one hand to be with the others and on the other hand tried to crawl away and hide. The actions of the representatives seemed to point to one of the grandmother's children having killed one of the others, perhaps by accident, and that this had been kept secret. Of course one needs to handle this sort of information lightly and keep the focus on the client's experience as to whether she feels relieved and more at ease, for example if from what she knows this might make sense.

A few months after the seminar the therapist let me know that the client with the counting compulsion had successfully moved to her new flat, and was able to let all the rubbish be thrown away. She did count a lot of things, but was able to throw them away herself. Previously that had been connected with a feeling of panic and a sense of being in mortal danger.

On the whole the therapist reported that she seemed very relieved and strong on the telephone. In the new flat things seem to have improved considerably and at the moment no new rubbish is accumulating. Now that her compulsion to count is slowly dissipating, she is becoming aware that she has had serious marital problems for years, which she now feels able to face.

In this case it seems that the counting compulsion is associated with the need not to forget and throw away something very precious – the dead child – thereby leading to the "messy syndrome".

Drug and Alcohol Addiction in Bonding System Traumas

Smothering internal suffering and turmoil with drugs is a common strategy in bonding system trauma. However, of course, no problem is ever resolved in this way, but the function of denial of reality that addiction provides is particularly applicable in connection with bonding system traumas which are founded on the need to keep the secret within the family. The addiction offers the escape from reality, a means of suppressing real feelings and replacing them with artificially created drug-induced feelings. The drug high replaces the dissociative mechanisms of psychological splitting when this no longer works.

Suicide in Bonding System Traumas

The motive for suicide in a bonding system trauma situation is usually to escape feelings of despair, guilt and shame. One could say that the perpetrator attempts to atone for his or her deed by taking his own life. Criminals are more at risk of suicide than others (Wolfersdorf, Grünewald, König, Hägele, 1997). The victims of acts that have been kept secret in order to preserve the family may also wish to die. Whether victim or perpetrator, in the collapse of the personality in a psychosis there is always the danger that the person will want to die as a deliverance from their suffering. Compulsory psychiatric hospitalisation along with compulsory medication is a frequent occurrence for those who resort to suicide. However, of course, suicidal ideation is not removed through psycho-pharmacology, it is just dulled. It can only disappear in the end through understanding the deeper causes for the psychosis. Especially for those who are not themselves perpetrators or victims and yet are entangled in the hidden family dynamics as mentioned above, it is more helpful to bring them out of these fatal entanglements. I have experienced many clients who, being entangled in a bonding system trauma, suddenly felt much better when they see that it is not they who are crazy, but that what happened in their family was crazy.

The search for a new self and world concept
What lies at the root of a bonding system trauma can shatter our trust in the institution of marriage and family. It is hard for us to accept the realities of some of the things that occur in families. We are more familiar nowadays with how prevalent sexual abuse and incest are, and it is also necessary for us to include the possibility of other crimes such as murder,

manslaughter, accidents that are covered up and other events that cause a family to collectively collude in silent secrecy. Even if the symptom carriers in later generations, who may indicate these prior events through their schizophrenic and psychotic episodes, are locked away in mental hospitals and their symptoms suppressed with medication, the issues will remain present and real. If as individuals or a society as a whole, we close our eyes to the realities that lie at the root of a bonding system trauma we are only creating an idealised image of people and the family as we think they should be, but in reality often are not.

A perspective that includes the notion of bonding system trauma and the possible trans-generational effects might initially lead us to have greater care and understanding when judging the behaviour of others. When we see and understand how far the array of entanglements often stretches within a family, one sees how easily neglected, deprived or abused children can themselves become perpetrators, thereby producing new victims who in turn can quickly become perpetrators, and so on. A better understanding might help us to be careful with judgements about the past and those who lived before us. Accepting reality makes one more merciful towards others and ourselves. We must not condemn the past in order to create a better future for ourselves. What we can also learn from events that cause bonding system traumas is how important real love between men and women, parents and children is, how necessary it is to take responsibility for our own deeds, and that we cannot sacrifice truth for loyalty. Even if it is hard, we must be prepared to bring to light the shadows of the past in order to become free of them, and not be condemned to repeat the same traumas over and over again.

8.4 Multiple and Sequential Traumas

One type of trauma often appears along with another. An existential trauma can be combined with a trauma of loss, for example when someone goes through a life-threatening accident in which he loses a relative, or when people in war not only have to endure fear for their life but also lose relatives, their goods and possession and their homeland.

Bonding system traumas can be coupled with existential trauma if, for example, sexual abuse is combined with the attempted murder of the child, or when an abused child is threatened with murder if she betrays the perpetrator. Existential fear can also arise when, for example, the child is older and wants to denounce the perpetrator and have him put on trial. Many victims of abuse and their mothers do not dare to go the police to report the abuse out of fear of being threatened with violence and murder, and this fear is not unfounded, as perpetrators of sexual abuse have more than proved their ability to exploit and abuse, and their unpredictability. Unfortunately this is often not taken seriously enough by the law. Inexperienced police officers and lawyers are frequently deceived by the perfectly constructed social façade of perpetrators.

In bonding system trauma the causal deed is also often coupled with loss, when, for example, a child dies and a parent is responsible for its death in some way. Because the responsibility is denied, mourning for the loss cannot take place.

In my book "Verwirrte Seelen" (Ruppert, 2002) I have given an example of a client whose bonding trauma (she was hated by her mother and sexually abused by her father) is coupled with deeds by her mother which led the whole bonding system to dissolve: the father of one of the client's sisters is unknown and unrecognised, and another child died in mysterious circumstances when very young (ibid.). As already mentioned in Chapter 2, traumatisation leads to bonding disorder which heightens the risk of further traumatisation. If a bonding trauma has irrevocably disrupted a mother-child relationship, then this is likely to perpetuate over many generations creating the basis for further traumas. Some families find themselves as a whole family in emotional turmoil that has persisted for generations finding expression in drug addiction, psychoses, suicide and criminal acts.

The more traumatisation a person experiences himself or herself, and the more traumas creating serious bonding disorders that afflict the family system, the greater the number of symptoms that the individual will suffer. Doctors, therapists or social workers are often confronted with a multitude of problems in one family, and the help that can be offered can only very slowly influence the various physical illnesses, emotional wounds and social entanglements positively.

Figure 4 summarises the four kinds of trauma that I have distinguished, the effect they can have on a person and how they can cause emotional illness over three generations through the psychological bonding between mother and child.

When looking at an individual case it is important to consider that various kinds of trauma can be present in a mother at the same time, and that the different effects of the individual traumas may be superimposed and intensified in the bonding with the child. If bonding trauma and existential and/or loss trauma are simultaneously present then the bonding trauma is likely to have the most severe effect on the emotional development of the child. Bonding traumas also seem to have more far-reaching effects over more generations.

Consequences of Trauma	... for the affected mother and her relationship to her child.	for children of that child – the following generation	for children in the third generation
In existential trauma	Split-off fear of death, over solicitous, restless-ness, fear of the future	Latent anxiety, sudden onset panic attacks and anxiety disorders	Mild forms of hyperactivity
In loss trauma	Split-off pain of loss, depression, lack of energy, low emotional ability to cope	Latent depression, sudden onset depression, medication addiction, suicidal ideation	Depression and latent suicidal ideation
In bonding trauma without experiences of other trauma	Internal emptiness, inability to bond with child or form relationships,	Narcissistic Personality Disorder, histrionic personality disorder	Mild forms of personality disorder
In bonding trauma with experience of sexual abuse	Borderline Personality Disorder, rejection of own children, not seeing when abuse to own children is taking place	Borderline Personality Disorder, serious drug addiction	Extreme forms of hyper-activity, Borderline Personality Disorder, Bulimia, compulsion to wash
In bonding trauma with experiences of violence	Split-off fear, rage and pain, multiple physical symptoms, violence towards one's own children	Antisocial Personality Disorder	Antisocial Personality Disorder
In bonding trauma with children from incestuous relationships (the child may live within the family or may be given away)	Split-off confusion, emotionless functioning	Denial of reality, latent Schizophrenia	Mania, Schizoaffective Psychosis
In bonding trauma with murdered children	Annihilation of all bonding feelings, escape into fantasy	Inner void, identity confusion, latent schizophrenia	Schizophrenia, Paranoid-hallucinatory Psychosis, anorexia, morbid obesity

Fig. 4: Consequences of the different types of trauma for the affected mothers and their children and their children's children.

PART II:
The Methodology of Systemic Constellations

9

Introduction to Systemic Constellations

9.1 The Constellations Process

Systemic Constellations as a method usually takes place in a group, often with people who don't know each other and who may not know the therapist. After an introductory round the first constellation can begin. I ask the participant who would like to do a constellation about their issue. It is only when a client has expressed a willingness to change something about him or herself that I can work with him or her. This principle is, in my opinion, valid for any form of psychotherapy. We must assume that all of us vacillate to some extent between the wish to change something in our life and our fear of losing the mechanisms we have always used to avoid and control embarrassing and painful emotions. The pressure of the suffering increases our willingness to change, but also increases our fear of losing control over our life. If a therapist does not see or cannot tolerate this ambivalence he or she may make one of the following two mistakes:

1. The therapist decides on behalf of the client what the issue is and what the outcome should be. By doing this the therapist positions him or herself as superior to the client and assumes responsibility for making the decision in the face of the client's ambivalence as to whether they want to change something about themselves or not.

2. The therapist rejects the client for having no clear outcome for the therapy and will not work with him or her. Here, too, the therapist positions him or herself above the client and relieves the client of making his or her own decisions. In doing this the therapist does not value the step that the client has already made by joining the group in the first place.

Both of these assume responsibility for the client and render the therapist more likely to become caught up with the client's systemic entanglements. The therapist who takes control over the therapy entangles himself because of his need to achieve something that the client is not yet ready for. The rejecting therapist on the surface may protect him or herself from that entanglement, but is very probably representing someone who is harsh and rejecting in the relational system of the client.

It is therefore advisable that the therapist and client work out together what is and what is not possible for the client at that particular moment. In my experience the client's presenting issue sets the frame for the particular change process he or she is willing to engage in at that time. This is why some issues seem less profound and some seem more profound, according to whether the client is able to take a larger step towards change or a smaller one. For the client at the stage that they are the step will always seem large. Through questioning the therapist discovers how far the client may be able to go. Even seemingly small steps can be immense if they encourage self-responsibility. Forcing the client into situations for which his present resources are insufficient would be irresponsible on the part of the therapist and likely to be fruitless.

I have realised that even while the constellation is in progress it helps for the therapist to keep checking with the client as to how he or she is doing and whether we should continue. It seems that even during the constellation the client continues his or her internal battle as to whether to face the frequently painful insights into his emotional life or to surrender to the desire to avoid this pain. The greater the traumatic splits within the client, the more one must take into account this vacillation. Particular care is advisable with some requests, for example if a mother or father wants to do a constellation on behalf of one of their children and is not willing to confront her own emotional wounds then the constellation cannot bring about a positive result. It would merely demonstrate clearly the entanglements in which mother, father and child are caught, without there being the possibility of finding a solution in the constellation. This is why it is not advisable to work with such client requests.

The best therapy for young children of course is that done by their parents (Dykstra, 2002, 2004). For the child to feel better it is the parents and not the child who need to be willing to face their issues.

Case Study 50:

Experiences of representatives

Bernhard writes about his experiences as a representative: "I gained a lot out of the constellations as a representative, and then started exploring my own issues. One thing that I understood was what happens to me when I have the sense that it's all up to me to resolve a difficult dynamic within my family: I am overstretched. The other thing was seeing and understanding the dynamic of abuse. In one constellation I took on the role of the son of a woman who was looking for help for him and his psychosis. It came out quite clearly that the issue was hers not the son's. That is, when she tackles her own issues and reveals herself to her son, then he can feel better. That is what actually happened in reality."

The Constellations Process

When I feel sufficiently clear about a client's issue and it seems that we can do a constellation, I ask the client about those major events in his family system which might be connected with the presented issue. This questioning is open to whatever might come from the client and is guided by trauma theory and hypotheses. I am interested in the existence of unstable bondings and traumatic events that might have led to the client's problems and symptoms. When I get a feeling for what might be relevant, I suggest what people or symptoms the clients might begin with. As a rule I only suggest a few people to begin with. In most cases these are a representative for the client themselves and for his or her parents.

The client chooses people from amongst the other group participants and places them according to his intuitive sense within the room. What the client demonstrates in the placing of the representatives is the direction in which the representatives are looking and the distance they are from each other. He or she simply allocates the representatives a position in the room; no gestures or body postures are used. I will usually wait for the representatives to arrive in their place, and then they will either move on their own initiative or describe their experience. I get an initial image of the emotional dynamics of the problem from the representatives' movements and described experiences. From the representatives' remarks, I may suggest to the client that he or she bring in further representatives.

All the representatives are free to make remarks or move at any time, and in this way the constellation develops to the point where the core emotional conflict that underlies the client's issue becomes visible.

At this point the process naturally starts to move the constellation in the direction of a solution. I always keep the client in view during the whole constellation paying close attention to his reactions. This allows me to see whether he or she is in resonance with what is happening in front of him or her. The client is free to add further information about the situation at any time. From time to time at certain points in the constellation I will ask the client whether anything important has occurred to her. Often the client, energised by what he or she sees happening in front of her, brings up new information or insight about her life or family history, and the representatives can then sense whether this fits with their experience or not. The representatives are also often able to sense whether something or someone is missing or whether further people need to be added in order to find a solution to the client's issue.

I invite the client to enter the constellation as him or herself when it seems likely that he or she would be able to experience a significant emotional process in direct contact with the people represented in the constellation. I usually ask the person who has represented the client up to this point to remain in the constellation as this person may continue to serve as a mirror for the client's internal state, and is usually experienced as a resource by the client.

The constellation is finished when the client has made a clearly recognisable developmental step, reflected in his behaviour and emotional and facial expressions. The representatives and the whole group can easily see this change in the client. At its best a constellation reaches a completely positive end when all the representatives of the different people feel at ease and in the right place in relation to everyone else, when their experience is congruent in the moment.

The Representatives

The client chooses the representatives. In a larger group, the choice is obviously greater. It is often the case that the client chooses people who are similar in some way to the person they are to represent, either in their appearance, the way they present themselves or in the more subtle signals that they unconsciously emit. The introductory round is important here since it is during this phase that the participants can get a sense of the other people in the group. They may unconsciously sense others in the group who may have similar traumatic experiences to themselves, and later they are more likely to choose them as representatives in their own constellation.

Many people report that they know in advance that they

will be chosen to represent a particular person. There seems to be an out-of-awareness yet highly effective transmission of information between the client and the participants from the beginning and during the selection process. It may be that the process of clarifying the issue with the client triggers emotional reactions in the participants that enable the client to resonate with them when selecting the representatives.

As previously mentioned, the representatives can move from their originally designated place, their movements showing in most cases quite clearly where the high emotional tensions are and where there are sympathetic or antipathetic reactions between representatives in the constellation. Sometimes representatives will have strong physiological reactions such as violent trembling, shortness of breath or become so weak and lacking in energy that they feel they will fall to the floor. These reactions in my experience clearly show symptoms of traumatisation leading to the question as to the cause of the trauma.

The representatives can describe whatever they experience in their place and in their contact with other representatives in the constellation. I do not judge as to what is right or wrong, good or bad in what they say, but try and allow the picture to emerge that can make some sense of the dynamics of the emotional conflict. The more people there are in a constellation, the greater the challenge to the facilitator to maintain an overview and see what is important and makes a difference, support the process to continue forward, or see where sequences of dynamics merely repeat themselves and do not move things forward.

For me, a significant principle in a constellation is to be willing to trust the experiences of the representatives as expressed either in words or in their body language. This is often not easy, since what the representatives sometimes say may sound improbable. Sometimes a representative may seem theatrically exaggerated, and sometimes representatives simply stand immobile for a long time and say nothing. The notion that a representative confuses his own issues and personality with what he is experiencing in his role also seems compelling. However, in my experience, trust in the remarks made by the representatives has always been rewarded, and a study we recently did on this issue supports this confidence (Ruppert, 2007). In the entire context of the constellation what the representatives experience in their roles always proves to be accurate, even if at first it does not seem to make sense. It is as though, through the co-operation of the representatives as a whole, a kind of co-consciousness evolves which allows the context, fragmented and shattered by the trauma, to be reconstructed with new coherence. This is most necessary when there are significant unspoken and hidden events in the family, as in a bonding system trauma. The representatives are then able to express something that the client is unable to access because of his or her inner dissociation from the experience of the trauma. The representatives can help the client find a way of accessing the split-off dissociated aspects of his personality.

Case Study 51:

A mouldy smell in the cellar

A week after her participation in a constellation a client wrote to me: "I would like to thank you again for my constellation. I was amazed and surprised when my representative mentioned the mouldy smell, and how accurately she described it. It mirrored exactly the fear I used to experience up to the age of 21. As a child I used to scream when I went down into the cellar and had to keep turning round because I had the feeling that someone was behind me. When it was dark I often hid behind corners on the streets because I felt someone was following me. I wasn't able to talk about this at the constellation. I'm sure it has something to do with my abuse. A whole chunk of my childhood is missing. It is simply eradicated. Many thanks to C., who so accurately got to the heart of my emotions" (Letter dated 8.8.2004).

In my view every representative will express certain aspects of an emotional event more or less clearly, depending on her own personal development. In my experience, in a constellation everyone always does this as well as she can. Trying to distinguish between what a representative senses in his role as representative and what he or she might be bringing into the situation from his own material is not helpful and will fail. What is his or her own, and what has been assumed in the role, cannot be separated theoretically, practically or methodologically. As a facilitator one either trusts that people do intuitively grasp unconscious aspects of other people to a sufficient degree relevant for therapy – and the practice of many people shows that this is the case, even if we don't fully understand it – or one does not trust this way of working. In my view one cannot usefully work with this method if one doesn't have trust in what the representatives express.

At the same time the facilitator should never try to convince the client that what the representatives are expressing is the only possible view of or even "the truth" in his family system. If a person wishes to do his constellation, he does it in the hope of finding out something new about himself and his family system. In doing so he runs the risk of seeing something that contradicts his expectations of the people in his system and their behaviour towards one another. That is not to say that either view is wrong. The client must remain free to make what sense seems right and plausible to him or her out of what he or she sees in a constellation. Clients in my groups may give a commentary during a constellation and, for example, say that they experienced their father differently to the representative's portrayal. I do not make any judgement of this, nor do I doubt what the representative is expressing at that moment. I allow both the remarks of the client and the portrayal of the representative to be just as they are. The whole process thus remains in a state of ambiguity, in which neither the client nor the representative feel wrong or shamed. This allows us to accept contradiction that is quite normal when dealing with traumatic events, and encourages new aspects to be brought to light. The responsibility for finding the solution to the issue remains with the client. Neither I as facilitator nor the representatives can or want to take this from him or her. Should representatives or other participants in the outer circle try to do this, I intervene so that everything is integrated in such a way as to widen the perceptual field further. The more that whatever surfaces in the constellation can be included without judgement or evaluation, the more intensive seems the impact of change at the end of a constellation – not only for the client, but for everyone who has taken part in the constellation. Even participants who sit in the outer circle, and have not taken a representative role are affected by the constellation.

The Therapeutic Stance

Facilitating this complex process that takes place simultaneously on several levels, requires the ability to keep focused on the client's issue. This involves a process of constantly formulating hypotheses about the dynamics of this particular emotional conflict, testing assumptions and, if necessary, letting them go, and taking on board what is required for the solution. As a facilitator one needs a lot of patience and the ability to refrain from any desire to steer the constellation in the direction one thinks right, that might fit with one's own model of the world. I see myself as an obstetrician for a process that gives birth to change under its own power, as long as the relevant prerequisite is given, namely that the client wants change. If this starting point is not present in the client, then the best facilitation skills won't help. This means that there is no point in suggesting a constellation to a person when he is not ready. One can draw a person's attention to the opportunity, but one should refrain from persuading her or putting any kind of pressure on her.

This prerequisite is of course true for all therapy. If the inner willingness to solve the problem is not present to some degree, the best therapist will not help. It is just a waste of

237

time for both sides and a waste of money for those who are paying. In people with addictions, for example this is the case. As long as they cling on to their addiction as a solution strategy they are unable to trust other solutions and don't believe in other ways out of their emotional turmoil. In traditional psychotherapy the issue is part of the therapy, and the therapist can keep testing whether their clients are really willing to change something or not. Doctors and social workers, who are often forced to work with people who really don't want to accept any help, even rejecting it, don't want to get well or be socially integrated, have the toughest job. Unfortunately it also happens that psychotherapists, doctors or social workers from their own sense of the hopelessness of the task, may eradicate their clients' hope of ever getting better again. It is likely that these therapists are those who have given up the hope of any chance of their own emotional healing. Then there are also the opposite situations, where a therapist may make promises of healing without any notion of how complex emotional change processes really are and what effort and strength it takes to overcome experiences of trauma and to free oneself from emotional entanglements.

Constellations in One-to-One Therapy

The constellations method can also be used in one-to-one therapy. Instead of using people as representatives in one-to-one therapy I use cushions of various sizes, shapes and colours. The client then stands behind the cushion that represents a person or other element in the constellation which is set out on the floor.

Experience shows that clients can gain a good understanding of their own psychological sub-personalities and can learn to differentiate between them in this way. When working with a particular issue, clients can empathise with the various positions and go through a process which brings about emotional clarification. As stated above, it is, of course, necessary for the client to be willing to let go of old survival patterns and to dare to try new ones. I recommend a book on family constellations in one-to-one therapy written by Ursula Franke (Franke, 2002). In my opinion it is not possible to find all the potential of a group constellation in one-to-one therapy or counselling; the more complex traumatisations and entanglements can only really be mapped out and disentangled in a constellation in a group. A constellations group is, in my view, both the fastest and most effective route.

9.2 Bert Hellinger and the Development of Family Constellations

Family constellations work was initially practised widely in Germany, and then travelled throughout much of the world. It has many adherents and supporters, and equally, there are some decided opponents of family constellations work. As a result of the positive experiences I have had with this method, obviously I belong to the supporters. At the same time I see many justified criticisms of how systemic constellations are sometimes carried out.

Bert Hellinger, the founder of family constellations, has more than most caused the psycho-social scene in Germany to move into this work and at the same time has stimulated much criticism. For a long time this theologist and past missionary, after he had turned to psychotherapy, was known only to a small circle of clients and therapists. He had learned and experimented with what was currently available in the western therapy world in the 1970's and 1980's: Freudian psychoanalytic interpretation, Janov's primal therapy, group therapy as practised by Carl Rogers, transactional analysis as espoused by Eric Berne, family therapy in the style of Virginia Satir, neuro-linguistic programming after Grinder, Bandler and Dilts. Finally, inspired by the practice of staging family dynamics as in Moreno's psychodrama, he found his own particular way of setting up family constellations. In contrast to family sculpting, originally developed by Virginia Satir, Hellinger prevented the representatives making any gestures or particular physical poses: "Some therapists let the client tell the participants what poses they should adopt, for example, to lean forwards or look in a particular direction. They call this family sculpture. I don't allow anything like that. For if someone [i.e. a representative] commits completely to what is happening, he will do everything and anything that is required on his own initiative." (Hellinger, 1994)

For a long time Hellinger would not commit to paper the ideas that guided him in his work. Eventually his companion from the early days, Gunthard Weber, persuaded him to present his principles and philosophy in the book entitled *Love's Hidden Symmetry* (Hellinger, Weber and Beaumont 1998). Here Bert Hellinger formulates his views on the principles that govern interpersonal relationships. He maintains that unconscious compensatory dynamics in families can be discovered through constellations: children try to carry heavy burdens of fate for their parents; those who have been excluded or forgotten are represented unconsciously by those born later and so on. He assumes the presence of a systemic unconscious that operates at a deep level, compelling some towards the repetition of terrible events in an attempt at rebalancing. Working with family constellations could help people to become aware of these "blind" attempts at balancing, thereby hopefully changing them to a better outcome.

"Movements of The Soul"

As Bert Hellinger himself developed he went further with the constellations work. Together with Hunter Beaumont he discovered in his work something that they called "movements of the soul". "I have observed representatives, when they are collected in themselves, suddenly go into a movement that they themselves are not doing. This is possible if the therapist holds back long enough and trusts the deep forces of the soul. In some constellations the therapist does not need to say anything, because something hidden emerges and comes to light from the movements of the representatives, finally leading

to solutions that could not be foreseen by any of the participants. ... the work with the movements of the soul demands
extremely close and concentrated attention, a parting from
habitual ideas, a renunciation of external direction, a willingness to let oneself be led by what is visible in the moment and
to trust oneself to the unknown " (Hellinger, 2001b).

In this way Hellinger developed the notion that the focus of
the work was not the working through of difficult emotional
dynamics with a client, it was instead enough to show her the
deep internal movements of her own soul, perhaps finding a
suitable sentence for her to release herself from entanglement
in the fate of her ancestors, accept her own fate and turn
towards her life.

In his search for deeper psychological meaning and forces,
Hellinger has gradually moved away from the traditional ideas of
psychotherapy. On completing some work with a client whose
sister is psychotic, he has said: "How can we arrive at a solution
here? Can we achieve it using therapeutic methods, with what we
have learned in psychotherapy or in psychology? Are any of the
concepts that we have learned applicable to what has happened
here? No, there is something completely different going on here.
Here something is emerging and coming to light that is an unbelievable force that can finally reconcile events that took place in
enmity: victims and perpetrators, both on the same level, neither
of them higher, neither lower. Only when these antagonists can
come together in the soul do we have access to the fullness of life
and to the fullness of love. These are the deep movements of the
soul" (Hellinger, 2001b).

Bert Hellinger no longer calls himself a therapist. He sees
himself as a philosopher: "I am actually a philosopher. I do
therapy as a sideline. This [work with constellations] is basically applied philosophy. I'm not really a therapist. But I
reflect on life. I would like to continue working in this way, in
the service of life as it is, without wishing it to be different."
He goes on to say "Philosophy means we look at life as a
whole and wait until it shows us something. Then we agree to
this" (Hellinger, 2003).

In line with this Hellinger has for some time called his work "applied philosophy" (Hellinger, 2003). He seeks out what is at work behind the superficial. He is a consistent thinker who treads his own path, undeterred. A person who at the end of his professional life has perhaps arrived cleansed at the place where he began: at his questioning and his search for God.

9.3 My own Journey as a Constellations Facilitator

In 1995 I began doing so-called "classical" family constellations. That is I would have a client place his whole family in a constellation, I organised the changing of positions and re-grouping of the representatives myself as the facilitator, and got the client, once he had taken up his own position in the constellation, to repeat the solution phrases and rituals given to us by Hellinger.

After a while I considered it increasingly clear that this "classical" procedure was really only suitable for a certain percentage of the issues that clients brought to seminars. Mostly this was emotional difficulties that have "trauma of loss" at their core. In such cases bringing in a representative for the deceased person stimulates the frozen unresolved grieving process and gets it moving again. The person who was left behind can, in the constellation, have a face-to-face conversation with the representative for the dead person and usually finds that the latter only wishes him or her well and is not at all angry about being dead while the other continues to live. One often can see in the constellation from the emotional responses of the representatives that the dead would rather have peace than be held onto by the living. One can suddenly understand that it makes the dead happy if their descendants carry on their life well.

I realised that a different kind of therapeutic support is required to overcome other kinds of trauma, most particularly "bonding trauma" and "bonding system trauma" since they are based on completely different kinds of emotional conflict, as discussed previously. I gradually developed my own kind of constellations work until eventually it reached the form that I currently practice today. The first new inspiration for me came from a seminar given by Bert Hellinger in Linz in 1999, where he demonstrated his work with the "movements of the soul". Combined with my interest in attachment theories and trauma theories this led to changes in my application of the constellations methodology. New problems brought by clients challenged and continue to challenge me in understanding the emotional connections better and in developing with my clients new techniques in the work. Dilemmas that I grappled with included: How can one take into account all the many different and frequently subtle splittings and traumatisations so that a positive change in the structure of the client's internal soul image really can take place? How can one meaningfully link newly discovered and resource-oriented strategies? How does one deal with extremely dissociated clients? How can perpetrators of crimes find peace in a constellation?

Critique of Hellinger's work

In the few personal meetings I have had with Hellinger I have come to know him as a person. He is constantly exploring, and is fascinated by what he discovers and continues to develop. In my eyes he was one of the first to step into unknown territory with constellations work. He leads, provokes and challenges.

If one observes Hellinger in his public appearances, one notices that from time to time he seems to be detached and distant. He has little interest in the concrete issues of those he is working with. He doesn't do much history-taking. He says what he thinks will help the client. He chooses the representatives, instead of the clients doing this for themselves. During the constellation he hardly allows the representatives to speak and directs them as to how they should move. He freely interprets what is happening in front of him according to the principles of his philosophy. At times his interpretations sound dogmatic and gloomy.

It is difficult to evaluate to what extent a therapy that seems to have such radical effects actually helps someone over time. Bert Hellinger does no long-term evaluations of his work and does not contract with researchers to do so. However, if people were not deeply moved and affected by the work, he would obviously have no supporters.

I have learned a great deal from Hellinger by participating in a number of his large group seminars. Without this opportunity I would not have found my own way to practise constellations work and I am very grateful to him for that, and to the many clients who dared to expose the deepest part of themselves in such a public forum thereby helping me to learn.

My own objection to Hellinger's work, particularly with clients who are suffering from bonding trauma and bonding system trauma, is that he does not work sufficiently with an understanding of trauma theory and dissociative processes, and thereby misses the client's real problems.

In liberal circles in Germany Hellinger has sometimes come under heavy fire. For some people Hellinger's ideas such as "Orders of Love" or "Happiness as a couple" found in his books are proof that an old patriarchal, undemocratic and misogynistic spirit is at work. Psychotherapists have also voiced other objections, "Criticism mostly focuses on the way he stages constellations, the absence of the integration of constellations into other processes, the public form of presentation in large groups, the founder himself as well as the dogmatic principles of systemic order and the positive solution" (Ritter, 2004). Some criticisms of Hellinger's work are certainly justified and it is up to Hellinger himself to answer these.

9.4 Method, Context, Theory and Facilitator

I think it is helpful to distinguish four aspects of family constellations:

- The distinctive aspects of the method itself;
- The situational context in which the method is employed;

- The theories linked with the method, and
- The personal and professional qualities of the person facilitating

Method, theory and facilitator influence each other recipro-cally and lead in each case to a very specific procedure (fig.4).

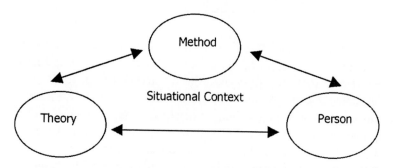

Fig. 4: Reciprocation between method, theoretical basis and personal qualities of the facilitator

Distinctive Aspects of the Constellations Method

In my view systemic constellations are an independent method, even if one acknowledges Jacob Moreno's (1889–1974) psychodrama and Virginia Satir's (1916–1988) family sculptures as historic precedents (Franke, 1996). There are currently various nomenclatures for this method.

Digression   6:   Family   Constellations,   Systemic Constellations, Systemic Structural Constellations etc...

Bert Hellinger talks about "family constellations", and in cooperation with Gunthard Weber he also coined the term "family staging" (Hellinger, Weber and Beaumont, 1998).
    Prof. Matthias Varga von Kibéd and Insa Sparrer have been particularly creative in their development of constellations

concepts and their own forms of constellations. They have developed "systemic structural constellations", "solutions-focused constellations", the "tertralemma constellation", and "belief polarities constellations" and many more (Sparrer and Varga von Kibéd, 2000). Theories of linguistic philosophy hallmark this autonomous approach to working with the constellations method.

The word "constellation" is often combined with the concept "system" or "systemic". This is for two reasons: one is that it expresses that not only families as a particular form of a human relational system can be the object of a constellation, but also other systems such as organisations – "organisational constellations" or political systems – "political constellations". The other is the linking of the constellations method with "systemic paradigms" in science. In the social sciences systemic thinking is differentiated from traditional approaches on several counts:

- Instead of ascribing attributes to individuals (e.g. clinical diagnoses), features of the system are highlighted as being relevant. Gregory Bateson proposed the famous "double-bind" hypothesis, according to which schizophrenia is the result of confusing communication in families (Bateson, Jackson, Haley and Weakland, 1956). A mentally ill person is thus regarded as the "symptom carrier" for the system.
- "Systemic thinking" is postulated as a new method of insight. Central assumptions are, for example, relinquishing causal-linear thinking in favour of accepting the reciprocal influence of subjects which interact with each other, or relinquishing the search for the "real truth" in favour of acceptance of subject-dependent constructions of reality. "Truth" would then be negotiated in a social context (Maturana and Varela, 1987).

246

The combination of the concept of a "system" with the constellations method has also led to controversies. Those who have been working for some time with the concepts of systemic theory and practice find the adoption of the concept by constellations practitioners ill-advised and stress the differences between a "systemic-constructivist" view and the phenomenological view of Bert Hellinger (Simon and Retzer, 2003).

The difference between the systemic-constructivist approach and the phenomenological constellations approach lies, in my opinion, in that the former works more with the concept of interaction, communication and conscious cognitive forms of reality perception, whilst in the latter the unconscious emotional human bondings find expression that are otherwise difficult to identify.

Representative Perception

The constellations method is based on the assumption of "representative perception" or the "ability of people to mirror relational structures appropriately" (Varga von Kibéd, 1998). This basic presupposition is breathtaking in its audacity if we compare it to our usual idea of the way information is passed from one person to another, i.e. the assumption that someone can only know something if we tell them; what we don't say, we don't communicate to anyone; we cannot know what no-one has told us. So, can someone who has never exchanged a word with me, who has never met me before, mirror me in a constellation to the deepest aspect of my soul? Can he or she know what specific relationship I had to my mother, my father and my siblings? Can he or she really sense my deeply buried fears and emotional distress?

My assumption about this is as follows: someone else can know what moves me emotionally only if I clear the path to this information. I assume this because I have experienced and tested it for myself. If a client, perhaps unconsciously, holds back certain important information the representatives in a constellation may only sense that there is something that is important that is not yet known. However, they cannot have any clarity about what this is. If the client provides the missing information or specifically allows within him or herself that anything that might be important may come to light in the constellation, then the information flows to the representatives again. Thus the client is consciously or unconsciously turning the light on and off in a constellation. He supplies the representatives with energy but can also withdraw this energy, just as if he were pulling the plug out of its socket. Thus if someone does not want to reveal a secret of their own or a secret in the family, then this cannot come to light in a constellation. The representatives sense the fact that something does not add up and is being kept secret, but at the same time their perceptions are clouded by the actions of the person doing the constellation, who transmits his defensive and repressive mechanisms as interference frequencies and thereby prevents the representatives from resonating with traumatic events in his past.

The representatives can only know what type of feelings and information is in the soul of the client. But, unlike the client, if they have the "permission" from the client, they are able to express the repressed, unconscious parts of the client's inner self, giving them voice in a way that the client is unable to. They can portray the representations of parents, grandparents, siblings and so on that the client carries deeply within him or her by giving them form. "The unconscious" of the client is thereby made conscious by the experiences of the representatives in a constellation.

Jacob Moreno, who originated psychodrama, stumbled onto the phenomenon of representative perception. He and his successors were amazed to discover that, in a psychodrama, the role players for people they had never known were "often so true to the real life circumstances, states and reactions of these others over such a long period of time ... that the actions that a psychodrama player displays often cannot be understood as something ensuing from an objective lack of knowledge of the circumstances" (Leutz, 1974).

How reliable is representative perception?
What seems unthinkable on the basis of our normal understanding of how information is passed from one to another
seems, after a period of experience with family constellations,
something completely self-evident. The representatives intuitively grasp the core of the emotional conflicts that are present
in a family. They mirror with great accuracy and detail what
has not been resolved over several generations. The proof for
this claim lies in the many thousands of experiences that
people have had all over the world of being a representative in
others' constellations. Everyone who has anything to do with
constellations can experience this themselves. Thomas Schäfer
writes: "although representatives are complete strangers, the
detail with which these people can portray the story of a family
is astonishing every single time. The representatives feel like
the real family members do" (Schäfer, 2000). Albrecht Mahr,
a constellations facilitator, thinks that the representatives in the
constellations can "through our perceptual ability to represent
or participate and empathise with the circumstances of other
members or forces in the system physically, emotionally and
mentally in the most appropriate way ... allow the unconscious
dynamic in a system to unfold in this way with astonishing
accuracy and reliability" (Mahr, 2003).

Jakob Schneider reflected on his experiences in representative roles and as a facilitator in an article in the "Praxis der
Systemaufstellung" (Schneider, 2001). He finds that the
authenticity of the representatives is not unqualified.
Sometimes a representative says or does something that is
anathema to the client, or the representative feels uncertain
about his own reaction. This throws up the question as to what
confusion there might be of the representative's own issues
with those of the person represented, and how to deal with
this. As I have stated above trustworthiness accrues from the
whole constellation situation, and representatives do, after all,
have their own idiosyncrasies and limits. On the other hand it
is repeatedly impressive for everyone to see the forces that can
and do take hold of a representative leading him or her to

make gestures or say words which are completely uncharacteristic of him or her under normal circumstances, and which involuntarily point out what is meaningful in the system. Schneider does not experience it as "something that falsifies constellations" when representatives frequently stress the similarity between the fate of the person they are representing and their own life (ibid.).

All in all Schneider experiences that "what representatives show and describe as felt processes is extremely enriching" and he recognises in these "a deep trust in a shared inheritance that connects and carries all of us, at least as far as it affects life and death, and goes beyond cultures" (ibid.).

As Matthias Varga von Kibéd states, every participant in a constellation has this ability of "representative perception" (Varga von Kibéd, 1998). Representatives get "extraordinarily intensive, sometimes gentle, sometimes intense, but very clearly internally experienced changes in their body perceptions and their feelings" (Varga von Kibéd, 2004). Representatives are able to relay correct information through the alien system by making their own body available as a "perceptual organ" (ibid.). A human being seems to be able to perceive as if he were an organ of the group or system (ibid.). If we assume the validity of "representative perception", then we would have to have perceptual abilities which "are specific ... only for me relative to the system to which I belong and perhaps also relative to a specific situation" (ibid.). Varga von Kibéd thinks that "this ability to assess relational structures in the environment is for a child vitally important for its survival" (ibid.) and forms in early child development.

I am particularly struck by the experience that occurs immediately before someone takes on a representative role that conflicts with their own current emotional state, where perhaps they spontaneously enter a state of sudden internal freezing with terror, or sudden feelings of rage and hate, or becoming deeply saddened and starting to cry. Images may suddenly appear in their minds which fit the family history of the person they are about to represent. The client choosing the representative in most cases makes confirmations like: just like my mother, just like my father .... But essentially it is only what his own soul is feeding into the constellation – without words and without conscious knowledge. The efficacy of the constellations method stands and falls in my opinion with the assumption that the representative can grasp the essence of the person he or she is representing, the very heart and soul of this person. If this were not the case, then this method would have little legitimacy or would be mere therapeutic role-playing. Throughout my extensive experience with constellations over many years I have collected sufficient empirical evidence that the method is sufficiently reliable and valid. That is, that different representatives in different constellations can discern the same basic bonding structures and conflicts within a client. The reliability of the constellating method can best be tested practically when one works with a particular client in different groups or with different family members at different times and with different groups. I have repeatedly experienced that different representatives make the same remarks about the same family members in different groups.

There is also a highly significant correspondence between family members in what they feel. Every family member has their own individual emotional reality about events in the family. But this reality is not an arbitrary image of reality, and the relevant facts of bonding and trauma. Facts will differ in their relevance for any specific individual. Thus a child can only be aware of certain aspects of his parents' internal psyche, whilst he obliterates others. But at the same time each individual accurately understands the core family dynamics from his or her own perspective.

Unintentionality

In order that hidden information may surface, representatives must be free from any intention to feel or experience anything specific. They must simply allow themselves to be taken by the experiences that they begin to sense in themselves. In a certain

251

sense they are channels through which a reality can manifest itself which cannot otherwise so clearly be expressed. The representatives should thus hold back from interpreting a contextual meaning onto their experience and feelings. Sometimes it is better to wait for strong impulses or to keep something suspended for a while. For many people being a representative is a wholly new experience that is contrary to their usual perceptual and thinking habits, and demands an explanation. As Varga von Kibéd deduces, constellating is a special form of a general principle of representational perception (Varga von Kibéd, 2000). A participant at a constellations seminar sent me a report about an experience that she had had in a theatre workshop. Here, too, she experienced how she was suddenly gripped by a force from which she could not extricate herself.

Case Study 52:

It happened to me

"Last Tuesday I was invited by a friend who is a drama teacher to take part in a play with him and other amateur actors. We practised portraying feelings. Then we started working on a play that had to do with a cowboy and his oxen. In great danger the cowboy makes his way through the swamps, has to walk very carefully and after his journey is both physically and emotionally completely exhausted by the effort. When it was my turn to play the scene as the cow-boy in front of the other participants, I felt as I had done in some of your constellations. I was no longer myself. I felt the danger so intensely that I began to tremble all over. I can hardly imagine ever being able to do that again – go on stage and start trembling. I don't know if you can understand what I'm trying to say: in the constellations – I can especially remember when I took the representative role for a partici-pant's alcoholic mother – I was influenced by gigantic forces as well. Before that I could never have imagined throwing myself on the floor in front of forty participants. But there was nothing I could do. It was as if something was pushing me down. How is that? What is going on with a representative? What is going on with an actor? Is it the same thing? Is it something different? That is really preoccupying my thoughts, especially as I keep asking myself: Did I just do that deliberately during the constellation seminar? Did I "act" that, because that was the way I thought an alcoholic mother would be? – Nonsense, how could I have known that? Or does one somehow know that? ... Up till now I had imagined that something external was influencing me. And now, in the play in the theatre (I have never acted before), the same experience. I don't need to do it intentionally and to act as if it were happening – at least partly – to me. Do you understand all that?"

Constellations as Challenge for our World Concept

Constellations work and the phenomenon of representative perception challenges us to rethink our view of the world. Finding new explanations which answer fundamental human questions more adequately probably means going beyond the classical physical model of an aimless world without plan, built of atoms and obeying so-called natural laws. There are hardly any physicists today who regard this model of the world as valid, but in some human and social sciences this mechanistic model is still the only imaginable one. There are, however, many alternatives. We have most certainly not yet arrived at an ultimate understanding of the world and reality.

.

Digression 7: Information in virtual worlds

What could characterise a new world model in which spirit and matter no longer exist separately? Following Laszlo it could derive from the following axioms (Laszlo 1997):

- *The universe consists of a quantum and supra-quantum field of matter-energy which is directly observable, and of a sub-quantum field of so-called virtual energy, which cannot be observed either directly or by means of instruments. Space, which up til now we have perceived as being empty, is thus in reality full.*
- *Materially visible or measurable energy bodies are electro-magnetic space/time models, which reproduce themselves in their surrounding universal energy field, leaving traces behind. Such energy bodies "in-form" the virtual sub-quantum fields surrounding them, i.e. they shape a specific form with its own specific informational content.*
- *Information imprinted on the energy field can spread everywhere and is not subject to the limitations of energy transfers by material bodies, which are limited by distances in time and space and consequently by the speed of light.*

If one starts with these assumptions, this might have consequences for what happens in the material world:

- *Everything that happens in the universe would be imprinted at every moment in the sub-energy field. There would be something like a universal memory for everything that is and that happens. Everything would potentially be connected to everything else.*
- *The electro-magnetic time-space matrices of energy bodies would resonate with this virtual energy field, retrieving information for themselves.*

- *If the human organism resonates with these virtual information matrices, then events that have already taken place could possibly be retrieved into current experience.*
- *Under certain circumstances, for example, if we clear the path to enable the process, other people might begin to resonate with energy fields that we have in-formed and thus come into contact with our past experiences.*
- *The past, in being retrieved out of the energy continuum into the material world and re-shaped, could not only be experienced, but also transformed.*

According to this model, the following may be happening in a constellation:

- *Like everyone else, a person with a constellation issue exists in an energy field, which penetrates him, and he resonates with whatever traces his past may have left behind.*
- *Bonding and trauma feelings have left particularly strong impressions in his virtual energy field.*
- *In formulating his current issue, he brings into the structure of his soul a process of resonance with whatever is relevant out of his past.*
- *The person doing the constellation places the representatives in his virtual field in such a way that they can resonate with his past and with whatever there is in his past that is having such an effect.*
- *By means of their own affective and perceptual structures, the representatives can bring the information stored in the virtual energy fields into their own experiences and express them through gesture and language.*

Of course these assumptions are only one possible hypothesis. Many others are conceivable.

Insight as a Dialogue with the World

The modern physical model implies that an objective under-standing of the world as was thought possible in the positivistic philosophy of the 19th century does not exist. There is no world that we, through our human understanding, can hold as "objective". Rather, insight develops from the dialogue between a human observer and what he observes. In this process the observer is mirrored in what he observes and vice versa. Whatever is measured scientifically is itself changed by being measured. Something for which we have no sensors or way of measuring cannot be identified by us. We remain blind to what we do not want to know or remember.

Consequently, those who for whatever reasons do not accept the phenomenon of constellations as reality and do not trust the method must remain excluded from its insights. The autonomy of this method can only be passed on through prac-tical experience. Whether we will find a theory in the foreseeable future which explains the representative phenom-enon is currently an open question. But even without a satisfying theory there is much that we do even though we cannot explain how it works. Our explanations for most processes are relatively superficial. The phenomenon of repre-sentative perception exists, there is no doubt of that, but as long as we don't really know how and why the representation of psychic structures functions, many different interpretations must be possible and the field must be open for discussion.

Therefore, on the one hand as long as the constellations method supports us to understand our human nature better and helps us when we suffer then, in my view, it is useful. On the other hand a healthy scepticism in the therapeutic application of this method is essential, because it seems so powerful and may be harmful to clients if not applied appropriately.

Contexts for Working with Constellations

I have already shown the context in which I work with constellations, however I think that it is possible to apply the method to a very wide field and we are only just at the beginning in terms of exploring the possibilities and limits. Unrealistic and erroneous expectations need to be guarded against, whilst expressed reservations and objections need to be taken seriously. Constellations can be done in one-to-one settings (e.g. client and therapist) or in small and large groups. In my view there are some contexts that are compatible with constellations, and some that are less compatible.

The individual setting

Although the particular strength of constellations, the work with representatives, is not available in individual settings, in my view one-to-one constellations work in therapy and counselling is very suitable. Since my experience, and that of others, shows that the client is entirely capable of feeling himself into constellation positions marked out by cushions, figures etc, good results can be achieved through this way of working.

Case Study 53:

I am normal

Martina is single and works as a clerk. In her spare time she has been studying philosophy enthusiastically for a good while. In one therapy session she complained that she was not being taken any notice of either in her job or in her studies. She did not feel seen, although she had often done things for other people. The balance between what she was doing for others and the attention she was receiving for it did not add up. We set up a small constellation of two markers, one for Martina and one for the part of her that doesn't feel seen (Figure 5).

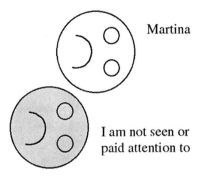

Fig 5. Martina (adult personality part) and the feeling of not being seen or paid attention to

Martina has a very bad relationship with her mother, whom she has always experienced as very child-like. When she connected with the position "I am not seen or paid attention to" she immediately went into a negative mood, which got worse and worse as she stayed there. She could not do anything to counter this feeling and felt helpless. I asked her to track the possible cause for this feeling, and it occurred to her that as a child she was once sent to play-school with infected tonsils. "My parents didn't take any notice of me. They just tied a scarf around my neck and sent me off." Other things occurred to her: her father was against her learning to play the flute as a child. Later she would have like to play guitar or the piano, but her father refused this as well. When I asked her why her father was against her doing this, she said that she suspected that he would have liked to go into further education himself, but that his parents had not supported him. I get Martina to place markers in the constellation to represent her father and her mother. In her father's place I asked her to see if she gets a sense of him and what motives he might have had in thwarting her wishes. In her father's place she immediately got in touch with the feeling that he experienced his mother as being too close to him, and that he found Martina to also be too close. As her father she felt watched and wanted to hide. I suggested that

Martina place a marker to represent this wish of her father's not to be observed, which she did. She felt even more uncomfortable when she stood in her father's position.

Martina then moved to the marker of "I am not seen or paid attention to". Here she felt completely spellbound by the cushion that represented her father's wish not to be paid attention to. She said: "In our family we all looked at our father because there was always something going on with him. He was always hiding something. I'm thinking now of his drinking and some strange money deals. It's precisely because he wanted to hide it that we looked all the more." Her father died in a drink-driving accident when Martina was 20.

Martina then formed the sentence: "I'm actually not worth being paid attention to. If you come from a family like mine, you can't be worth anything."

Next I asked Martina to place a cushion in the constellation to represent the statement "I am not worth being paid attention to." She stood on this place and immediately her self-doubt and self-criticism intensified. "If you come from such an anti-social family, then you have no right to find a husband who offers something better." I asked her what might help this part in her. After thinking about it briefly she said: "If things were normal. If I had the feeling that I was normal." I suggested that she place a cushion to represent the feeling "I am normal". Immediately she said that as the part of "I am not worth being paid attention to" she began to feel better, she could relax. Martina then went towards the position "I am not seen or paid attention to" and she immediately became calmer. "I can feel now that's it's quite normal to need to be seen and be paid attention to." (Figure 6)

In the place of her adult "Martina" part she initially wondered why it was so important to be "normal", yet at the same time she did not want to be bothered with worrying about it. However, she realised that it was helpful for these "child" parts of herself if they felt they were "normal". She

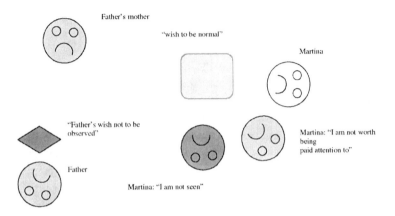

Father's mother

"wish to be normal"

Martina

"Father's wish not to be observed"

Father

Martina: "I am not seen"

Martina: "I am not worth being paid attention to"

Fig. 6: Martina integrates the parts "I am not paid attention to or seen" and "I am not worth being paid attention to"

re-arranged the constellation a little and went to the place of each of her two personality parts to confirm the congruity of the constellation. Returning to the position of her adult self, she now felt in contact with her child selves.

Constellations in groups

In my view groups of up to forty people over several days are straightforward. With this size of group it is still possible for everyone to introduce themselves and say why they are there. Also with groups of this size or smaller either a written or verbal contract setting out the conditions for the work can easily be agreed with all participants.

With larger groups there has to be a distinction between those who want to do a constellation and those who are there to gain experience as representatives or as observers. Experience of this work shows that every participant usually gains something, whether from doing their own constellation, from experiencing being a representative or through experiencing the process from outside as an observer. There is ample opportunity at the beginning and between constellations for all participants to say something about themselves, to support the facilitator in the work or to ask questions.

In very large groups, more than fifty participants, these opportunities are no longer so freely available. The influence of the individual on the process diminishes, and the facilitator becomes the more central figure. It then depends very much on the personality style of the facilitator as to how far she encourages the inclusion of the group into the work and to what extent she can include any questions or concerns about each piece of work.

For anyone doing a personal constellation, large and more anonymous groups mean that she may be in danger of exposing too much of herself in such a public forum. In a large group it can be more difficult for there to be an intensive exchange between the person doing the constellation and the facilitator.

Within the organisational and business arena there are other situations in which working with constellations can be very difficult. These include groups in which participants are professionally dependent on one another (e.g. manager and employees) or where there is a strong hierarchical relationship between participants and facilitators (teachers and pupils). In such cases the constellations method should only be utilised by independent facilitators and only for such issues that can be addressed by not impinging directly on the work relationship.

Constellations are suitable for therapy as well as counselling settings. However the intention should made clear before commencing work. It is possible in a counselling situation, without going too deeply into emotional issues, to show the client that more intense psychotherapy might be useful to him.

Digression 8: Advice, counselling or psychotherapy

New discoveries and innovations tend to be accepted by the traditional institutions and by people who work with accepted methods only with reservations. Some strongly reject innovations if their own theoretical training and practice is called into question. I am convinced that, professionally applied, constellations are a very effective psychotherapeutic intervention, and can be usefully combined with other methods.

Most people who decide to do constellations for their own journey have a fine instinct for what will help them further and what will not. There are, however, also situations where facilitators are not up to dealing with the complex emotional dynamics that a client brings. Thus in a constellation clients can be stripped of their old defensive mechanisms without gaining new strategies to overcome their problems.

Constellations in social work

For psychotherapists and counsellors constellations are a unique diagnostic instrument for understanding how mental conflicts arise and develop in complex relationship systems. Thus in this simple form constellations can be used for case analysis in many psychosocial fields and offered in life coaching. I am constantly surprised how much clients can get from even a short constellation, and how quickly their relationships can improve as a result.

Case Study 54:

Lucas and hyperactivity

One of the most gratifying outcomes of a small study on hyperactivity syndrome was that the parents, teachers and social educators who work with hyperactive children were, apparently for the first time, able to understand the child better. It was important to represent the symptom hyperactivity and the child with two representatives, that is, separately. When interviewed three months after the constellation, it was ascertained that "Mr and Mrs Huber, Lucas's parents, experienced great relief in the constellation. They were able to understand Lucas and his emotional world better, and that he felt restricted and burdened. Mrs Huber can now tolerate the closeness of her son much better, whilst Mr Huber can see his son as separate from the hyperactivity. He can see him as Lucas, who is carrying a huge burden around with him. They no longer see their son's behaviour as malicious, reacting more calmly and being able to get more in touch with their son. The boy seems much more balanced" (Schwer, 2004).

Cecilia Pänzinger, a student of mine, proved how useful constellations can be in social work and the psychosocial field in her dissertation. With the help of a constellation she analysed the situation of a boy in a village for fostered children. "The follow-up meeting with the social work team and the foster mother showed that the constellation of the work relationships had proved very helpful for everyone. In the constellation people had the opportunity to step out of the situation, see it from the outside and from another point of view. It was good that all the team members were there and went through the experience together. The constellation gained more strength in this way. It is consistently in everyone's awareness, they talk about it, and the feelings that came up come up repeatedly. In Martin's case (one of the fostered children) a kind of common denominator arose. The foster mother felt very well represented by her representative. The constellation made her very aware of the significance of the child's father. It also helped her to realise that she had been too matter-of-fact and unemotional with the child. She realised that she could allow herself to show her emotions far more, and now does this. The social worker V. realised that Martin was being constantly pushed aside. He now had greater understanding for Martin's restless states and aggression, and can accept these now without getting annoyed. V. has found his own place in the system and enjoys having an image for this. He also sees it as a further advantage of the method that a constellation allows people not only to observe a situation, but also to feel their way into it" (Pänzinger, 2004).

Applied with the necessary care constellations can be extremely useful outside the therapeutic setting in many areas of social work or teaching (e.g. Döring-Maijer, 2004; Franke-Gricksch, 2001; Knorr, 2002; Schricker, 2001; Ulsamer, 2001).

Theoretical Orientation

How someone applies the constellations method depends on the theoretical orientation of the therapist. There is no constellation that is free of a basic psychotherapeutic theory, even if Bert Hellinger seems to imply this when he talks about a "phenomenological attitude" on the part of the facilitator, that they must be without intention, free of fear or even empathy for the client so that reality can reveal itself as it is. However strongly we may value an open and non-judgemental attitude, it is impossible not to be impacted by and have views and ideas about what one sees, nor to have expectations of what will happen next. One can learn by experience to linger in a state of simple non-assessing perception longer before making an intervention. Experience with meditation techniques helps this. However, one cannot separate observation from thinking and feeling.

So that we can be seen to be open about what we are doing and that we are not trying to manipulate it, it seems necessary to me to disclose the theories and hypotheses as to what one perceives in a constellation, and these must be up for discussion. It should not only be possible to test one's own theories empirically in a constellation, but also through argument in professional discourse. The way in which someone perceives a client's issue and the techniques that he applies in a constellation are closely dependent on the theories he holds about emotional and psychological phenomena, on his model of illness as well as his ideas about emotional and psychological health.

Essentially many theories can be combined with this method. Everyone will see, to a certain degree, his own theories confirmed in the application of this method. This is also usually true for other methods. The constellations method cannot therefore be used as proof for the accuracy of any particular theory. The basic theory in itself must be consistent and as free from contradiction as possible. Theoretical discussions need to be on the theoretical level and methodological discussions on the methodological level.

Professional Competence

The personality of the counsellor is of particular importance in the professional fields of counselling and psychotherapy. What has a therapist/counsellor learned? What knowledge does he possess, what experience, what skills? Can he work with a group? Does he know how to moderate a group discussion?

Being able to facilitate a constellation competently is one aspect of a more comprehensive psychotherapeutic and counselling competence. I think that all therapeutic approaches have their strong points, and these can be utilised by therapists and counsellors from different theoretical approaches and models. I personally consider the following helpful:

- The ability to maintain "evenly suspended attention", as it is taught in psychoanalysis.
- Active and empathic listening, as recommended in client-centred therapy in the sense of Carl Rogers.
- Attention to body movements and minimal body signals, as recommended in neuro-linguistic programming (NLP).
- Concentrating on achievable (part) goals, as is practised in behavioural therapy.
- Inner direction and orientation of the client to solutions for his emotional conflicts, as recommended in systemic therapy approaches.
- The ability to lead and structure groups in the tradition of group dynamics.

- Working with resources, as recommended in trauma therapy methods.

Constellations can, when properly applied, utilise and combine in their own particular way many helpful elements from existing therapeutic approaches:

- Constellations "mirror" a client's emotional reality in a graphic and comprehensive way. Just as Rogerian client-centred therapy recognised that a therapist helps a client to gain clarity about himself if the therapist reflects back his feelings, so too the behaviour of the representatives in a constellation reflects back to the client many indications about his inner self. No therapist could reflect back to the client the complexity of feelings in the multiple relationships as clearly as representatives can. Constellations also show the many levels of a soul or psychic structure much more accurately than an individual therapist would be able to do. However, for this to be achieved, the facilitator must hold back her interpretations and allow the representatives to speak for themselves. She must keep the developing process as free as possible from external influences, and this includes any rushed interpretations by the therapist.
- A principle of systemic therapy says that the system is its own best descriptor and holds the potential for its own self-preservation as well as any appropriate adjustment to environmental conditions. A constellation in this sense can be seen as its own focussed systemic description of a client. Constellations can thus find solutions in the most complicated emotional entanglements, which even a very experienced therapist would not be able to suggest to his client. However, it requires a great deal of patience on the part of the facilitator not to follow his own ideas immediately, but to give the constellation the time it needs to get to the heart of the problem and then to find a way out. The intervention of the therapist, who is outside the

system, is necessary to expand the system by including those elements that need to be seen to provide the total context within which the problem first arose. He also has to intervene when he sees that the system has caught itself up in a paradox that it cannot resolve by itself.

- Psychotherapeutic work in groups increases the potential of finding in other people a mirror for understanding one's own psyche. I can confirm from my own constellations groups the experiences of Anne Ancelin Schützenberger when she says "I find that the energy that circulates in a group, together with the group dynamic, help a person to specify their problem, to bring it to light and sometimes be able to talk about it. I have noticed in work with small groups that the memory of one person triggers the memory of another. We support each other reciprocally, warm each other, and the memories return. One remembers, glances back, looks and talks. And finally, after two or three intensive sessions, which can each last two or five days, the members of this geno-social programme group are better able to understand their families, their family myths, their family system and the family history, as well as their own identity and what is stopping them from being who they really are." (Schützenberger, 1998) To utilise these special qualities of a group, a warm-hearted and open relationship is needed between the facilitator and the group members. Without this mutual understanding no meaningful work is possible.

Blind spots
Personal competence is just as important as professional competence. One of the biggest blocks for members of the psychotherapeutic and psychosocial professions in recognising and understanding the emotional wounds in their clients is rooted, in my opinion, in not having dealt with their own trauma and bonding disorders sufficiently. Many people avoid doing so all their lives. Those who do not want to explore their

267

own blind spots and are not prepared to know them, can, in my opinion, only be of limited use to others. They will always be in danger of identifying too strongly with the problems of their client so that entanglement must follow. Solutions are thus more likely to be hindered than promoted by the therapist.

It is justifiable to assume that those who choose to work in the psychotherapeutic and social work fields are likely to have their own emotional wounds. This is not to object to those working in this field, but to assert that anyone who refuses to confront the unintegrated parts of their own identity as part of their professional training and supervision cannot claim to be working professionally.

My personal supervision issues as well as my supervision work with experienced therapists have shown me time and again how closely one's own blind spots and difficulties in therapeutic work are linked to the problems of our clients. These blind spots may also unconsciously make the therapist attractive to the client, because both have a common theme, a similar form of trauma. This may support the start of the therapeutic relationship well, but at the same time the entanglement will at some point threaten the relationship.

Case Study 55:

A common fate

Maria is an experienced therapist. In a supervision group she presented the case of a client who was very depressed and with whom she felt very blocked. She herself felt paralysed by the client's hopelessness. In the constellation it emerged that the client's mother and Maria's mother had both lost their husbands in the war. This resulted in depression in both the mothers, which was then transferred to their daughters. Once this entanglement became clear to Maria and she understood her own issue and began to resolve it in a constellation, she was able to continue working with the client.

The method of family constellations is gaining increasing attention also in the field of social work, serving as a background for professional self-reflection for social workers. Valentina Haberling has carried out in a diploma dissertation a small study about the phenomenon of representative awareness. In talking about her own work as a social worker she concludes that: "Only a social worker who has become aware of himself through doing family constellations is able to recognise others for how they are. 'Helping' out of an unequal position and with the hidden motives of not having to look at one's own problems or for other compensatory reasons can be harmful both for the helper, e.g. as in burn-out syndrome, and for the person looking for help, who is unable to get out of the role of being small and weak. According to Hellinger a helper should 'say goodbye to the idea that he might have been, so to say, chosen by a higher power to improve the world .... He has not been chosen. In this respect he is on the same level as the client' (quoted in Neuhauser, 1999). Also: 'He is great who feels equal to others. This greatness connects all people with humility and love' (Hellinger, 2001a). A social worker who approaches his client with respect and from a systemic perspective can see and take into account his [the client's] fate as well as his family's. This enables him to act in the interests of the person seeking help" (Haberling, 2004).

Thorough training as well as a willingness to continue one's education is fundamentally important for therapists and counsellors. The human psyche and soul are far too complex for anyone to think that they have thoroughly understood them, packing them away into theoretical boxes. A willingness to have feedback on one's work in supervision and inter-vision [peer supervision], and, whenever necessary, to undertake appropriate personal work, is part and parcel of the quality standards in the psychosocial professions. The efficacy of using one's own method when working with oneself should be self-evident for therapists and counsellors who work with constellations.

9.5 A Small Research Study on the Effectiveness of Constellations

Interviews with Participants in Constellations Seminars.

For his diploma dissertation Bozo Maric, a student of mine, questioned twelve people who had done constellations with me in various seminars about their experiences. He asked them questions about the issues they had brought to the seminar, about their impression of the facilitator, of the representatives and the whole group and what the results were for them (Maric, 2003). Their answers showed how comprehensively participants undertake the whole process of a constellation: how thoroughly they consider their issue for a constellation, how carefully they choose the representatives, how intensely they experience the process from outside the constellation and what it is like when they take their place in the constellation.

All those questioned reported that they had gained new insights through the constellation. It was interesting that those who had attended constellations seminars more frequently were able to describe their developmental processes in considerably more detail than those who had attended less frequently. Thus familiarity with the method seems to help.

As previously described, the appropriate starting point for a constellation is the foreground issue. This determines how much someone can and wants to achieve through a constellation, and participants in Bozo Maric's questionnaire reported that they also experienced this as important. One respondent found it very helpful, for example, that I helped her to go deeper into her original issue: "That was exactly the right thing to do, as I had been staying on the surface myself. Franz Ruppert's first intervention was to have me formulate the issue again. I had sent him several emails, then said something about my situation at the seminar, but then he asked again: 'What can we do for you?' In the follow-up session I asked him: 'I have got much further than I originally intended, but what made you get me to formulate my issue again?' He said: 'I saw the despair in your eyes, that was the energy to go further.' This intervention was important. In eye-contact with me he noticed that I was longing for something else. That is why he told me that he could see the despair in my eyes, and so we realised that there was something else going on here. Through this brief moment of eye-contact I was able to go deeper. In the beginning he had asked me to formulate the issue. I had finished. Then he looked at me and (I thought: Here we go!) asked me: 'Now tell me how you really are.' Then I was able to formulate the issue differently. From that moment on I was able to go deeper" (ibid.).

The choice of representatives is seen by all those questioned as relatively uncomplicated. The first impression that forms in the introductory round is sufficient as a selection aid. A fairly brief evaluation takes place to ascertain whether the person in question is suited for a particular representative role: "... I simply chose people who reminded me of the persons. Who have certain characteristics, facial features, sometimes it is their figure, sometimes just external aspects, but in the main it's character traits that simply remind me of that particular person. That's why I choose them as representatives" (ibid.).

As the seminar continues participants come to know each other better, as people with their own personal stories, in their representative roles, in the chats during the breaks. This allows the criteria for the selection of representatives to broaden. "In the constellation that went before I saw her and I thought: 'Actually I am just as much on the ropes as she is.' There was something symbiotic, we had something in common, and that's why I chose her to represent me. She reminded me of how I do things and how I behave. Externally we are not at all alike. But we're similar types, the way she deals with things, the way she sees some things seemed very similar to me. Or maybe it's because I saw myself in her, and that's why I chose her" (ibid.).

It is important to ascertain whether the constellation and the representatives reflect a situation for the person doing the constellation that he experiences as his own or not. Those who have done several constellations develop more trust in the method because they have already experienced the accuracy with which constellations portray their relationships. "For me it was very important what the individual representatives, the individual people, said in their roles, because my experience to date has been that it fitted 'one to one'. That what I have experienced in life fits with what has happened in the constellations. It was often the case that certain behaviours or sentences that people in my life have said were said by the representatives" (ibid.).

The reliability of the constellation in the sense of its congruity with experienced reality becomes apparent in that the people whose constellation it is experience the representatives' behaviours and statements as similar to those of the real people. The constellation also enables the person to gain a new point of view. While originally only able to see certain people through the filter of their own experiential matrix, they can then see that this person has quite different, possibly even opposite features as well. What follows describes a constellation about a student's work experience: "Well, it was like this: I sat there and had to agree with how the representatives were behaving. They behaved exactly like it was in my work experience. The only thing that surprised me was the position of my instructor. That she opposed the situation with such vehemence and force. I hadn't experienced her like that, and the funny thing was that for a long time afterwards I thought about always having seen her as weak, as a duckling that I had to protect. And she wasn't like that, so that preoccupied me. And the funny thing about that is that today I really see her like she was in the constellation. She is actually like that, I had just never seen her that way. I had had a different perception of her from the way she really was. It's not that she has changed in any way because of the constellation, but I see her now as she really is. She isn't small, she isn't shy, she isn't weak. She isn't any of these things. I imposed those interpretations on her, perhaps in order to make myself seem bigger in comparison" (ibid.).

It also doesn't seem to be contradictory that representatives can reflect people they don't know so accurately, and at the same time recognise what of their experience has to do with their own personal story. Some people experience the representative role as very revealing for their own questions: "I notice more and more that I sometimes find answers for myself when I stand there as a representative. Then I sometimes have the feeling that I can see the answers just as or even more plainly. Or it's exactly the same as in my own constellation, which I find absolutely amazing. I see a development there, that stuff I have experienced as a representative that was heavy, that I couldn't even imagine, then I did my own constellation, then afterwards was a representative again in another constellation which was very heavy, too, and then slowly I began to realise that the three constellations where I had been a representative formed a kind of line, like a red thread, where I realised things about my own story or about my family story, or about my own blockages. That's what I find totally amazing. That that's a part of the process, too" (ibid.).

Participants who are also familiar with "classic family constellations" appreciate the style of work I have developed with "the movements of the soul". They find it more helpful for the resolution of emotional entanglements. "I have also known other facilitators who did more of a compensatory constellating, this classic family constellation where the facilitator walks around and puts the people into positions and then constructs solution structures. The main advantage in this [Ruppert's] way of working, as I see it, is that it is not constructed, but the space stays free for the movements of each individual. The representatives can move around, they can act verbally and through movement. This moves away from the inflexibility of classic constellations. I am convinced that this method supports the process. The other is pure bonding work, resource orientation, and here we have a process orientation which starts at the point where there is a psychic knot which is longing for its solution" (ibid.).

Some people who have done several constellations experience this as an intensely personal development in their whole relational field: "I sense that this has taken me forward personally and professionally. I sense that I have become softer, I have the feeling that I can approach people more readily, whereas before I would have kept my distance. I have experienced this constellation as a process. As a process I understand it inasmuch as I saw a thread right from my first constellation through to the final image in the last constellation. There were levels: levels of self knowledge and levels of resolution. There are smaller units of solutions that do not take me any further, but that are necessary. I have the feeling that the issues that I formulated for myself have expanded from session to session, from month to month. More and more new horizons opened up right up to the final image. And they are all organically connected. I have the impression that there is no separation of private and professional, both are connected, linked, and there is an effect on both social levels. On all social levels, whether it's about work or family. I experience that as a new warmth, in the family as well, and people who I didn't know particularly well have suddenly phoned me. That would have been unthinkable before" (ibid.).

A fresh look at the parents is very significant in overcoming bonding disorders: "What I experienced is that we are all connected, in some way connected, in all our limitations, and that parents are limited, that our expectations of parents are too great. It has become clear to me that one must simply see it this way. We can't do everything ourselves, and our parents are not omnipotent and we can't demand from them more than they can achieve" (ibid.).

The group and the development of a sense of belonging during the seminar is also very significant for those doing a constellation. "The most important aspect is this solution-oriented approach in the constellation, that I experience as incredibly freeing. People come together in their suffering and pain and are safe in the group, respected, protected, appreciated and one shares their fate and empathises. And that gives the feeling that we belong together" (ibid.).

The word "fascinating" keeps coming up when evaluating the potential of the constellations method. People clearly find something very significant for them. Young and old come closer in this way: "What fascinated me so much in constellations work: the first time that I took part all the people were rather older than me, some were even very old. In my first constellation there was someone who was 70–75, who had been through the war. I had problems with this. Anyway, he sat on the chair and began to cry. There was another older man there who broke down in tears. That was what moved me so much. I was so fascinated that people who are so staunch in life can come out of themselves through this method and allow this feeling to be let out and let go of. That fascinated me about this work and I wanted to come again and be there again when so many older people came out of themselves. That people like that can display and express such feelings in a circle of total strangers! These are often people who find this really difficult and who have always played the tough business man and then can strip it all away in a circle like this. I was fascinated that this is a method which can trigger something like this without tying you to a chair and beating it out of you. Not forced, not tense, but so gently. This method works gently and carefully with the person's story and yet can release huge emotions. Till now I have only known sledgehammer methods, beat it out of you and scream it out, make a hullabaloo and you're rid of it. And that works, too. It works this way, too. And it works with people who all their lives have hidden behind it all and tried to build a wall around it, and then someone comes along, asks three questions, looks at the circle and sparks off something like this" (ibid.).

Feedback from Workshop Participants

In the end every therapeutic intervention is measured by its success, but how can we adequately evaluate this? In my opinion there are two criteria: the client's sense that they are feeling better than they did before the therapeutic intervention of a constellation, and by the disappearance of the symptoms of psychological confusion. Fear, depression, confusion and compulsive or addictive behaviour should not occur any more, or at least not to the same intensity as before. The client should have better ways of dealing with the symptoms. A serious psychological disorder clearly cannot be healed by one constellation. Deep psychological and spiritual change processes take time. Depending on the kind of traumatisation and bonding disorder, different problems need to be the subject of discussion and careful scrutiny, which then works towards revealing the core trauma layer by layer. Through each successful therapeutic step new energy is freed for the next step.

I receive ongoing feedback from my clients about their development. This has taught me to ascertain what can and what cannot be realistically achieved by means of a constellation. Many clients report a surge of energy after a constellation, and then it must be understood that, depending on the particular central trauma, further previously split off personality parts may dare to emerge. For example a small, helpless child that can only express its emotional pain through illness may begin to show. After a good constellation experience a client is more able to deal with such new emergent parts. Whatever emotional experiences follow will point to the next therapeutic step. The client should be prepared in advance for the various phases that can take place after a constellation.

The following report stems from a client who originally did a constellation because of suffering from episodes of psychotic confusion. She has a therapist near her home and travels a great distance specifically to do her constellations. After one constellation she went through a phase in which other split-off personalities emerged. Because of her previous positive experiences in the constellation she was able to manage the crisis. The experience she gained from being a representative gave her the understanding that in the end only she could help herself. After the family entanglement that was the background to her psychosis had been clarified in two constellations, and she had worked through the bonding disorder with her mother and father, she then had the courage to deal with the trauma of her sexual abuse. She now takes more care of her mental and physical health than she did before, and feels that everything that she has been doing for her own health since her first constellation makes sense.

Case Study 56:

Going forwards step by step

"Two months have passed since the constellation in June, and I want to let you know what has happened for me in the meantime. Three or four days after my return ... I felt a real surge of energy which made me feel much more alive. About two or three weeks after the constellation I was really floored by a nasty 'flu which lasted 2–3 weeks, and which affected me psychologically when it resulted in a deep depression. Towards the end of this 'flu phase I felt so bad one afternoon that I went to my doctor's surgery and asked the receptionist if the doctor could give me a so-called emergency injection as I was feeling so bad psychologically. A distant acquaintance had once told me that he had been given an injection like this in a similar situation to tide him over. I was told that in acute situations an injection of "imap" was possible, but the receptionist could not explain what exactly it was. So I left the surgery to think it over and perhaps return. I went into the nearest chemist's and asked the assistant to look up "imap" on the computer. She explained that it was a neuroleptic. You can imagine that all my alarm bells started ringing when I heard the word 'neuroleptic'.

"I went home and rang my therapist, a friend and my brother, which gave me short-term relief. That evening I went to bed early and picked one of my many books (about Hawaiian shamans) and then went to sleep at around 4 a.m. As unbelievable as this might sound, reading that book calmed me down so much that the next day the crisis was over.

"In the meantime I've come to believe that the content of the book was immaterial. It probably could just as well have been one of my many other books. I now believe that above all else it was the shock of realising that I had nearly had myself injected with a neuroleptic, that I grasped perhaps subconsciously that nobody other than I myself could help me in this situation. I can't really judge the extent to which the June constellation played a role here, only that the constellation brought a great deal of movement into an image that had been completely frozen.

"Since then, in spite of a relatively stable basic state, I still have ups and downs from time to time. I have started applying for jobs and sorting out my affairs little by little. I am still bothered by the mess, which has reached enormous proportions over the last two years. But hopefully that can be sorted out step by step.

"I have calmed down a bit as far as the subject of men is concerned, that is, I am not so massively thrown off balance and can get a grip much more quickly. It's only sometimes when I really like a man that I suddenly feel intense physical restlessness/anxiety/fears, and then I think that after the next planned constellation in December this will get a lot better. Although I suspect that the constellation issue will work out far more complex than I can see at the moment, I am really eager to do this constellation. I suspect that the sexual and physical violence in my childhood has affected many more areas than just my love-life with men. Constellations like the ones that you do (greatest possible freedom for representatives and participants doing the constellation) I now hold to be the most effective method for emotional development. The danger in one-to-one therapy of the therapist muddling things with his own issues is reduced to practically nil in this method. In my current view I am fairly certain that doing the constellation with you and coming out of my pathogenic family enabled me to grasp the initiative to do something fundamental for my own mental and physical health."

In her next constellation she saw that the abuse by her father was rooted in the fact that neither he nor her mother had known who their own parents were. Neither of them had grown up with their own mother and neither knew their father. They had then expressed their helplessness and despair in their behaviour towards their children. Once these connections became clearer in the constellation, the client began to dare to feel loving feelings towards her parents.

10

Constellations in Therapy of Bonding Disorders and Trauma

On the level of the soul, people are multi-generational beings. Psychological and emotional illness arises, as a rule, in the context of more than one generation. Traumatic injuries evolve as an inability of the parents to form relationships and the resulting bonding disorder between parents and child. These bonding disorders hinder the development of a stable personality structure and further increase the risk of the person concerned suffering traumatic wounding themselves. A constellation can make visible in all its complexity the chain of traumatisation, bonding disorders and entangled relationships that lead to illness over several generations. Acknowledging the reality of these contexts helps us better understand the basic causes of psychological disorders.

Seeing oneself as part of a human bonding system from the outside as one does in a constellation can be very helpful for many people. The constellation greatly expands the possibilities for such awareness of ourselves by comparison with other available opportunities for obtaining open, honest and real feedback.

10.1 Therapy of Bonding Disorders

So can we also advocate constellations for use in therapy for serious psychological disorders? I am persuaded that this is possible so long as we are aware of the cross-generational association of trauma and bonding disorders. Using constellations for serious mental and emotional wounding, without an understanding of the structure and dynamics of psychological disorders and of entanglements of the psyche, will either fail to bring lasting therapeutic success or, in worse cases, produce greater confusion and exacerbate the problem.

Using "classic" family constellations in groups offers, in my experience, the best chance of healing the effects of loss trauma in the second and third generation. For example, when the mother of a client suffers because of the death of her brother in the war and identifies her son with this dead brother in that she gives him the same name, the resulting emotional entanglement is relatively easy to resolve for the client through a constellation. It provides him with an image and suggests an emotional impression of how a resolution of the identification with his uncle might be possible. The constellation offers a 'healing image' that can work in the client's soul. The way in which this happens is, amongst other things, through:

- looking at the other person,
- addressing the person by his or her name ("You are "X" the brother of my mother who died early."),
- the naming of this person's fate and its significance for others ("You died early and it was hard for my mother. She couldn't forget you. Her heart stayed with you."),
- presenting a positive relationship ("Please look on me and my life to come in a friendly light."),
- withdrawing with love and respect for the fate of this person,
- turning towards the mother and father.

The fundamental principle of this work is that it re-starts the frozen feelings flowing between people who are bonded. The essential goal in addressing loss trauma must be carrying through the grieving process in the family system to its conclusion, so that the way becomes free for the children to form a secure attachment with their parents. As long as the parent is tied emotionally to a person who is dead, they are unable to open their hearts fully to their children. Their feelings are frozen by their sense of deep pain. Their despair is often directed as an accusation towards the dead person for having deserted them. If these feelings can be seen and acknowledged, then ultimately love, warmth and joy in life can flow towards the children. In many cases this step is only successfully taken when the parents are able for the first time to turn towards their own parents, and because they can now sense love for themselves, they become freed in their feelings to turn fully towards their own children. For example, reconciliation is needed between the grandmother and her daughter in order for good feelings to flow from one to the other and thence to the granddaughter.

The success of the whole process is demonstrated, above all, by the client taking the first steps of his own accord to go towards his own parents. At the conclusion of a successful constellation, the client often lies sobbing in the arms of the representatives of his parents. The original love of the child for his parents and his inherent need for support and security from his parents are given a platform to express themselves through the constellation. The successful movement towards his parents forms the basis for him to become autonomous and to feel that he is a person in his own right. The parents' experiences, the cause of their suffering, can be left with them. The child no longer needs to be sad with them when they suffer, or to live in constant anxiety and worry that they need him to keep them alive, to keep them from leaving or dying. From out of the symbiosis of the 'we' arises the duality: 'I and you'.

Case Study 57 shows a successful development in the relationship between a client and her mother. The relationship was burdened because of several early deaths in the mother's family of origin. The client had internalised the suffering of her mother, which provided the only emotional access to her mother.

Case Study 57:

"It helps when you carry your own grief."

A client wrote me the following letter: "After our last session my mother rang me and asked how I was. I said: 'Things are not very good. I still feel very entangled with the dead children in our family.' She answered: 'I'm sorry that the whole burden has landed on you.' In a later conversation she said that she would like to take some of the load off my shoulders. I was amazed and said spontaneously: 'It will suffice if you carry your own grief.'

"I am happy that I can at last be honest with myself and with her, without feeling that this will overtax her and something bad will happen. It's wonderful how my mother has actually changed in reality."

The therapist or counsellor who supports people in shunning their parents, or even despising them, does them a disservice, especially when clients already expect people to judge their parents as they do; the therapist should not entangle herself in these cases. The rejection of our parents signifies a rejection of our own self or a core part of our self, because on a soul level every child's identity is composed of their mother and father. The therapist who disrespects the client's parents implicitly disrespects the client. Possibly she sees herself as a better father or a more caring mother for the client. In this way she unavoidably involves herself in the client's negative transference and becomes entangled with him. This gives rise to client dependency on the therapist and to prolonged therapy leading to unsuccessful outcomes.

The movement towards the parents is a gradual process of clearing and releasing particularly when the parents have not seen the child in his very being, ignored, injured and even tormented him. The hurt child within the client needs opportunities to express his anger and disappointment in relation to his parents. Only in this way can the way be cleared for peaceful feelings towards the parents. So a person should not be made to bow before his parents in a constellation for example, or visibly to subjugate himself in any way. In this I agree with the view of Hunter Beaumont: "When you speak to people about their negative experiences of constellations and really hear what they have to say about what was negative, it becomes clear: exactly this point is often misunderstood by the client. The 'you must' is not ... heard as an offer, but rather the super-ego is directly addressed and thereby clients feel constrained to subjugate themselves. This doesn't achieve anything. It only makes the situation worse" (Beaumont, Madelung, De Philipp and Schneider, 2004).

Turning towards our parents and thereby towards our own deepest self is the end result of a successful therapy. Thanking our parents for the gift of life that they have passed on to us can be a closing gesture of reconciliation and respect. It has not the least bit to do with subjugation. Keeping a respect even for those who mistreat and abuse others, will only happen when the therapist understands why people become perpetrators and how victims can themselves in turn become perpetrators. If the therapist makes judgements too quickly she will have no chance, in my opinion, of helping people with serious psychological injuries to overcome their often massive bonding disorders in relation to their parents.

However an accepting and non-judgemental stance sets a difficult challenge for the therapist. Sometimes the situation appears to be hopeless. The relationship between parent and child is totally frozen. But trust in therapeutic work can sometimes work miracles. Constellations can give access to powerful, persuasive energy for the soul to be able to act and move on.

Case Study 58:

"Thus our mother-daughter relationship has grown more genuine."

Vanessa originally sought therapeutic support for her professional problems. As she gradually admitted, these problems had their emotional roots in her early childhood experiences. There was, amongst other things, evidence of possible sexual interference. As became clear in more than one constellation, her mother had also possibly endured sexual abuse from her father. As these links became clearer, the client was in a position to re-establish the contact with her mother that had been broken off many years before. Overtures were made but the relationship remained as before full of tension and unsatisfying and bewildering.

At the request of the client I telephoned her mother. In this phone call I developed the impression that the mother's lack of response related to her guilt feelings and that she was avoiding a confrontation of her own psychological problems.

Vanessa did a further constellation, which showed that her mother's mother was possibly the child of an incestuous relationship between her father (the great grandfather of the client) and his daughter. As this secret came to light, an intensive encounter arose between the client, the representative of the mother and the representative of the grandmother in the constellation. Several months later Vanessa informed me of the following: "Today I had a very good encounter with my mother. Much has changed with her. In the meantime she has also done a constellation and seen the same things as revealed themselves in my constellation. And she not only saw all the problems but also how my representative and I were totally positive in our approach towards her. I had the impression that this experience with the constellation was very important to her. I could then tell her everything that came to light in my constellation. She accepted everything very calmly and with interest. Through our addressing the secret, our mother-daughter relationship has become, while not free from tension, at least more genuine."

A constellation cannot change another person than the client, for example a parent. The client may be able to see them from a different perspective and see aspects that previously were hidden from her. She may see the help and support that she requires in order to extricate herself from her trauma. We are more easily able to maintain contact with the part of our parent's personality that has remained healthy. A constellation set up by the child cannot remove the split in the structure of the parent's personality. This can only be achieved by the parent him or herself through their own therapy. But a constellation *can* enable the child to heal the negative and confused image she has of her parents and separate herself from their confusion. If therapeutic steps are to have a healthy effect then they must not idealise reality, instead setting forth clearly what was and is, and trusting the soul's positive movement to mourn the misfortune that is past and thereby find peace. With eyes focussed on a reality that is not idealised a person can discover her own strength and so begin to live her own life properly.

Case Study 59:

Living one's own life

Her entanglement with her grandmother had almost caused this client to go mad because she had become a substitute for a child of the grandmother's that was conceived through a rape and not allowed to live. After the resolution of this unhealthy entanglement, she recognised how little she herself had lived up to now. She also became aware of why she had adopted a child in addition to having three of her own. The adopted child represented her mother's sibling, the child who had not been allowed to live. The client felt as if she had lived through and for other people. "Now I see for the first time how, up to now, I have lived through my children." It now became painfully clear to her that she too had not been allowed to live her childhood. She was finally able to draw a line between herself and the needs and demands of others and to live her own life. Her daughter who, up to now, had tried to substitute for the client's mother could now also be released from her role.

10.2 Trauma Therapy

The movement towards the mother and the feeling of having a secure and supportive bond with her is often, in my experience, the most decisive step of all in therapy. However, with bonding trauma, and bonding system trauma in particular, this step is not easy to achieve. In either case it must initially be established what the issue within the family system is. The incidents or events that caused these traumas are as a rule denied, hidden and split off. A woman who has been sexually abused by her father cannot be expected to lie in her father's arms at the conclusion of a constellation. In the attempt to reconcile himself with his parents, a client who comes from a system with a guilty secret, might be confronted with such emotional confusion that, in the worst case, he succumbs to a psychotic episode. It is therefore essential before the constellation to have absolute clarity concerning the client's symptoms and history of illness. There is a pressing need for increased diagnostic ability amongst constellations facilitators. If it emerges that the client's symptoms of illness are linked to one or more forms of trauma then the procedure of a constellation must be adjusted accordingly. Only with this careful adjustment can constellations be an instrument of healing and relief, especially in cases of serious psychological disturbance.

The symptoms that prompt clients to seek therapy often turn out to be split off parts of their own personality as a result of traumatisation, or split off parts of the personality of the parent with whom the client is bonded. Anxiety, depression or physical complaints are the client's unconscious protective mechanisms against the flood of traumatic memories whether his or his parents'. He seeks therapy wishing to be free of the symptoms, while of course the process of the therapy opens him up to the dismantling of these protective mechanisms. So the purpose of a constellation is not to eradicate symptoms but rather to bring them to light together with their meaning and function. Only then do preferable solutions to the problem become clear.

Case Study 60:

Restlessness and sleeplessness

A client wanted to understand what the cause of her restlessness and difficulty with sleep were, that she had suffered since she was a child. A constellation crystallised the following for her: the function of her restlessness was to express her anxiety about her father who was at risk of suicide. Her hyperactive behaviour served to occupy her depressed father as an attempt to keep him alive.

In the constellation the representative for the restless part of her finally became peaceful when the representative for the father was able to move towards his own parents' representatives. This was made possible when the representative for his mother was released by another representative portraying her lack of feeling that had been caused by an earlier trauma.

If one allows the representatives in a constellation to express feelings freely one can relatively quickly arrive at the heart of the traumatic issue for the client and his family. If the facilitator does not appreciate this the constellation can lead to an uncontrolled re-traumatisation of the client. However if properly set up and interpreted with informed eyes this type of constellation can become a very specific variation of trauma therapy and a very effective method of psychotherapy, combining the healing of traumatic wounds and the resolution of entanglements at the soul level.

At present only a few therapists working with the constellations method are attempting to bring concepts of trauma to bear in their work, so we have to learn from others engaged with trauma work. Peter Levine and Fred Gallo are two prominent people who have developed trauma specific theory and derive their trauma therapy from this. (Appendix 5).

Constellations, provided they are consciously set up with this focus, embody many principles that prove to be effective in the various forms of trauma therapy:

- controlled re-playing of the trauma situation,
- the possibility of achieving distance from the trauma situation through the observation of representatives from the outside,
- making visible the splitting-up and splitting-off of the client's own personality,
- slowing down of the chronological re-playing of the trauma so that spontaneous dissociation from the trauma situation can be avoided,
- the provision of emotional resources,
- the building of healing images,
- the participation of the entire body in the transformation process,
- the gradual release of physical and emotional blocks,
- the possibility of spontaneous dispersal of energy,
- social support through a group of well-meaning people.

With clients who have themselves experienced trauma, the constellation must be meaningfully embedded within the totality of a trauma-specific treatment. In this way, overcoming the trauma in cases of complex traumatisation can proceed successfully via a combination of individual and group therapeutic measures and assistance. In this, it is essential that the bonding disorder be kept in view as much as the trauma experience. In cases of complex traumatisation, which may stretch over several generations, an isolated treatment of the bonding disorder would be just as inadequate as an exclusive concentration on overcoming the individual trauma experience itself. Both must come together. The disentangling of traumatic injuries from the bond with the father succeeds, in my experience, only when the client has clarified and healed the bond to the mother. So sexual abuse can mostly only be worked on when the broken trust in the mother has had a chance to re-establish itself.

Control and Trust

Trauma therapy makes a paradoxical demand on clients. They must give up their attempts at control and dissociation from the trauma memory, which, up to this point, was the only strategy they thought helpful. Many clients with trauma experiences find giving up their mistrust and control strategies extremely threatening. They link the abandonment of these strategies directly with powerlessness and the surrendering of the self. They have to learn that their defence and withdrawal strategies cannot help them any more; letting go of these strategies in therapy doesn't mean a repetition of the powerlessness of the original trauma situation, but rather represents the only real chance of healing and appropriately controlling their inner processes themselves. Only then can they accept the support offered that would help them take charge of their chaotic feelings.

The Constellations Process in Bonding Trauma Situations

The most important pre-condition for working with a client with serious bonding disorders and psychological injuries, apart from their readiness to change their situation, is enough stability and support. I question clients thoroughly as to whether they feel able to handle what may come to light or

290

whether there is something they still need to put in place in order to get to grips with their trauma. When they are ready for the next step I ask them about their concerns and keep these in mind as the focus of the constellation.

In the setting up of a constellation the client lays out what he wishes to look at and what he feels able to handle. He signals the start and defines when it is enough for him. During the constellation the therapist must keep the client in mind and recognise whether he is involved or not. The behaviour of the representatives will show if the client dissociates, in which case the constellation should be interrupted and the therapist should discuss with the client how to proceed. Is this the right point at which to stop or is there further work that can be done? In this way the client learns to recognise the point at which he bails out and dissociates from his feelings.

As a rule I start the constellation with a representative for the client and a representative for the problem (for example a headache). In most cases it becomes clear that the headache for example is connected to other physical and emotional symptoms, and often represents an in-between symptom that acts as a barrier between the traumatised and the untraumatised parts of the personality. Next I ask the client to choose representatives for the symptoms that have emerged from the statements of the first representative. By this process the client has many representations in the constellation. The various parts of the personality are separated from each other due to the trauma, and will not be in good contact with each other. The focus is to clarify the function of these different parts and the nature of their relationship with each other.

In this way, a dynamic procedure takes place in which the representatives of the symptoms go through a process of change. Step by step the trauma that lies at the root of the client's symptoms becomes visible, along with the people in the client's bonding system who are involved. This gives rise to a complex formation of the representatives of people and parts of their personality, which helps in understanding the traumatic event as it affects the intra- and inter-personal dynamics, and in its symptomatic compensatory forms. At the same time a process of change is set in motion by the interactions of the representatives between themselves, in which the client can participate as he observes and comments from outside the constellation. The extent to which this occurs can be checked out by visual contact with the client and questioning after the constellation ends.

At the conclusion of such a constellations process, the split off parts of the client's personality should have a better connection with each other, and be able to support and stabilise each other. The trauma feelings that have been taken on by the client should have been reassigned to the person to whom they originally belonged.

A process such as this takes time and may last between 90 and 120 minutes. Measured against a life to date which may have involved many seemingly fruitless attempts at freeing oneself from difficult symptoms, without ever realising that they were rooted in trauma and serious bonding disorder, this is a very short amount of time. Serious traumatisation and bonding disorders will not be healed in one constellation, but as long as the work heads in the right direction, every step is valuable. An image still stays in my memory, for example, of the constellation of an experienced psychotherapist who, through this work, was ready and able, for the first time in her life, to look at her sexual abuse without plummeting into blind activity and fury at her feeling of vulnerability, or, finding all restriction unbearable, into her impulse to flee from confrontation with the reality of her soul.

Principles of the method
When discussing this type of method, the following principles are important:

- The client lays out the limits as to how far the therapeutic work can proceed at that moment in relation to whatever she has identified as the issue for the constellation. Only in the context of the resources that support her and a sense of safety in that moment will she be able to risk something new, something that may initially cause her anxiety and panic.

- She must be able to cut short the constellation at any time, or to withdraw if her anxiety as an observer threatens to overwhelm her.

- The participants in the group must have the freedom to decide whether they wish to take on the role of representative or not. The facilitator should inform them that they may get out of their role at any time if it becomes too stressful for them.

- The representatives must be completely free to say everything that they feel, and to move in the space as their impulse takes them.

- Representatives must undertake not to act out violence towards other representatives.

- The suggestions of the representatives should take precedence over the facilitator's hypotheses.

- Sentences that have been given by the facilitator are suggestions only, which do not have to be repeated by the representatives and which they may change around at any time, as seems appropriate to them.

- The most important task of the facilitator is to keep the process free of outside disturbance for the representatives. He or she must keep the process in motion through the addition of further representatives, in such a way that, on the one hand, the trauma and bonding disorders can be clearly recognised while on the other, resolutions for the different emotional conflicts can gradually unfold.

- A particular task of the facilitator is to intervene with appropriate suggestions that will support the client at appropriate times.

- The facilitator must keep in contact with the client at all times, and be aware as to whether the constellation that is unfolding is useful for her or not.

Trauma and serious bonding disorder put people in a vulnerable and helpless state. Therapy should therefore aim to help them regain control of their lives, their thoughts and feelings. The sufferer must see the split-off parts of his personality and enter into emotional contact with them in the most anxiety-free way possible. In order to re-enter into a traumatic situation involving uncontrollable feelings, a client will only give up his mistrust in an atmosphere of the greatest possible safety. He needs a context in which his self-protective instinct can take a step back, in which he can relax his body and tolerate new perceptions and experiences of relationship. In addition he needs to trust his therapist, the group and the method. Nothing crucial can occur without this basic trust. The client must know that he has a choice: he can remain in his usual state or he can decide to risk something new. Only when he himself, and no one else, resolves to risk a step towards change, does the full responsibility that he carries for the decision enable him to grow.

Therapeutic trauma constellations work is therefore not compatible with an authoritative and strongly confrontational style of facilitation; at the same time the renunciation of psychiatric, psychological and psychotherapeutic theory and their substitution with philosophical, religious and spiritual frameworks of thinking are also not helpful. Philosophical knowledge and spiritual understanding do not in themselves heal traumatic injuries, even if the perception of a greater or wider context is ultimately indispensable for opening up the space we need in order to release ourselves from the obsessions and restrictions created by our attempt at managing our trauma.

Therapy for Sexual Abuse

Therapists need to pay particular attention to the complex entanglements occurring in cases of sexual abuse, which has such a strong taboo attached to it that, even in psychotherapy, we may choose other apparently more easily handled symptoms as the central focus of the therapy, rather than engaging with the client's sexual abuse. The client, who is often already uncertain about her buried memories, unfortunately then gets the impression that her experiences of abuse must not be significant if they are not addressed, or are pushed aside, even by an experienced therapist. Diminishing the abuse ignores its ability to traumatise and fosters illusions about how easily its severe consequences may be overcome.

If the therapist is afraid of the entangled dynamics of sexual abuse then the client will also become afraid and be unable to open up; on the other hand, the over–dramatisation of the abuse by the therapist is also not helpful and indicates a lack of understanding of the issues.

The necessity of addressing sexual abuse openly must be combined with a consideration of the client's damaged boundaries in relation to shame and of what resources he or she may have for trauma integration. For example, the therapist should not exert pressure if abuse has not been mentioned by the client, even when she has well-founded reasons for believing that an experience of abuse is at issue. The appropriate healing step is to find and confirm the truth: if the sexual abuse did take place or not. If it took place then the client should be able to say overtly what was dreadful about that. The abused victim always remains innocent of the event even if the child may feel guilty. Their love for their parents must be respected, their anxiety and worry about preserving the family system must be acknowledged.

Entangled feelings need time to resolve themselves through a recognition of the realities of the whole family system. For example the client may come to recognise how, as a child, he unconsciously became entangled in the traumatised relationship of his parents. Responsibility for the abuse of a child of course remains with the perpetrator, and his act cannot be excused or diminished, even if it is the consequence of his own traumatisation. Accordingly at some stage the client must fully understand the guilt of the perpetrator and others who hold some responsibility even when he feels love and compassion for them.

It takes an enormous weight off the shoulders of an abused

child if the perpetrator takes responsibility for their actions, particularly when it is the child's own father. Unfortunately few people who have been responsible for sexual abuse are capable of this: to admit to the act and say to the child, "I am sorry, and you are not responsible in anyway". If this were possible then there might possibly be a chance of the relationship between perpetrator and victim being put straight again. If the perpetrator on his part is able to clarify his own disturbed bonding with his mother, which is likely to be part of the underlying causality, then there is a greater chance of his taking appropriate responsibility for his actions.

The client is not always simply a victim, often being split within him or herself, there being parts of him or her that excuse the abuse, or even actively contrive it. It is exactly this 'perpetrator loyalty' in the victim that needs to be brought to light in therapy for them to be able to change (Huber 2003b). Only in this way can a client:

- relinquish his or her inappropriate feelings of guilt to the perpetrator,
- relinquish his or her tendency to self punishment,
- withdraw from those people who are no good for them,
- develop healthy contact with other people little by little.

This work, including the 'perpetrator loyalty' issue, generally succeeds well in constellations.

Case Study 61:

"Life may just simply be."

We have discussed Laura and her experiences of trauma and the trauma within her family system many times in this book. It is only because Laura doesn't give up that she is able, step by step, to gradually free herself from her wounds and entanglements: "Through the individual sessions, that were of the greatest importance for my safety and protection, fragments of the trauma came to light. Like pieces of a great puzzle, smells, feelings and images appeared, quite independently of each other. It was in the family constellation that the pieces of the puzzle first fitted together as a whole, and I began to understand. The constellation work gave me the opportunity once again to enter into the experience and feel the pain and sorrow. Only then did I realise that I could trust my feelings. Even if the scars remain in my soul for a lifetime, the feeling of being bad, worthless, unworthy of love and guilty has come to an end. The constellation work revealed the cause of my anxiety, panic attacks, crying fits, my tendency to demand too much of myself and my thoughts of suicide. I could also recognise the repeated pattern within my family system: the chronic sexual abuse of my grandmother, the missing bond between my parents and their respective mothers, who were traumatised themselves.

"My whole life took on a different quality. All at once the perpetual stress stopped and clarity emerged that I had never known before. I have suddenly realised that life may just simply be and I don't need to fight every day against windmills. I can better listen to and sense inner peace. My constant companions were headaches, sadness and a frequent trance like state. They have increasingly bidden me farewell."

The following is Laura's description of a process that she experienced during and after a constellation: "In one constellation the little, helpless child in me surfaced and I could really only see the ruins that lay in front of me. I had panic anxiety and the feeling that I couldn't bear myself any longer. It was very helpful that some one sitting next to me was able to support me. Buried images, feelings and sentences once heard, came to the surface. I have managed quite well to cope with this. I have allowed the deep pain. Amongst the many alter-personalities there is a therapist in me. I am now much better. I still swing up and down acutely but I can cope with this."

At the same time Laura sees that her own therapy is the

most effective therapy for her children: "I also have the feeling at last that I am not at the mercy of life and that I can really protect my children. I am happy that I have gone along this path. Only in this way could I save my son for whom I felt such anxiety. Years of therapy did nothing for him. After I had worked on myself, his psychotic outbreaks, aggression, depression and permanent talk of suicide ceased step by step. He is now a completely changed person, who can laugh, find fun in life, and approach other people. His mental and emotional as well as his physical symptoms had made a normal school day all but impossible. The somatic complaints such as stomach-ache, constant nausea, vomiting and diarrhoea have now vanished."

Often further traumas lie behind sexual abuse within the family. Disclosure of the transgenerational entanglements in trauma processes, in the course of constellations, creates a better understanding of these unconscious dynamics. Sexual abuse can thereby take its appropriate place in the entirety of what has happened in a family. The relationships between men and women and between parents and children have often been violent and confused for generations. There are children from incestuous relationships and children who have been secretly given away or even murdered. Children are often not allowed to know who their real mother or father is. No one is then in their right place in the bonding system. Parents become children and children become parents. There are no healthy boundaries only symbiotic fusion on a soul level in a tangle of anxiety, anger, shame, guilt and powerlessness. Out of such victims grow perpetrators, who in turn create new victims.

Overcoming the multi-faceted physical, mental and emotional consequences of sexual abuse requires as a rule, intensive psychotherapeutic and trauma-therapeutic work and the process usually takes several years. Clients must learn to speak openly about the abuse and to accept that the manifold problems that they have experienced in life up to now have a causal relationship to the abuse. Thus they learn, step by step to assign their physical and psychological symptoms and their relationship difficulties to the nature of the sexual abuse. Gradually they can recognise:

- the extent to which they have up to now oscillated backwards and forwards between pushing aside and running away and plunging into feelings of anxiety and vulnerability;
- how effectively their mechanisms have functioned in separating them from their feelings;
- how much they now have to struggle to reconnect with themselves and their feelings, demanding too much of themselves as a result, and falling into escape or addictive processes.

The process of regaining a stronger sense of self can be very painful as clients gradually come to recognise how little they were in contact with their feelings, their bodies, other people and their surroundings in their previous life. Clients, who already have children of their own, begin to have a sense too of how much they have expected of their children, and still expect of them in terms of colluding with their attempts to repress the memories of the sexual abuse. Concern about the well-being of one's child can be a great motivator in inducing one to confront one's painful past. When clients learn to treat themselves with love more, this allows the love to flow to their children. The release of anxiety and energy blocks in the body can be supported by appropriate physical treatments such as massage and yoga. In this way clients gradually learn to withstand a reversion to old patterns of entanglement and can use the energy that is freed up from repressing the trauma for further work. The reading of books, as 'Ways to Self-healing' demonstrates, can be helpful in this process (Bass and Davis, 2004).

Coming to Terms with Reality

Trauma results in reality disappearing into the unconscious. Trauma therapy therefore means reconstructing this missing reality and bringing it into consciousness again, a reclaiming of reality. Everything that takes place in reality appears in a constellation. To work with people who suffer from serious psychological problems, one must understand that it is the reality that vanished through experiences of trauma and later come to the surface that must be looked in the eye. I have more than once seen how a client's symptoms originated from the madness of a satanic cult or a Nazi crime – unimaginable to many people. The effects of ritual violence or Nazi crimes are so devastating at the level of the soul that they have powerful effects over many generations. Only when the victims of such madness receive affirmation that someone has done something terrible to them, and that it is not they who are crazy but the perpetrators, is it possible for a healing process to begin in the soul. Constellations groups can constitute a form of sympathetic public forum where the truth can be affirmed for the victim. They can achieve a lot for the victim in the confirmation that they are believed and in supporting them to feel what is normal and what is not. The client can learn within a group of people who are also prepared to confront socially repressed realities, once again to trust her own perceptions and feelings.

The Courage to Unlock the Secret

Dealing with trauma in bonding systems represents a special challenge, often being concerned with secrets that have been guarded by generations to protect themselves and in the belief that this would also protect their descendents from social disgrace. What then can provide a motive to reveal such a secret? It appears, and has been shown to me in many constellations, that the only motive is love for children and grand children. Only when the keepers of the secret can see clearly that silencing the truth does not help their descendents but harms them greatly, can they be induced to speak. This can happen in a constellation; as it unfolds in the constellation that there is a secret in the family, I often let the client go towards the representative of the keeper of the secret. The client can then reassure the keeper of the secret that it is only by revealing the secret that he, the client, can be helped to overcome his grave psychological problems. If the client himself is ready for the secret to be revealed and can feel love for the keeper of the secret then, in my experience, whatever is most important will unfold. Everything that has significance for the client in the bonding system is held in the client's soul, and at the deepest part of himself it is ultimately his decision whether a secret should come to light or not.

I have developed this process in such a way because I suspect that what is often lacking is the permission to know something consciously; that we all know everything that is significant to us in our soul, we just don't have conscious access to it. I work with the hypothesis that anyone who is ready can discover through a constellation the things that are essential for the rehabilitation of their soul. In my opinion, in the search for truth a client cannot be at variance with her family system. By bringing the truth to light she serves everyone in the system in the depths of their souls and lays to rest old traumas. She interrupts unhealthy practices, unresolved problems and emotional confusion that otherwise simply extend their reach down from generation to generation and pull others into the same abyss.

11
Future Considerations

My work with constellations makes it increasingly clear to me that current psychotherapeutic theories only touch the surface of our exceptionally complex emotional and mental processes. If we talk about psychological problems we must, in my opinion, initially discuss the realities that cause these problems and which severely damage bondings between parents and children. It is only after that that we can consider the person's intra-psychic or physiological attempts to cope with the consequences. Symptoms, which are the manifestations of coping with trauma and bonding disorders, are visible signs and pointers to the nature of the underlying injuries and entanglements. Symptoms in this sense are not illnesses to be done away with by whatever therapy so that the client may be healthy again. Some symptoms are, for example, the only, albeit totally confused, emotional bridge that connects a child with his mother at the level of the bonded soul. Some symptoms can be seen as attempts at self-healing, the better to come to terms with traumatic experiences through dissociative processes. Symptoms therefore have a creative aspect to them, which are for us to understand. Even, say, the self-destructive behaviour of an abused child makes sense when it is seen as a protective measure. A person who can no longer feel anything and inwardly shuts down might be protecting himself from a situation in which his repressed hate expresses itself in a more extreme way, for example, by committing murder or suicide. To become mentally and emotionally healthy is therefore not a question of fighting or suppressing symptoms, but rather of transforming those symptoms which have arisen, in a process of common recognition, understanding and mutual support.

With the concept of multi-generational systemic psycho-traumatology I am trying to articulate these connections. A start has been made, but the voyage of discovery is certainly not at an end. There are many discoveries still to be made concerning the soul, the mind and the emotions. Socially accepted theories of "psychological illness" and the way they are handled constitute a yardstick of the openness with which individuals in a society face themselves and others, and are in a position to realistically see and reflect on their own humanity. Currently problems and realities in many places are still veiled by ideologies, which are tied to questions of power, ideological and economic interests. Even in science and psychotherapeutic practice there are often considerable restraints in dealing with realities, and thus with coming to grips with the traumatic life experiences of clients and the unambiguous identification and clarification of the often hopeless entanglements between men and women, and parents and children.

For the situation to change, besides greater theoretical clarity about the causes of serious emotional illness, new systems of assistance will have to emerge to enable emotional growth from trauma and bonding entanglements accumulated over generations, with greater readiness to face the profound individual and social consequences of trauma and bonding disorders. Also professional helper groups, who normally themselves suffer with trauma and bonding disorders, must initially go through the experience of coping better with their own trauma. It is only then that they can seriously recommend or give this type of help to clients: help that has helped them out of their own constrictions of their soul.

I am increasingly convinced, from my work with seriously

psychologically disturbed clients, that if everyone were able to speak about what turns them into perpetrators or victims (something that is often relegated to the unspeakable), then psychiatry in its current form would soon become redundant. And if parents could succeed in facing and resolving their own traumas and entanglements, that would be the best possible therapy for their own children. At the same time it would also be the most effective preventative measure for sparing the next generation hate, despair, instability, confusion and violence.

Considering the supreme importance of secure maternal bonding for the healthy emotional development of a child, society should do everything conceivable to create circumstances that are stress and anxiety free for mothers and newborn infants. That is the primary preventative measure for avoiding mental and emotional disorders, violence and crime. The provision of secure bonding for a child is more important than the existence of doctors, psychiatrists, teachers, social workers, policemen or judges for secure and healthy social relations.

Shared concern and engagement with the causes of psychological injuries, entanglements and their trans-generational after-effects, as expressed in the constellations work of small groups of individuals willing to change, can in my opinion, create a new consciousness for the flourishing and creative living together of men and women, parents and children and people in society.

What we do today can still have an impact in a hundred years' time. We bear the responsibility for good as well as bad. We should jointly re-align the polarities of man and woman, perpetrator and victim, power and impotence, in order to find new solutions. To understand perpetrators helps victims. To acknowledge helplessness allows an opening for help. Truth makes madness disappear. Love heals injuries of the soul. Healing only happens when the soul is really touched.

Appendices

Appendix 1: Post Traumatic Stress Disorder – DSM IV 309.81

A. The person has been exposed to a traumatic event in which both of the following have been present:

(1) the person experienced, witnessed, or was confronted with an event or events that involved actual or threatened death or serious injury, or a threat to the physical integrity of self or others (2) the person's response involved intense fear, helplessness, or horror. **Note:** In children, this may be expressed instead by disorganized or agitated behavior.

B. The traumatic event is persistently re-experienced in one (or more) of the following ways:

(1) recurrent and intrusive distressing recollections of the event, including images, thoughts, or perceptions. **Note:** In young children, repetitive play may occur in which themes or aspects of the trauma are expressed.
(2) recurrent distressing dreams of the event. **Note:** In children, there may be frightening dreams without recognizable content.

305

(3) acting or feeling as if the traumatic event were recurring (includes a sense of reliving the experience, illusions, hallucinations, and dissociative flashback episodes, including those that occur upon awakening or when intoxicated). **Note:** In young children, trauma-specific re-enactment may occur.

(4) intense psychological distress at exposure to internal or external cues that symbolize or resemble an aspect of the traumatic event.

(5) physiological reactivity on exposure to internal or external cues that symbolize or resemble an aspect of the traumatic event.

C. Persistent avoidance of stimuli associated with the trauma and numbing of general responsiveness (not present before the trauma), as indicated by three (or more) of the following:

(1) efforts to avoid thoughts, feelings, or conversations associated with the trauma

(2) efforts to avoid activities, places, or people that arouse recollections of the trauma

(3) inability to recall an important aspect of the trauma

(4) markedly diminished interest or participation in significant activities

(5) feeling of detachment or estrangement from others

(6) restricted range of affect (e.g., unable to have loving feelings)

(7) sense of a foreshortened future (e.g., does not expect to have a career, marriage, children, or a normal life span)

D. Persistent symptoms of increased arousal (not present before the trauma), as indicated by two (or more) of the following:

(1) difficulty falling or staying asleep

(2) irritability or outbursts of anger

(3) difficulty concentrating

(4) hypervigilance
(5) exaggerated startle response
(American Psychiatric Association, 1994)

Appendix 2: Panic Disorder – DSM IV 300.01
Panic attacks are not currently a coded disorder. The DSM IV describes a panic disorder as a clearly defined episode of intense anxiety and uneasiness in which at least four of the following named symptoms abruptly occur, reaching a high point within ten minutes:

(1) Palpitations, heart pounding or accelerated heart beat
(2) Sweating
(3) Trembling or shaking
(4) Shortness of breath or smothering
(5) Feeling of choking
(6) Chest pain or discomfort
(7) Nausea or abdominal distress
(8) Dizziness, unsteadiness, light-headedness, faint
(9) Derealisation (feelings of unreality) or depersonalisation (feeling detached from oneself)
(10) Feelings of losing of control or going mad
(11) Fear of dying
(12) Parasthesias (numbness or tingling sensations)
(13) Hot flushes or cold shudders.

Although a panic attack as a rule reaches a high point within ten minutes, it may take hours for the person to feel back to normal (American Psychiatric Association, 1994).

Appendix 3: Depression
In ICD-10 (Dilling, Mombour and Schmidt 1993, s. 139ff.) a distinction is made between light, middle grade and severe (with and without psychotic symptoms) episodes of depression. "The indications of a depressive episode (F 32) are: ... low spirits, loss of interest, joylessness, reduction in drive, reduction in energy, heightened fatigue, diminished level of activity. Other common symptoms are:

- Reduced concentration and attention
- Reduced self-esteem and self-confidence
- Feelings of guilt and worthlessness (even in light depressive episodes)
- Negative and pessimistic perspective on the future
- Thoughts of suicide, self-harming and attempted suicides
- Disturbed sleep
- Low appetite."

(World Health Organization, 1992)

Appendix 4: Dissent among Experts as to the Gruesome Reality of the Concentration Camps

"In Germany of all places concentration camp victims were for many years denied the acknowledgement that their suffering was occasioned by trauma. The accepted opinion of academics referred to the work of Bonhoeffer and Stier (1926) and to a fundamental decision of the Third Reich's insurance office ... according to which a traumatic neurosis did not fall into a category that warranted disability benefit because it was accepted that a person's psyche could restore itself in practically limitless ways after psychological stress. Similar theses were still being advocated in 1982 by the behavioural biologist Hemminger.

"In the sixties this resulted in dissent between experts in Germany (documented by Pross 1988). Several experts began to distance themselves gradually from the prevailing academic opinion that traumatic disturbances were either genetically determined or merely the inventions of scroungers, and to acknowledge the intolerable reality of the concentration camps and their long-term traumatising effects. These included Wetzlaff (1958, 1963), who correctly described the aggravating symptomatic as 'experience reactive personality change'" (Fischer and Riedesser, 1999).

Today it is a matter of scientific certainty that the concentration camp prisoners found themselves in a traumatising situation. Many people died or killed themselves while on the way to the camps because the threat and the fear of death were so menacing. For some the survival strategy involved acting as underlings for the Nazis to order about. They supervised, frightened and murdered the camp inmates. 'Identification with the aggressor' and putting oneself entirely in his or her power are survival mechanisms that have also been observed in existentially threatening situations, for example among hostage victims.

Other concentration camp prisoners managed to survive from one hour to the next through encystment in the "state of an automaton". Not thinking, not feeling but only doing what was asked of them – for many this was the only possibility if they were to avoid dying immediately or exposing themselves to the danger of being summarily murdered. This encystment is not a passive process. It requires enormous psychic energy to bring about such a task of adaptation in such an extreme situation. This became clear when people no longer managed to keep up the performance: "After several months of imprisonment in the concentration camp, dying took on a different and ever more frequently encountered form: this was the development into a so-called 'Muselmann' state.* With the first cases of death in the camp, it was the trauma that had lead immediately to death, a pattern that is wide spread in the animal kingdom (Meerlo, 1959; Seligmen, 1975). In the case of a 'Muselmann', on the other hand, death first arose when the collected emotional resources became exhausted; the process of dying followed an observable pattern, in which the behaviour necessary for survival was given up. Occasionally these people became gripped by an unfocused outbreak of anger when faced with imminent death, directed at any one who happened to be nearby regardless" (Krystal and Farms, 2000, p. 845).

The most important protection against premature death proved to be the maintenance of relationships between people in the concentration camps. Those who did not focus entirely

---

* A Nazi concentration camp term for a prisoner suffering from extreme starvation.

on their own survival but rather, were prepared to share what little there was with others, could also count on the loyalty of others. The backing of a group, which preserved a sense of belonging, helped many to endure the extreme situation.

After liberation, the survivors of the concentration camps had to survive survival. Many had a sense of survival guilt, which is a deep feeling of guilt in relation to those others who had not survived – in relation to their dependents, friends and companions. They were apathetic, inwardly frozen, they withdrew and could no longer find pleasure in anything. Again and again they were overcome by fear and states of agitation. Images of their dreadful experiences flooded in and could not be suppressed. Many lapsed partially into states resembling psychosis and had the feeling that they were still in the camp and still being persecuted.

In the case of Jewish survivors of the National Socialist genocide we can see the attempts that were undertaken on a collective level to cope with an existential trauma. So in the first instance there was an impulse among the survivors to gather together again. The families and dependents who remained tried to find each other again. Then, together with their surviving companions, fixed groups were formed, which offered mutual stability and support. Marriage contracts were hurriedly arranged, primarily between the survivors. The trauma of persecution was talked through again and again within familiar and trusted circles and in this way an attempt was made to reconstruct and to emotionally integrate it. Words often failed however, and silence reigned. Non-verbal communication was sufficiently eloquent for those who understood the message. But this locked the memories in nonetheless and there remained things that no one spoke about (Grünberg, 2000).

Appendix 5: Trauma Theories and Trauma Therapy
There is no unified provision of trauma therapy. Different authors develop distinct views on trauma and derive their current trauma therapy procedures from these:

- Peter Levine starts from the point of view that a trauma situation mobilises a great deal of stress energy that cannot be utilised. These energy excesses become frozen in a trauma situation into numbness and immobility ("shock"). Levine refers to observations of animals that show how, when faced with the danger of death, an animal will fall into a state of numbness. If it survives, however, it will use up the excess of energy in violent muscle movements, for example in shivering. If the dispersal of this energy after a trauma situation is blocked, then, according to Levine, the numbing reaction becomes fixed, the alarm reaction continues and the result is a persistent anxiety block. "The 'freezing' reaction in animals is usually limited. With people it is much harder to release the state of numbness, because the mobilised energy is bound up in the nervous system of the client through anxiety. A vicious circle is created that hinders the natural cessation of the 'freezing' reaction. In the same way that terror and anger have played a role in the numbing reaction, so they also have a hand in sustaining it later on – even though there no longer exists any real threat" (Levine, 1998). The transformation of the trauma experience can be brought about, according to Levine's experience, if the person is again brought in touch with the original trauma situation and the immobilisation reaction on a physical level is brought to an end. "Somatic experience is a gentle, gradual method of transforming a trauma. With the help of a holistic inner awareness, the controlling energies that are bound up in the trauma symptoms can be mobilised. This process resembles the successive layers of an onion, which, as they are removed, reveal the traumatised heart" (ibid.). In my opinion Peter Levine's assessment has most bearing on existential traumas where the aspects of bonding and relationship are not so prominent.
- Francine Shapiro, according to her own assertions, discovered quite accidentally how movement of the eyes

to and fro can make stressful feelings disappear. She developed a method on this basis, which she called 'Eye movement and desensitisation and reprocessing' (EMDR) (Shapiro and Forrest, 1998). The method quickly gained a worldwide following (Manfield, 2000). She became acknowledged among experts (Lamprecht, 2003). "EMDR not only allows people to recover from their trauma but guides them as well to a feeling of joy, openness and deep connection with themselves and their lives. The development of EMDR is a real quantum leap in relation to the healing of trauma and dysfunctional fixations" (Parnell, 1999). This method too seems to have the greatest success in the treatment of mono-traumas, that is, for example, one-off existential traumas.

- Adherents have also found methods that relate to the energetic paradigm of psychology and to the hypothesis of interpreting psychological problems as manifestations of energy interruptions in the body (Gallo, 2000). According to these, it is then attempted in therapy to release these energy blocks, for example by putting pressure with the finger on supposed meridian points in a specific order (Kaufmann, 2002).
- Gottfried Fischer, Professor at the University of Cologne and editor of the periodical for Psychotraumatology, Science of Psychotherapy and Psychological Medicine, is working on a comprehensive psychodynamic understanding of the causes and consequences of trauma and the possibility of overcoming them. Together with Peter Riedesser he has written a manual on psycho-traumatology that, to my eyes, points the way (Fischer and Reidesser, 1998). He has also developed a detailed therapy manual on the treatment of psycho-traumatic disturbance, which is being tested practically in a clinic (Fischer, 2000; Bering, Horn, Spiess and Fischer, 2003).
- Worthy of mention too are trauma-specific therapy assessments in the tradition of hypnotherapeutic concepts. Maggie Phillips and Claire Frederick have gathered an

abundance of important findings through professional contact with so-called dissociative images of disturbance, which pay particular attention to the outcomes of the processes of splitting on a soul level in the client (Phillips and Frederick, 2003).

- Finally, as an eminent trauma specialist, Michaela Huber should be mentioned. She has been instrumental in bringing about a better understanding of extreme trauma-tisation in victims of sexual and ritual violence and makes full use of her many experiences in the treatment of such cases (Huber, 1998). She pays particular attention to the existence of the so-called perpetrator-introjects in the victims of sexual and sadistic violence that hinder or scupper the success of therapy over long periods. In both her published works she sets out established concepts in an attempt at providing a better understanding of the causes and consequences of trauma. She describes a number of tested trauma specific treatment techniques (Huber, 2003a, 2003b).

The body of trauma-specific literature is increasing. The classic texts, that have come primarily from the United States (Herman, 2003; Putnam, 2003; van der Kolk, McFarlane and Weisaeth, 2000), can now be supplemented with a list of publications from other researchers and psychotherapists (amongst others Eckhardt-Henn and Hoffman, 2004; Hirsch, 2004; Reddemann, 2004; Sachse, 2004). Successful practitioners are in a position to make a suitable choice from the body of different theories and methods (e.g. Kraemer, 2003).

Bibliography

Abraham, N. & Torok, M. (1994). The Shell and the Kernel. Chicago: Chicago University Press.

Ainsworth, M. (1973). The Development of Infant-Mother Attachment. In B. M. Caldwell & H. N. Ricciuti (eds.), Review of Child Development Research (vol. 3). Chicago: University of Chicago Press.

American Psychiatric Association (1994) (ed.). Diagnostic and Statistical Manual of Mental Disorders (4th edition). Washington, DC: APA.

Antonovsky, A. (1979). Health, Stress and Coping: New Perspectives on Mental and Physical Well-being. San Francisco: Jossey-Bass Wiley.

Antonovsky, A. (1987). Unravelling the Mystery of Health: How People Manage Stress and Stay Well. San Francisco: Jossey-Bass Wiley.

Bäuml, J. (1994). Psychosen aus dem schizophrenen Formenkreis. Ein Ratgeber für Patienten und Angehörige. Heidelberg: Springer Verlag.

Bäuerle, S. & Moll-Strobel, H. (2001). Eltern sägen ihr Kind entzwei. Trennungserfahrungen und Entfremdung von einem Elternteil. Donauwörth: Auer Verlag.

Bauer, J. (2005). Warum ich fühle, was du fühlst. Intuitive Kommunikation und das Geheimnis der Spiegelneurone.

Hamburg. Hoffmann und Campe.

Bar-On, D. (2003). Die Last des Schweigens. Gespräche mit Kindern von NS-Tätern. Hamburg: edition Körber-Stiftung.

Bass, E. & Davis, L. (2004). The courage to heal. A guide for women survivors of child sexual abuse. New York: Harper & Row Publishers.

Bauer, J. (2002). Das Gedächtnis des Körpers. Wie Beziehungen und Lebensstile unsere Gene steuern. Frankfurt/M.: Eichborn Verlag.

Bateson, G., Jackson, D., Haley, J. & Weakland, J. (1956). Toward a Theory of Schizophrenia. Behavioral Science, 1, 251–264.

Baxa, G., Essen, C., Kreszmeier, A. (Hrsg.) (2004). Verkörperungen. Heidelberg: Carl-Auer-Systeme Verlag.

Beaumont, H., Madelung, E., De Philipp, W. & Schneider, J. R. (2004). Gespräch zum Thema »Die Verneigung«. Praxis der Systemaufstellung, 1, 36–41.

Bentall, R. B. (2004). Madness Explained. Psychosis and Human Nature. London: Penguin Books.

Bering, R., Fischer, G.& Johansen, F.F. (2005). Neurobiologie der Posttraumatischen Belastungsstörung im Vier-Ebenen-Modell. Zeitschrift für Psychotraumatologie und Psychologische Medizin, 2, S. 7–18.

Bering, R., Horn, A., Spieß, R. & Fischer, G. (2003). Forschungsergebnisse zur Mehrdimensionalen Psychodynamischen Traumatherapie (MPTT) im multiprofessionellen Setting. Zeitschrift für Psychotraumatologie und Psychologische Medizin, 4, 45–59.

Berth, H., Albani, C., Stöbel-Richter, Y., Geyer, M. & Brähler, E. (2004). Arbeitslosigkeit als traumatisches Ereignis: Ergebnisse einer Repräsentativerhebung. Zeitschrift für Psychotraumatologie und Psychologische Medizin, 3, 21–31.

Binion, R. (1978). Hitler among the Germans. New York: Elsevier.

Bock, T. (1999). Lichtjahre. Psychosen ohne Psychiatrie. Krankheitsverständnis und Lebensentwürfe von Menschen mit unbehandelten Psychosen. Bonn: Psychiatrie Verlag.

Bohleber, W. (2000). Die Entwicklung der Traumatheorie in der Psychoanalyse. Psyche, Sonderheft Trauma, Gewalt und Kollektives Gedächtnis, 797–839.

Bonhoeffer, K. (1926). Beurteilung, Begutachtung und Rechtsprechung bei der sogenannten Unfallneurose. Deutsche Medizinische Wochenzeitschrift, 52, 179.

Bowlby, J. (1973). Attachment and Loss, Vol. II. Separation: Anxiety and Anger. New York: Basic Books.

Bowlby, J. (1995). A Secure Base. London: Routledge.

Bowlby, J. (1998). Attachment and Loss, Vol. III. Loss: Sadness and Depression. London: Pimlico, Random House.

Boszormenyi-Nagy, I. & Spark, G. M. (1993). Invisible Loyalties. New York: Harper & Row.

Brachatzek, C. (1991). Das betäubte Geschlecht – Frauen und Medikamentenabhängigkeit. In H. Neubeck-Fischer (Hrsg.), Frauen und Abhängigkeit (S. 183–189). München: Fachhochschule, Fachbereich Sozialwesen.

Breggin, P. R. (1996). Giftige Psychiatrie. Was Sie über Psychopharmaka, Elektroschock, Genetik und Biologie bei »Schizophrenie«, »Depression« und »manischdepressiver Erkrankung« wissen sollten! Heidelberg: Carl-Auer-Systeme Verlag. Englische Ausgabe: Toxic Psychiatry. New York: St. Martin's Press.

Bretherton, I. (2002). Konstrukt des inneren Arbeitsmodells. Bindungsbeziehungen und Bindungsrepräsentationen in der frühen Kindheit und im Vorschulalter. In Brisch, K. H., K. E. Grossmann, K. Grossmann und L. Köhler (Hrsg.), Bindung und seelische Entwicklungswege. Stuttgart: Klett-Cotta Verlag.

Brisch, K. H. (1999). Bindungsstörungen. Von der Bindungstheorie zur Therapie. Stuttgart: Klett-Cotta Verlag.

Brisch, K. H. (2003). Bindungsstörungen und Trauma. In K. H. Brisch und T. Hellbrügge (Hrsg.), Bindung und Trauma (S. 105–135). Stuttgart: Klett-Cotta Verlag.

Brisch, K. H., Grossmann, K. E., Grossmann, K. & Köhler, L. (Hrsg.), (2002). Bindung und seelische

Entwicklungswege. Stuttgart: Klett-Cotta Verlag.

Brisch, K. H. and Hellbrügge, T. (2006). Kinder ohne Bindung. Stuttgart: Klett-Cotta Verlag.

Brisch, K. H. and Hellbrügge, T. (2007). Die Anfänge der Eltern-Kinder-Bindung. Stuttgart: Klett-cotta Verlag.

Brizendine, L. (2006). The Female Brain. New York: Morgan Road Books/Random House.

Butollo, W., Hagl, M. & Krüsmann, M. (1999). Kreativität und Destruktion posttraumatischer Bewältigung. Forschungsergebnisse und Thesen zum Leben nach dem Trauma. Stuttgart: Pfeiffer bei Klett-Cotta.

Chamberlain, S. (1996). Aus der Kinderstube der Herrenmenschen. Psychosozial 63, 95–114.

Chalmers, A.F. (1999). What is this Thing Called Science? Queensland: University of Queensland Press.

Colbert, T. C. (1999). Broken Brains or Wounded Hearts. Santa Ana: Kevco Publishing.

Decker, O., Brähler, E. & Radebold, H. (2004). Kriegskindheit und Vaterlosigkeit – Indizes für eine psychosoziale Belastung nach fünfzig Jahren. Zeitschrift für Psychotraumatologie und Psychologische Medizin, 3, 33–41.

Deutsche Hauptstelle gegen die Suchtgefahren (Hrsg.), (2004). Jahrbuch Sucht. Geesthacht: Neuland Verlag.

Dilling, H., Mombour, W. & Schmidt, M. H. (Hrsg.) (1992). Weltgesundheitsorganisation – Internationale Klassifikation psychischer Störungen. ICD-10 Kapitel V (F), Klinisch-diagnostische Leitlinien. Bern: Huber Verlag.

Döring-Meijer, H. (Hrsg.). Systemaufstellungen. Geheimnisse und Verstrickungen in Systemen. Ein neuer dynamischer Beratungsansatz in der Praxis. Paderborn: Junfermann.

Dulz, B. (2000). Über die Aktualität der Verführungstheorie. In O. Kernberg, B. Dulz und U. Sachsse (Hrsg.), Handbuch der Borderline-Störungen (S. 11–25). Stuttgart: Schattauer Verlag.

Dykstra, I. (2002). Wenn Kinder Schicksal tragen. Kindliches Verhalten aus systemischer Sicht verstehen. München: Kösel Verlag.

Dykstra, I. (2004). Die Seele weist den Weg. Aufstellungsarbeit mit Kindern und Jugendlichen. München: Kösel Verlag.

Eckhardt-Henn, A. & Hoffmann, S. O. (2004). Dissoziative Bewusstseinsstörungen. Theorie, Symptomatik, Therapie. Stuttgart: Schattauer Verlag.

Engelmann, B. (1983). Bis alles in Scherben fällt. Wie wir die Nazizeit erlebten. München: Goldmann Verlag.

Freud, S. (1972). Totem und Tabu. Frankfurt/M.: Fischer Taschenbuch Verlag.

Fischer, G. & Riedesser, P. (1998). Lehrbuch der Psychotraumatologie. München: Reinhardt Verlag.

Fischer, G. (2000). Mehrdimensionale Psychodynamische Traumatherapie MPTT. Manual zur Behandlung psychotraumatischer Störungen. Heidelberg: Asanger Verlag.

Franke, U. (1996). The River Never Looks Back. Heidelberg: Carl-Auer International.

Franke, U. (2002). In My Mind's Eye. Heidelberg: Carl-Auer International.

Franke-Gricksch, M. (2001). "You're One of Us!". Heidelberg: Carl-Auer International.

Fricke, S., Schmidtke, A. & Weinacker, B. (1997). Epidemiologie von Suizid und Suizidversuch. In T. Giernalczyk (Hrsg.), Suizidgefahr – Verständnis und Hilfe. (S. 25–33). Tübingen: dgvt-Verlag.

Fröhlich, U. (1996). Vater unser in der Hölle. Ein Tatsachenbericht. Seelze-Velber: Kallmeyer'sche Verlagsbuchhandlung.

Fröschl, M. (2000). Gesund-Sein. Stuttgart: Lucius und Lucius Verlag.

Gallo, F. (2000). Energy psychology. Explorations at the Interface of Energy, Cognition, Behaviour and Health. Boca Roda: CRC Press LLC.

Gardner, R. A. (2002).: Should Courts Order PAS-Children to Visit/Reside with the Alienated Parent? American Journal of Forensic Psychology, 3, 61 – 106.

George, C. & Solomon, J. (1989). Internal Working Models of

Care-giving and Security of Attachment at Age Six. Infant Mental Health Journal, 10, 222–237.

Giernalczyk, T. (Hrsg.) (1997). Suizidgefahr – Verständnis und Hilfe. Tübingen: dgvt-Verlag.

Glöer, N. & Schmiedeskamp-Böhler, I. (1990). Verlorene Kindheit. Jungen als Opfer sexueller Gewalt. München: Verlag Antje Kunstmann.

Gribbin, J. (2001). In Search of Schrödinger's Cat. London: Wildwood House.

Grossmann, K. E., Grossmann, K., Winter, M. & Zimmermann, P. (2002). Bindungsbeziehungen und Bewertung von Partnerschaft. In K. H. Brisch, K. E. Grossmann, K. Grossmann und L. Köhler (Hrsg.), Bindung und seelische Entwicklungswege (S. 125–164). Stuttgart: Klett-Cotta Verlag.

Grossmann, K. & Grossmann, K. E. (2004). Bindungen – das Gefüge psychischer Sicherheit. Stuttgart: Klett-Cotta Verlag.

Grubrich-Simitis, I. (1979). Extremtraumatisierung als kumulatives Trauma. Psychoanalytische Studien über seelische Nachwirkungen der Konzentrationslagerhaft bei Überlebenden und ihren Kindern. Psyche, 33, 991–1023.

Grünberg, K. (2000). Zur Tradierung des Traumas der nationalsozialistischen Judenvernichtung. Psyche, Sonderheft Trauma, Gewalt und Kollektives Gedächtnis, 1002–1037.

Grünwald, M. & Hille, H.-E. (2003). Mobbing im Betrieb. München: C. H. Beck Wirtschaftsverlag.

Haberling, V. (2004). Verknüpftes Universum. Das Phänomen der repräsentierenden Wahrnehmung in der Aufstellungsarbeit. Diplomarbeit: Fachhochschule Hildesheim, Fachbereich Sozialpädagogik.

Harrer, J. (1940). Die deutsche Mutter und ihr erstes Kind. München.

Harlow, H. F. & Zimmermann, R. R. (1958). The Development of Affectional Responses in Infant Monkeys. Proceedings of the American Philosophical Society, 102, 501–509.

Hayward, J. (1998). Letters to Vanessa: On Love, Science, and Awareness in an Enchanted World. Shambhala Publications.

Heiliger, A. (2000). Täterstrategien und Prävention. München: Verlag Frauenoffensive.

Hellinger, B. (1994).: Love's own Truth. Heidelberg: Carl-Auer International.

Hellinger, B., Weber, G. & Beaumont, H. (1998). Love's Hidden Symmetry. Phoenix, Arizona: Zeig, Tucker & Co.

Hellinger, B. (2001a). Die Quelle braucht nicht nach dem Weg zu fragen. Ein Nachlesebuch. Heidelberg: Carl-Auer-Systeme Verlag.

Hellinger, B. (2001b). Liebe am Abgrund. Ein Kurs für Psychose-Patienten. Heidelberg: Carl-Auer-Systeme Verlag.

Hellinger, B. (2003). Ordnungen des Helfens. Ein Schulungsbuch. Heidelberg: Carl-Auer-Systeme Verlag.

Hellinger, B. (2004). Gottesgedanken. Ihre Wurzeln und ihre Wirkung. München: Kösel Verlag.

Hellinger, B.. (2005). In eigener Sache und: Nur die Liebe hat Zukunft. Praxis der Systemaufstellung, 1, 7–12.

Herman, J. (2003). Trauma and Recovery. Philadelphia: Basic Books.

Hesse, E. & Main, M. (1999). Second-Generation Effects of Unresolved Trauma in Non-Maltreating Parents: Dissociated, Frightened, and Threatening Parental Behaviour. Psychoanalytic Inquiry, 19, 481–540.

Hesse, E. & Main, M. (2002). Desorganisiertes Bindungsverhalten bei Kleinkindern, Kindern und Erwachsenen – Zusammenbruch von Strategien des Verhaltens und der Aufmerksamkeit. In K. H. Brisch, K. E. Grossmann, K. Grossmann und L. Köhler (Hrsg.), Bindung und seelische Entwicklungswege (S. 219–248). Stuttgart: Klett-Cotta Verlag.

Hirsch, M. (2004). Psychoanalytische Traumatologie – das Trauma in der Familie. Psychoanalytische Theorie und Therapie schwerer Persönlichkeitsstörungen. Stuttgart: Schattauer Verlag.

Holmes, J. (2002). John Bowlby & Attachment Theory. New

York: Routledge.

Huber, M. (1995). Multiple Persönlichkeiten. Frankfurt/M.: Fischer Taschenbuch Verlag.

Huber, M. (2003a). Trauma und die Folgen. Trauma und Traumabehandlung, Teil 1. Paderborn: Junfermann Verlag.

Huber, M. (2003b). Wege der Traumabehandlung. Trauma und Traumabehandlung, Teil 2. Paderborn: Junfermann Verlag.

Hüther, G. & Bonney, H. (2002). Neues vom Zappelphilipp. ADS: verstehen, vorbeugen und behandeln. Düsseldorf: Walter Verlag.

Hüther, G. & Krens, I. (2005) Das Geheimnis der ersten neun Monate. Unsere frühesten Prägungen" Düsseldorf: Walther Verlag.

Jacobsen, O. (2003). Das freie Aufstellen. Gruppendynamik als Spiegel. Karlsruhe: Olaf Jacobsen Verlag.

Janus, L. (1997). Wie die Seele entsteht. Unser psychisches Leben vor und nach der Geburt. Heidelberg: Mattes Verlag.

Jung, C. G. (1979). Der Mensch und seine Symbole. Olten: Walter-Verlag.

Kastner, H. (2000). Von einem Tag zum anderen. Wie vom sexuellen Missbrauch Betroffene überleben. Dettelbach: Röll Verlag.

Kaufmann, R. (2002). Ängste, Phobien und andere unnötige Lasten. Energiefeld-Therapie (EFT) als Anleitung zur Selbsthilfe. Heidelberg: Asanger Verlag.

Kessler, N. (Hrsg.) (1997). Manie-Feste. Frauen zwischen Rausch und Depression. Drei Erfahrungsberichte. Bonn: Psychiatrie Verlag.

Kind, J. (1996). Suizidal. Göttingen: Verlag Vandenhoek & Ruprecht.

Knopp, G. (2001). Die große Flucht. Das Schicksal der Vertriebenen. München: Econ Verlag.

Kolodej, C. (2003). Bonding: The Beginnings of Parent-Infant Attachment. New American Library Trade.

Klöckner, F. (2005). Hat das „Lebensborn" Projekt heute noch Auswirkungen? Bindungssystemtraumata unter dem Mehrgenerationenaspekt und ihre Konsequenzen für die

Theorie und Praxis der Sozialen Arbeit. Diplomarbeit. Katholische Stiftungsfachhochschule München.

Kloiber, A. (2002). Sexueller Missbrauch an Jungen. Kröning: Asanger Verlag.

Knorr, M. (2002). Der Ausgleich zwischen Täter und Opfer – eine heilende Begegnung. Praxis der Systemaufstellung, 2, 50–55.

Kraemer, H. (2003). Das Trauma der Gewalt. München: Kösel Verlag.

Kreisman, J. J. & Straus, H. (2005). Sometimes I Act Crazy. Living with Borderline Personality Disorder. New Jersey: John Wiley & Sons.

Krystal, H. & Farms, B. (2000). Psychische Widerständigkeit: Anpassung und Restitution bei Holocaust-Überlebenden. Psyche, Sonderheft Trauma, Gewalt und Kollektives Gedächtnis, 840–859.

Krystal, J. H., Karper, J. P., Seibyl, G. K., Freeman, G. K., Delaney, R., Bremner, J. D., Heninger, G. R., Bowers, M. B. & Charney, D. S. (1994). Subanesthetic Effects of the Noncompetitive NMDA Antagonist, Ketamine, in Humans: Psychotomimetic, Perceptual, Cognitive and Neuroendocrine Responses. Archives of General Psychiatry, 51, 199–213.

Laessle, R. G. (1994). Essstörungen. In H. Reinecker (Hrsg.), Lehrbuch der Klinischen Psychologie (S. 363–390). Göttingen: Hogrefe Verlag.

Lamprecht, F. (2003) (Hrsg.). Behandlung psychotraumatischer Belastungsstörungen mit EMDR. Zeitschrift für Psychotraumatologie und Psychologische Medizin, Heft 3.

Laszlo, E. (1997). The Creative Cosmos: A Unified Science of Matter, Life and Mind. Edinburgh: Floris Books.

Lebert, N. & Lebert, S. (2002). Denn Du trägst meinen Namen. Das schwere Erbe der prominenten Nazi-Kinder. München: Goldmann Verlag.

Lehmann, A. (1993). In der Fremde ungewollt zuhaus. Flüchtlinge und Vertriebene in Westdeutschland 1945–1990. München: C. H. Beck Verlag.

Levine, P. A. (1998).: Waking the Tiger; Healing Trauma. California: North Atlantic Books.

Leutz, G. (1974). Das klassische Psychodrama. Theorie und Praxis. Berlin: Springer Verlag.

Lilienthal, G. (2003). Der »Lebensborn e.V.« Ein Instrument nationalsozialistischer Rassenpolitik. Frankfurt/M.: Fischer Taschenbuch Verlag.

Mahr, A. (2003). Konfliktfelder – Wissende Felder. Systemaufstellungen in der Friedens- und Versöhnungsarbeit. Heidelberg: Carl-Auer-Systeme Verlag.

Mahr, A. (2005). How the Living and the Dead Can Heal Each Other. The Knowing Field, 6, 4–8.

Manfield, P. (Hrsg.) (2000). Extending EMDR. A Casebook of Innovative Applications. New York: W.W. Norton & Company.

Maric, B. (2003). Welche Wirkungen haben Aufstellungen? Supervisionsaufstellungen aus Sicht der Aufstellenden. Diplomarbeit: Katholische Stiftungsfachhochschule München.

Maturana, H. & Varela, F. (1987).: Tree of Knowledge: Shambhala Publications.

Meerloo, J. A. M. (1959). Shock, catalepsy and psychogenic death. Int. Record Med., 172, 384–393.

Metzdorf, M. (2001). Sozialpädagogischer Umgang mit sexuell missbrauchten BewohnerInnen in einer betreuten Kinder- und Jugendwohngruppe. Diplomarbeit: Katholische Stiftungsfachhochschule München.

Mentzos, S. (Hrsg.) (2000). Psychose und Konflikt. Göttingen: Vandenhoeck & Ruprecht.

Moser, T. (1996). Dämonische Figuren. Die Wiederkehr des Dritten Reiches in der Psychotherapie. Frankfurt/M.: Suhrkamp Verlag.

Müller, U., Schröttle, M., Glammeier, S. und Oppenheimer, C. (2004). Lebenssituation, Sicherheit und Gesundheit von Frauen in Deutschland. Eine repräsentative Untersuchung zu Gewalt gegen Frauen in Deutschland im Auftrag des Bundesministeriums für Familie, Senioren, Frauen und

Jugend. Universität Bielefeld (ohne Verlag).

Neuhauser, J. (Hrsg.) (1999). Supporting Love. How Love Works in Couple Relationships. Heidelberg: Carl-Auer International.

Niederland, W. G. (1980). Folgen der Verfolgung. Das Überlebenden-Syndrom. Seelenmord. Frankfurt/M.: Suhrkamp Verlag.

Oerter, R. & Montada, L. (Hrsg.) (1995). Entwicklungspsychologie. Weinheim: Psychologie Verlags Union.

Pänzinger, C. (2004). Sind Arbeitsbeziehungsaufstellungen hilfreich in der stationären Kinder- und Jugendhilfe? Zwei Fallstudien über Elternarbeit in SOS-Kinderdorffamilien und Darstellung der Konsequenzen für die Soziale Arbeit. Diplomarbeit: Katholische Stiftungsfachhochschule München.

Parnell, L. (1999). EMDR – der Weg aus dem Trauma. Über die Heilung von Traumata und emotionalen Verletzungen. Paderborn: Junfermann Verlag.

Pawlowski, H. M. (2001). Zum Verhältnis von Ehe, nichtehelichen Lebensgemeinschaften und gleichgeschlechtlichen Lebenspartnerschaften – Abschied von der bürgerlichen Ehe. (S. 10–25). In Bäuerle, S. und Moll-Strobel, H. (Hrsg.), Eltern sägen ihr Kind entzwei. Donauwörth: Auer Verlag.

Phillips, M. & Frederick, C. (2003). Healing the Divided Self. New York: W.W. Norton & Company.

Pross, C. (1988). Wiedergutmachung: Der Kleinkrieg gegen die Opfer. Frankfurt/M.: Athenäum Verlag.

Putnam, F. W. (2003). Diagnosis and Treatment of Multiple Personality Disorder. The Guilford Press.

Rahn, E. & Mahnkopf, A. (2000). Lehrbuch Psychiatrie für Studium und Beruf. Bonn: Psychiatrie Verlag.

Raschke, P. (1994). Substitutionstherapie. Ergebnisse langfristiger Behandlung von Opiatabhängigen. Freiburg i. B.: Lambertus Verlag.

Reimer, H. (2002). Das heimatlose Ich. Aus der Depression zurück ins Leben. München: Kösel Verlag.

Reddemann, L. & Sachsse, U. (2000). Traumazentrierte Psychotherapie der chronifizierten, komplexen Posttraumatischen Belastungsstörung vom Phänotyp der Borderline-Persönlichkeitsstörungen. In O. Kernberg, B. Dulz und U. Sachsse (Hrsg.), Handbuch der Borderline-Störungen. (S. 11–25). Stuttgart: Schattauer Verlag.

Reddemann, L. (2004). Psychodynamisch Imaginative Traumatherapie. Stuttgart: Pfeiffer bei Klett-Cotta.

Reemtsma. J. P. (2002). Im Keller. Reinbek bei Hamburg: Rowohlt Taschenbuch Verlag.

Reißer, R. (2002). Königsmord am Starnberger See. Wie und warum Ludwig II. am 13. Juni 1886 sterben musste. München: Buchendorfer Verlag.

Riedesser, P. (Hg.) (2004). Traumatisierung bei Kindern – Entwicklungslinien der Diagnostik und Therapie. Zeitschrift für Psychotraumatologie und Psychologische Medizin, 4, 5–6.

Ritter, R. (2004). Boom mit Hellinger. Die Sehnsucht nach Ordnung und Lösung. Psychotherapeuten Forum, 5, 17–25.

Rizzolatti, G., Fadiga, L., Fogassi, L. & Gallese, V. (2002). From Mirror Neurones to Imitation: Facts and Speculations. In A. Meltzoff and W. Prinz (eds.), The Imitative Mind. Cambridge: University Press.

Rogers, C. (1994). Client-Centered Therapy. Boston: Houghton Mifflin Co.

Rüggeberg, S. & Rüggeberg, A. (2003). Werkstattbericht zur Mitwirkung von Tieren in Familienaufstellungen. Praxis der Systemaufstellung, 2, 85–89.

Ruppert, F. (2001). Berufliche Beziehungswelten. Das Aufstellen von Arbeitsbeziehungen in Theorie und Praxis. Heidelberg: Carl-Auer-Systeme Verlag.

Ruppert, F. (2002). Verwirrte Seelen. Der verborgene Sinn von Psychosen. Grundzüge einer systemischen Psychotraumatologie. München: Kösel Verlag.

Ruppert, F. (2002a). Psychosis & Schizophrenia: Disturbed Bonding in Family Systems. Systemic Solutions Bulletin, 3, 12–19.

Ruppert, F. (2007). Wie zuverlässig ist die Aufstellungsmethode? Praxis der Systemaufstellung, 2, 76–92.

Sachsse, U. (2004). Traumazentrierte Psychotherapie. Theorie, Klinik und Praxis. Stuttgart: Schattauer Verlag.

Saß, H., Wittchen, H.-U. & Zaudig, M. (1998). Diagnostisches und Statistisches Manual Psychischer Störungen DSM IV. Göttingen: Hogrefe Verlag.

Satir, V. (2002). Selbstwert und Kommunikation. Stuttgart: Pfeiffer Verlag.

Schäfer, T. (2000). Was die Seele krank macht und was sie heilt. München: Knaur Verlag

Schechter, D. S. (2003). Gewaltbedingte Traumata in der Generationenfolge. In K. H. Brisch und T. Hellbrügge (Hrsg.), Bindung und Trauma (S. 235–256). Stuttgart: Klett-Cotta Verlag.

Schechter, D. S., Coates, S. W. & First, E. (2003). Beobachtungen aus New York. Reaktionen von psychisch vorbelasteten Kindern auf die Anschläge auf das World Trade Center. In K. H. Brisch und T. Hellbrügge (Hrsg.), Bindung und Trauma (S. 224–234). Stuttgart: Klett-Cotta Verlag.

Schlötter, P. (2005). Vertraute Sprache und ihre Entdeckung. Systemaufstellungen sind kein Zufallsprodukt – der empirische Nachweis. Heidelberg: Carl-Auer-Systeme Verlag.

Schlosser, R. (2003). Von Auschwitz zu Familienaufstellungen: Die Reise einer Seele in Richtung Versöhnung. In A. Mahr (Hrsg.), Konfliktfelder – Wissende Felder (S. 136–159). Heidelberg: Carl-Auer-Systeme Verlag.

Schuengel, C., Bakermans-Kranenburg, M., van Uzendoorn, M. & Blom, M. (1999). Unresolved Loss and Infant Disorganization: Links to Frightening Maternal Behaviour. In J. Solomon und C. George (Hrsg.)., Attachment Disorganization. New York: Guilford Press.

Schmideder, H. (2002). Die Mädchen des Pfarrers. Sexueller Missbrauch in der kirchlichen Jugendarbeit. Chronik einer

Aufdeckung. München: Verlag Frauenoffensive.

Schmidt, C. (2004). Das entsetzliche Erbe. Träume als Schlüssel zu Familiengeheimnissen. Göttingen: Verlag Vandenhoeck & Ruprecht.

Schneider, J. R. (2001). Beobachtungen zur Rolle des Stellvertreters. Praxis der Systemaufstellung, 1, 23–27.

Schricker, G. (2001). »Ich fühle mich wie zerrissen«. Engagement und Ordnung in der Schule. In G. Weber (Hrsg.), Derselbe Wind lässt viele Drachen steigen (S. 269–277). Heidelberg: Carl-Auer-Systeme Verlag.

Schützenberger, A. A. (1998). The Ancestor Syndrome. Transgenerational Psychotherapy and the Hidden Links in the Family Tree. London: Routledge.

Schwer, B. (2004). Kann die Systemische Psychotraumatologie Betreuern und Eltern beim Umgang mit hyperaktiven Kindern helfen? Einsichten gewonnen aus Familienaufstellungen an einer Heilpädagogischen Kindertagesstätte. Diplomarbeit. Katholische Stiftungsfachhochschule München.

Seligman, M. E. P. (1975). Helplessness: On Depression, Development, and Death. San Francisco: Freeman.

Shapiro, F. und Forrest, M. S. (1998). EMDR. The Breakthrough Therapy. Philadelphia: Basic Books.

Shaw, J. (2002). Odysseus in America. Combat Trauma and the Trials of Homecoming. New York: Scribner.

Shaw, J. (2003). Achilles in Vietnam. Combat Trauma and the Undoing of Character. New York: Sheldrake, R. (2003). Der siebte Sinn des Menschen. München: Scherz Verlag. English Version: The Sense of Being Stared At. New York: Crown Publishing Group.

Sparrer, I. & Varga von Kibéd, M. (2000). Ganz im Gegenteil. Tetralemmaarbeit und andere Grundformen systemischer Strukturaufstellungen. Heidelberg: Carl-Auer-Systeme Verlag.

Spitz, R. & Wolf, K. (1946). Anaclitic Depression. Psychoanalytic Study of Children, 3, 313–342.

Stamm, B. H. (2003). Sekundäre Traumastörungen. Paderborn: Junfermann.

Stern, D. (2003). The Interpersonal World of the Infant. New York: Basic Books.

Stier, E. (1926). Über die sogenannten Unfallneurosen. Leipzig.

Stricevic, J. (2002). Folgen traumatischer Kriegs- und Nachkriegserfahrungen kroatischer Soldaten. Befragung von Betroffenen. Welche Aufgaben ergeben sich daraus für die Soziale Arbeit? Diplomarbeit Katholische Stiftungsfachhochschule München.

St. Just, A. (2005). Relative Balance in an Unstable World. A Feminine Perspective on Individual and Social Trauma.

ten Hövel, G. (2003). Liebe Mama, böser Papa. Eltern-Kind-Entfremdung nach Trennung und Scheidung: Das PAS-Syndrom. München: Kösel Verlag.

Terr, L. (1991). Childhood traumas: An outline and overview. American Journal of Psychiatry, 1, 10–20.

Thomas, C. A. (2003). Krieg beenden, Frieden leben. Ein Soldat überwindet Hass und Gewalt. Berlin: Theseus Verlag.

Tisseron, S. (2000). Phänomen Scham. München: Reinhardt Verlag.

Tisseron, S. (2001). Die verbotene Tür. Familiengeheimnisse und wie man mit ihnen umgeht. Reinbek bei Hamburg: Rowohlt Taschenbuch Verlag.

Troje, E. (2000). Die Weitergabe psychischer Inhalte von Generation zu Generation und ihre potentielle Auswirkung auf die Entstehung einer Pychose. In S. Mentzos und A. Münch (Hrsg.), Die Bedeutung des psychosozialen Feldes und der Beziehung für Genese, Psychodynamik, Therapie und Prophylaxe der Psychosen (S. 26–52). Göttingen: Verlag Vandenhoeck & Ruprecht.

Trossman, B. (1968). Adolescent Children of Concentration Camp Survivors. Canadian Psychiatric Ass. Journal, 12, 121–123.

Ulsamer, G. (2001). Der Ansatz von Bert Hellinger in der praktischen Sozialarbeit. Praxis der Systemaufstellung, 2, 38–41.

Van der Kolk, B., McFarlane, A.C. & Weisaeth, L. (Hg.) (2000). Traumatic Stress. The Effects of Overwhelming Experience on Mind, Body and Society. New York: The Guilford Press.

Van der Kolk, B. (2000). Der Körper vergisst nicht. Ansätze einer Psychophysiologie der posttraumatischen Belastungsstörung. In B. van der Kolk, A.C. MacFarlane und L. Weisaeth (Hg.), Traumatic Stress (S. 195–220). Paderborn: Junfermann Verlag.

Van Kampenhout, D. (2003). Images of the Soul: The Working of the Soul in Shamanic Rituals and Family Constellations. Phoenix: Zeig, Tucker & Theisen.

Varga von Kibéd, M. (1998). Bemerkungen über philosophische Grundlagen und methodische Voraussetzungen der systemischen Aufstellungsarbeit. In Weber, G. (Hrsg.), Praxis des Familien-Stellens. (S. 51–60). Heidelberg. Carl Auer-Systeme Verlag.

Varga von Kibéd, M. (2000). Unterschiede und tiefere Gemeinsamkeiten der Aufstellungsarbeit mit Organisationen und der systemischen Familienaufstellungen. In G. Weber (Hrsg.), Praxis der Organisationsaufstellungen (S. 11–33). Heidelberg: Carl-Auer-Systeme Verlag.

Vershuren, H. A. & van Buren Molenaar, M. (2005). Body-oriented Interventions in Family Constellations. The Knowing Field, 6, 30–32.

Von Bülow, G. (2004). Erfahrungen bei der Integration der Mehrgenerationen-Perspektive in die psychoanalytische Arbeit. Praxis der Systemaufstellung, 1, 18–28.

Watkins, J. G. & Watkins, H. H. (2003). Ego States Theory and Therapy. New York: W.W. Norman & Company.

Welzer, H., Moller, S. und Tschuggnall, K. (2002). »Opa war kein Nazi«. Nationalsozialismus und Familiengedächtnis. Frankfurt/M.: Fischer Taschenbuch Verlag.

Wenzlaff, U. (1958). Die psychoreaktiven Störungen nach entschädigungspflichtigen Ereignissen. Die sogenannten Unfallneurosen. Berlin: Springer Verlag.

Wieck, W. (1992). Männer lassen lieben. Die Sucht nach der

Frau. Frankfurt/M.: Fischer Verlag.

Willi, J. (2002). Psychologie der Liebe. Stuttgart: Klett-Cotta Verlag.

Wolfersdorf, M., Grünewald, I., König, F. & Hägele, U. (1997). Suizidprävention in der Notfallpsychiatrie. In T. Giernalczyk (Hrsg.), Suizidgefahr – Verständnis und Hilfe (S. 115–135). Tübingen: dgvt-Verlag.

Worden, J. W. (1999). Beratung und Therapie in Trauerfällen. Ein Handbuch. Bern: Hans Huber Verlag.

World Health Organization (ed.) (1992). ICD-10: International Statistical Classification of Diseases and Related Health Problems (10th revised edition). Geneva: World Health Organization.

Zimmer, K. (1998). Erste Gefühle. Das frühe Band zwischen Kind und Eltern. München: Kösel Verlag.

Index

Green Balloon Publishing
is an imprint of Constellations Work Trainings UK Limited.

Next Publication:

In the Presence of Many
The Practice of Systemic Constellations
in the Individual Setting

Vivian Broughton

Due for Publication: 2009

---

www.greenballoonbooks.co.uk

CWT Ltd - P O Box 4215 - FROME - Somerset - BA11 5WU - UK
+44 (0) 1373 836694
Info@greenballoonbooks.co.uk

LaVergne, TN USA
11 December 2009
166774LV00003B/1/P